BLACKSTONE'S GUIDE

The Domestic Violence, Crime and Victims Act 2004

BLACKSTONE'S GUIDE TO

The Domestic Violence, Crime and Victims Act 2004

Elizabeth Lawson Q.C.
Melanie Johnson
Lindsay Adams
John Lamb
and
Stephen Field

OXFORD
UNIVERSITY PRESS

*This book has been printed digitally and produced in a standard specification
in order to ensure its continuing availability*

OXFORD
UNIVERSITY PRESS

Great Clarendon Street, Oxford OX2 6DP
United Kingdom

Oxford University Press is a department of the University of Oxford.
It furthers the University's objective of excellence in research, scholarship,
and education by publishing worldwide.
Oxford is a registered trade mark of Oxford University Press in the UK
and in certain other countries

Reprinted 2012

British Library Cataloguing in Publication Data
Data available
Library of Congress Cataloging in Publication Data
Data available
ISBN 978-0-19-928189-3

Contents—Summary

Visit the Blackstone's Guide Series website: www.oup.com/uk/law/practitioner/bgseries

Contents

Contents

Foreword

The Criminal Justice Act 2003 is one of the most far-reaching statutes affecting the administration of criminal justice ever enacted. Judges are currently learning to master some of its most important and difficult provisions in a series of residential seminars run by the Judicial Studies Board. While we were still anticipating the implementation of the 2003 Act, the Domestic Violence, Crime and Victims Act 2004 received Royal Assent in November. We must hope that the respective implementation dates for both Acts will not follow the haphazard and uncertain arrangements which have made it so difficult for the practical application of legislation in this field to be rapidly appreciated and understood.

Perhaps the most significant long-term feature of the 2004 Act is that it will have an impact on both family and criminal courts. As the authors explain, breach of a non-molestation order will be prosecuted as a criminal offence. Family practitioners will therefore need to give unequivocal advice to their clients about the possible consequences of such breaches. Criminal practitioners will need to learn more about the process which has led up to the non-molestation order, and the courts themselves will have to appreciate the distinction between a non-molestation order and an undertaking to desist from conduct which would justify such an order. I welcome sensible steps which will reduce what can sometimes be the over-compartmentalization of criminal and family justice. It will be interesting to watch further developments.

The Domestic Violence, Crime and Victims Act 2004 is a significant, major criminal justice statute, perhaps illustrated by its range. For example, it covers both murder and common assault. In relation to murder, a new offence addresses the evidential difficulty of establishing which of two adults responsible for the care of a child caused its death, when one did, and it has not hitherto been possible to establish by admissible evidence which of them was responsible. This will link with the reforms of the rules relating to hearsay evidence in Chapter 2 of the Criminal Justice Act. At the other extreme, common assault becomes an arrestable offence, and it will be open to a jury to convict of common assault on an indictment alleging more serious offences of violence. These are two highlights among many, which are neatly identified in the Contents page and carefully summarized in the Introduction.

This Guide has been written for practitioners with backgrounds and experience in both family and criminal law, who will shortly have to grapple with the new provisions, and their impact on both substantive and procedural law. The text is clear and easily assimilated, and the authors have been at pains to identify or illustrate, as appropriate, the links between this legislation and the earlier provisions which it either replaces, or amends, or extends. They have also drawn attention to aspects of the legislation where express provisions are absent, and the relevant law will have to be analysed and developed by judicial decision.

At a time when the relentless pace of legislation relating to the criminal justice system in particular shows no sign of abating, this Guide will prove invaluable, and those who use it will, I am confident, discover a stimulating and highly practical analysis of the 2004 Act.

Right Hon Lord Justice Igor Judge
February 2005

Table of Cases

References are to Paragraph Numbers

Table of Primary Legislation

References are to Paragraph Numbers

Table of Secondary Legislation

References are to Paragraph Numbers

Table of Rules of Court

References are to Paragraph Numbers

Table of Abbreviations

CCR	County Court Rules 1981
CDA 1998	Crime and Disorder Act 1998
ECHR	European Convention on Human Rights
FLA 1996	Family Law Act 1996
FPC(MP)R 1991	Family Proceedings Courts (Matrimonial Proceedings, etc) Rules 1991
FPR 1991	Family Proceedings Rules 1991
MCA 1980	Magistrates' Court Act 1980
PACE 1984	Police and Criminal Evidence Act 1984
RSC	Rules of the Supreme Court

1

INTRODUCTION

A. SUMMARY

The Domestic Violence, Crime and Victims Act 2004 was introduced in the **1.01** House of Lords on 1 December 2003. It was stated to be the 'the most radical overhaul of domestic violence legislation in 30 years'.[1] During its passage through Parliament the Act grew, incorporating clauses which had nothing whatever to do with domestic violence or with each other. The long title has nearly doubled since introduction. When the amendments were debated it was commented that many organizations outside Parliament were saying: 'This appears now to be less of a domestic violence Bill than a general crime Bill'.[2]

Indeed, some commentators have made the point that it is in fact the annual **1.02** Criminal Justice Act. It repeals and replaces previous criminal justice legislation which has never been brought into force, it corrects errors and omissions in recently passed statutes, and it is the repository for ill-assorted pieces of legislation which failed to find a statutory home elsewhere. Indeed, Baroness Warmsley commented: 'the Home Office must have a very large and dusty box of Christmas baubles in its attic. It seems to raid that box very frequently to hang them on any unsuspecting passing Bill'.[3]

More troubling to those who are concerned about civil liberties, or ensuring a **1.03** fair trial, the Act continues to erode requirements which have hitherto been regarded as fundamental to a fair trial. That the Home Office Minister could

---

[1] *Hansard*, HL col 950 (15 December 2004).
[2] *Hansard*, HL col 1423 (11 March 2004).
[3] *Hansard*, HL col 216 (2 November 2004).

describe the measures as 'to close loopholes where offenders were currently escaping justice', is surprising to say the least.[4] The gradual chipping away at the requirement for jury trial continues with the proposals for the trial of sample counts, or for the judge to decide whether the defendant is unfit to plead. More seriously, the removal of the requirement that the prosecution has to prove which of two individuals committed a crime, and that they may be required to give evidence against themselves when the Crown cannot establish a case for them to answer, in the case of the new offence of causing the death of a child or vulnerable adult, sets a potentially dangerous precedent. Whilst some of these changes may be defensible in the context in which they are passed, the possibility for the practices being extended to other areas is a real and dangerous one.

1.04   The Act is unusual in the way that it incorporates civil and criminal law. The fact that breach of a non-molestation order will become a criminal offence means that criminal practitioners will need to understand the basis on which a non-molestation order is made; equally, family practitioners will need to advise clients as to the potential criminal repercussions of submitting to a non-molestation order.

B. THE DOMESTIC VIOLENCE PROVISIONS

1.05   In its final form, the Act does not live up to its billing as the most radical overhaul of domestic violence legislation in thirty years. The Domestic Violence provisions are contained in Pts I and II of the Act. Section 1 amends the Family Law Act 1996 to make the breach of a non-molestation order a criminal offence. Sections 2, 3, and 4 extend the provisions of the Family Law Act 1996 to same-sex couples and to those who have had an intimate personal relationship with each other which is or was of significant duration.

1.06   Section 5 of the Act creates a new offence of causing or allowing the death of a child or vulnerable adult. Section 6 sets out the changes in evidence and procedure in England and Wales for the new offence. One of the most controversial changes in procedure is that at the defendant's trial, the question of whether there is a case for the defendant to answer on the charge of murder or manslaughter, is not to be considered before the close of evidence.

1.07   Section 9 of the Act provides for the Secretary of State to set up multi-agency domestic homicide reviews in cases where the death of a person aged 16 or over has or appears to have been caused by violence, abuse, or neglect from a relative, partner, or member of his or her household.

1.08   Section 10 of the Act provides for common assault to become an arrestable offence. The provisions of s 11 allow for common assault and other lesser

---

[4] *Hansard*, HL col 949 (15 December 2003).

offences to be an alternative verdict to the count charged, without the alternative count having to be included on the indictment.

Section 12 amends the Protection from Harassment Act 1997. The court will **1.09** have the power to make restraining orders when a defendant is convicted of any offence, not just an offence under the Act or when a defendant is acquitted. Section 13 makes similar provisions in relation to Northern Ireland.

There is no statutory definition of domestic violence. Various agencies, includ- **1.10** ing the Home Office and the Crown Prosecution Service, each have their own different definitions. Whether a single definition should be used by all agencies was debated in Parliament, but rejected by the Government. The amendment to include a definition was withdrawn.[5]

There was no legislation specifically against domestic violence until the **1.11** Domestic Violence and Matrimonial Proceedings Act 1976. Until then, remedies to protect women and children against domestic violence had been developed by the judges. In 1989 the working paper 'Domestic Violence and Occupation of the Family Home' was published. The paper was followed by a report from the Law Commission in 1992 'Family Law: Domestic Violence and the Occupation of the Family Home'. The concern identified was that remedies for domestic violence varied depending on the court, and that different criteria were applied.

This led to the introduction of Pt IV of the Family Law Act 1996 which **1.12** provided a consistent set of remedies giving all family courts the same jurisdiction to make non-molestation and occupation orders.[6] The Family Law Act 1996 came into force on 1 October 1997. Since then, awareness of domestic violence and the social problems it causes has increased. Those social problems range from health care to housing. In June 1998 the British Medical Association published 'Domestic Violence: A Health Care Issue', reporting on the impact of domestic violence on health.

Apart from the new offence of causing or allowing the death of a child or **1.13** vulnerable adult, the domestic violence provisions arose out of the Safety and Justice consultation paper published in June 2003. Views on extending the availability of non-molestation and occupation orders under the Family Law Act 1996 were canvassed. Other proposals included the provision for Domestic Homicide Reviews, for common assault to become an arrestable offence and to extend the powers to make restraining orders under the Protection from Harassment Act 1997.

The new offence of causing or allowing the death of a child or vulnerable **1.14** adult arose out of the difficulties highlighted in cases of a child's death where the prosecution were unable to show when the injury was inflicted or by whom. In July 2002 the NSPCC held a seminar which led to a working group entitled 'Which one of you did it?'. An informal consultation paper circulated by the

---

[5] *Hansard*, HL col 1223 (11 March 2004).
[6] Subject to FLA 1996, s 59 which does not allow the magistrates' court to deal with disputes over whether or not a person has a beneficial right to occupy the property.

Law Commission was followed by the publication of a consultative report in April 2003.[7] The Law Commission made recommendations, accompanied by a draft bill in their final report published in September 2003,[8] and concluded that the rules of evidence and procedure in criminal trials posed an obstacle to the effective investigation, identification, and punishment of those guilty of causing death or injury to the most vulnerable members of society. The Law Commission's consultative report provided the framework for the provisions in the Act. The Act departs from the recommendations by excluding cases where a victim suffers harm which does not result in death, and the Act also includes vulnerable adults as victims. The definition of a vulnerable adult has been left to the court.[9]

1.15   Common assault, etc as an alternative verdict was an amendment proposed in the House of Lords. It did not arise from a consultation process. The amendment deals with the situation where the prosecutor and judge have overlooked the necessity of including a specific count of common assault in the indictment if the jury were to be asked to consider it as an alternative verdict.

C. THE CRIMINAL JUSTICE PROVISIONS

1.16   The criminal justice provisions are contained in Pt II of the Act. Sections 14 to 16 introduce the concept of surcharges as an additional penalty in criminal proceedings. The proposal for surcharges arose out of the consultation paper 'Compensation and Support for Victims' published in January 2004. Section 14 adds a surcharge to any conviction in the courts. Section 15 adds a surcharge to penalty notices for disorderly behaviour and s 16 allows a higher fixed penalty to be issued where the defendant has committed repeated road traffic offences within the last three years. The Government justified the late amendment to the Act as 'The revenue recovered would be paid into the victims' fund to provide support and services to the victims of crime. That would fall within the territory currently covered by Part II of the Bill'.[10] The late amendment provoked criticism in the House of Lords where it was stated to be an 'illogical and half baked proposal'.[11]

1.17   Sections 17 to 20 of the Act provide for trial by jury of sample counts only where the number of counts included in the indictment makes a trial of all the counts impracticable. It is a two-stage process. The first stage is to take place before a judge and jury with an indictment containing sample counts; should a

---

[7] Law Commission, *Children: Their Non-accidental Death or Serious Injury (Criminal Trial), A Consultative Report* (Law Com No 279, April 2003).
[8] Law Commission, *Children: Their Non-accidental Death or Serious Injury (Criminal Trial)* (Law Com No 282).
[9] *Hansard*, HL col 333 (21 January 2003).
[10] *Hansard*, HL col 193 (19 January 2004).
[11] *Hansard*, HL col 221 (4 November 2004).

defendant be convicted of one or more counts on that indictment then a second stage of trial may follow. The defendant would be tried by a judge alone in relation to scheduled offences linked to a sample count on which the defendant had already been convicted. Before 1998, prosecutors had framed indictments by including a small number of specimen or sample counts, said to be representative of offences of a like kind committed by the defendant. When passing sentence the court took account of the isolated instances specified in the counts and also of the conduct of which, on the evidence adduced by the prosecution, those counts were representative. That was challenged in *R v Kidd*[12] when the court concluded that the practice was inconsistent with the principle that a defendant should not be sentenced for offences which he had neither admitted nor of which he had been found guilty. Concerned that a defendant should be sentenced for the totality of his offending, the Law Commission published a report in 2002[13] as to how this might be achieved. Sections 17 to 20 are based on the recommendations of the Law Commission that there should be a two-stage process.

Sections 22 to 26 provide for the procedure and powers of the court in cases where the defendant is unfit to plead or there is a finding of insanity. The provisions allow for a finding by a court and not a jury on whether a defendant is fit to plead and findings as to whether the defendant did the act or omission charged against him. The proposals were considered in January 2000. Lord Justice Auld began a review of the criminal court to consider the practices, procedures, and rules of evidence applied by the criminal courts at every level. The report was published in October 2001.[14] Many of the recommendations were implemented in the Criminal Justice Act 2003. The recommendation that a judge and not a jury should determine the issue of fitness to plead was to be in the draft Mental Health Bill published in June 2002. That bill did not proceed, therefore the recommendations were included in this Act. **1.18**

Miscellaneous provisions are contained in ss 27 to 31 of this Act. Section 27 provides for further powers to be given to authorized officers executing warrants. The power to make disclosure orders for the purpose of executing warrants and the use of information supplied under disclosure orders are provided for in s 28. The procedure on breach of a community penalty as contained in Sch 5 to this Act is put into effect by s 29 of the Act. Section 30 contains a minor amendment to s 58(13) of the Criminal Justice Act 2003 in relation to 'applicable time' for prosecution appeals. Section 31 gives effect to Sch 6 of the Act. Schedule 6 contains amendments in respect of intermittent custody, which amends the Criminal Justice Act 2003. The miscellaneous provisions did not arise from any consultation process. The amendments were put before the House of Lords on 11 March 2004. **1.19**

---

[12] [1998] 1 WLR 604.
[13] *The Effective Prosecution of Multiple Offending* (Law Com No 227).
[14] Auld LJ, *Review of the Criminal Court of England and Wales* (October 2001).

D. VICTIMS

1.20 A statutory Code of Practice for victims is provided for by s 32 of the Act. The procedure for issuing the code is prescribed by s 33. Non-compliance with the code does not of itself give rise to either civil or criminal liability, although if there is otherwise civil or criminal liability, the failure to comply with the code is admissible in evidence, and the court may take it into account: s 34. Under s 35 of the Act, victims of a sexual or violent offence have the right to make representations or receive information concerning licence conditions or supervision requirements where the offender has been sentenced to imprisonment or detention. Corresponding provisions in relation to an offender subject to a hospital order, hospital direction, or a transfer direction are contained in ss 36 to 44. Section 45 provides the interpretation of ss 35 to 44.

1.21 Section 47 gives effect to Sch 7 which amends the Parliamentary Commissioner Act 1967 to allow for investigations by the Parliamentary Commissioner in respect of complaints arising from the duties imposed by the code of practice and the duties of the local probation boards under ss 35 to 44 of the Act.

1.22 A Commissioner for Victims and Witnesses is provided for by s 48. The general functions of the Commissioner are set out in s 49. Section 50 requires the Commissioner to give advice to ministers when requested. Section 51 sets out the restrictions on the exercise of the Commissioner's functions. Section 52 defines the meaning of victims and witnesses in respect of ss 48 to 51. Section 53 gives effect to Sch 9, which specifies the authorities within the Commissioner's remit. Section 54 provides for the disclosure of information in respect of compliance with the code of practice for victims, compliance with ss 35 to 44, and the functions of the Commissioner.

1.23 Section 55 imposes a duty on the Secretary of State to appoints a Victims' Advisory Panel. Section 56 allows the Secretary of State to pay grants to assist victims, witnesses, and other persons affected by offences. Section 57 allows for the recovery of criminal injuries compensation from offenders.

1.24 Part III of the Act arose out of recommendations from the 'Justice for All' White Paper and the National Strategy 'A New Deal for Victims and Witnesses' published by the Government in July 2003. The 'Justice for All' White Paper suggested that there should be a statutory code of practice for victims to replace the non-statutory Victims Charter. The Victims Charter explains what happens after an offence has been reported to the police and the standard of service which should be expected. The Victims Charter also placed responsibility on the probation service to contact the victims of life-sentence prisoners to ascertain whether there were any concerns about conditions attached to an offender's release.

E. COMMENCEMENT AND TRANSITIONAL PROVISIONS

The Domestic Violence, Crime and Victims Act received Royal Assent on 12 **1.25** November 2004.

At the time of writing there is no date fixed for the implementation of any of **1.26** the provisions. The Home Office said on 6 January 2005: 'Although the measures will have different commencement dates the Government expects implementation to be rolled out from April 2005'.

Schedule 12 deals with the transitional provisions. They are not retrospective. **1.27** In essence, they all relate either to acts committed after the Act comes into force, or, where there are procedural changes, to the situation being dealt with after the Act comes into force.

2

CHANGES TO THE LAW ON DOMESTIC VIOLENCE[1]

A. SUMMARY

The main aim of the changes made in the Domestic Violence, Crime and Victims Act 2004 is to change the climate of tolerance towards domestic violence and to ensure that it is treated with the same seriousness as any other crime.[2] To that end, the Act inserts a new s 42A into the Family Law Act 1996 which makes breach of a non-molestation order a criminal offence. The police are given power to arrest for common assault. It also extends the Family Law Act 1996 to same-sex couples and to those who have had an intimate personal relationship with each other which is or was of significant duration. **2.01**

---

[1] Note: In this book the respondent/defendant is referred to by masculine pronouns for stylistic convenience. It should be read as including the feminine. Whilst most domestic violence is committed by men against women, there are also cases where men experience violence from a partner, and it is not our intention to ignore that reality.

[2] The Crown Prosecution Service reissued its guidance on the prosecution of offences of domestic violence 'Policy for Prosecuting Cases of Domestic Violence' on 1 February 2005 available at www.cps.gov.uk.

2.02   It will remain possible to deal with a breach of a non-molestation order by issuing and serving an application for committal, but it will no longer be possible to attach a power of arrest to a non-molestation order. A power of arrest may still be attached to an occupation order. Once a person has been convicted, he cannot be dealt with for contempt of court in respect of the same breach of the injunction, and if he is dealt with for contempt, he cannot then be convicted in respect of the same breach.

B. THE NEW CRIMINAL OFFENCE: (1) THE CONDUCT REQUIRED

2.03   The new s 42A(1) of the Family Law Act 1996 provides that 'A person who without reasonable excuse does anything that he is prohibited from doing by a non-molestation order is guilty of an offence.' It applies only to conduct on or after the commencement of the section.[3] A person guilty of an offence under this section is liable, on conviction on indictment, to imprisonment for a term not exceeding five years, or a fine, or both, or on summary conviction, to imprisonment for a term not exceeding twelve months,[4] or a fine not exceeding the statutory maximum or both.[5] The effect of making the maximum sentence five years is to make any breach of a non-molestation injunction an arrestable offence. Proceedings in respect of the offence are criminal not family proceedings.[6] If the respondent has a public funding certificate for the injunction, this will not cover the criminal proceedings for breach.

2.04   The first ingredient of the offence is that the person has done something that he is prohibited from doing by a non-molestation order. A non-molestation order is defined by s 42 of the Family Law Act 1996 as

an order containing either or both of the following provisions—
(a) provision prohibiting a person ('the respondent') from molesting another person who is associated with the respondent;[7]
(b) provision prohibiting the respondent from molesting a relevant child.

By s 42(6), a non-molestation order may be expressed so as to refer to molestation in general, to particular acts of molestation, or to both.

2.05   A non-molestation order is often coupled with an occupation order. This

---

[3] Schedule 12(1) to the Act.
[4] Six months in relation to an offence committed before the commencement of s 154(1) of the Criminal Justice Act 2003 (Sch 12(1) to the Act).
[5] FLA 1996, s 42A(5).
[6] FLA 1996, s 42A(6).
[7] Associated persons are defined in ss 62(3)–(6) and 63(1) of FLA 1996. The Act amends the definitions to include first cousins (Sch 10) and those who have or have had an intimate personal relationship with each other which is or was of significant duration (s 4). 'Cohabitants' now includes same-sex couples (s 3).

includes an order prohibiting the respondent from returning to the home, or excluding him from a defined area around the home. The Act does not make it a criminal offence to breach an occupation order. Such orders are made under other sections of the Family Law Act 1996,[8] and not s 42. Sometimes non-molestation orders are currently drafted so that the prohibited acts of molestation include returning to the home. It is arguable that this practice should cease, since it will now have the effect of making criminal that which Parliament has decided should not be a criminal offence. Occupation orders will continue to be enforced by committal, and a power of arrest may be attached to them. As to some of the consequences of this, see paras 2.59 to 2.63 below.

There is no statutory definition of molestation, and it is not an easy word to **2.06** define. In *Vaughan v Vaughan*[9] the court approved the definition in the *Shorter Oxford Dictionary*: 'To cause trouble; to vex; to annoy: to put to inconvenience'. In *Davis v Johnson*,[10] it was said by Lord Salmon to include acts and threats of violence and 'a multitude of other things'. It is not limited to behaviour which is itself tortious or otherwise unlawful.[11] In *Johnson v Walton*,[12] it was said that molestation was any conduct which causes such a degree of intentional harassment as calls for the intervention of the court.

It follows that molestation includes not only actual or threatened physical **2.07** violence, but also conduct which may not in itself be criminal or otherwise unlawful. One of a series of amendments that was proposed during the passage of the bill, was to define domestic violence and then substitute for 'does anything' the words 'commits an act of domestic violence'.[13] The Government opposed the amendments. The debates in committee show that there was considerable difficulty in defining domestic violence in a way that was both comprehensive and workable, and it appears that no satisfactory definition could be agreed. The change would also have produced a narrower offence than the Government's definition which survives in the Act.

One immediate difficulty is that, whilst for lawyers and the courts 'non- **2.08** molestation order' is a convenient shorthand phrase, 'molestation' and 'molesting' are not widely used or understood words in everyday speech. When they are used, it tends to be in the context of sexual molestation, especially against children. The average respondent, served with an order preventing him from 'molesting' his partner and children, may genuinely not understand, unless he is

---

[8] Sections 33(3), 35(5), 36(4), or 38(3), depending on the legal basis upon which the home is occupied.

[9] [1973] 1 WLR 1159, CA.

[10] [1979] AC 264, HL, 341.

[11] *Burris v Azadani* [1995] 1 WLR 1372, CA.

[12] [1990] 1 FLR 350, CA.

[13] HC Standing Committee E *Hansard*, col 18 (22 June 2004) *per* Under-Secretary of State for the Home Office, Paul Goggins. The debate on the definition of domestic violence begins at col 8. A similar debate took place in the House of Lords in the Grand Committee on the Bill, *Hansard* Vol 656, cols GC207–19 (19 January 2004).

legally represented, that that means he may not ring her up with angry and abusive demands to know why she has taken him to court.

2.09   Non-molestation orders are therefore commonly drawn to restrain the respondent from specific acts of behaviour, some of which are already criminal offences and others which are not. Thus, a respondent may be restrained from using or threatening violence against the applicant, or he may be ordered not to communicate with her at all, except through her solicitor. At present, there tends to be a standard basic formula for such orders, with additional restraints included if the need for them is established by the evidence. It remains to be seen whether the creation of a criminal offence means that the courts will be more careful to include in the non-molestation order only conduct that the evidence shows the respondent has committed or is likely to commit. What is apparent is that the drafting of non-molestation orders will require even greater care in the future than it does at present, so that it will be quite clear to the respondent on the face of the order what he may or may not do.

2.10   During the course of the debates on the bill, the Government made it clear that it was not its intention, in creating a criminal sanction for breach of a non-molestation order, to raise the standard of proof required for the making of a non-molestation order to the criminal one.[14]

2.11   There may be another consequence of creating the criminal offence. In *Wookey v Wookey, Re S (a minor)*,[15] the Court of Appeal considered whether or not an order should be made either against a minor or where the respondent was incapable within the *M'Naughten* rules of understanding what he was doing or that it was wrong. The court held that an order should not be made in those circumstances. In the case of a patient, the respondent's condition would be a complete defence to an application to commit. The order would not operate on his mind to affect his conduct, and so he would not be capable of complying with it. Similarly, the court considered that an injunction should not have been made against a boy of 16. Under the restrictions on custody then in force for juveniles, a court could only commit to prison a juvenile who had attained the age of 17. Since the court could not enforce the order against a 15-year-old by committing him to prison, the court held that the order should not have been made. The effect of criminalizing the behaviour is that the court now has a much greater range of sanctions open to it than imprisonment. The rationale for not making an order against a 15-year-old can no longer stand. The position is different in relation to a patient. There a balance has to be struck between laying open to criminal sanction someone who is incapable of regulating his conduct in accordance with the order, and the wider powers which the criminal courts have to deal with those who are unfit to plead or have a defence of insanity (see s 24 of the 2004 Act and Chapter 9).

---

[14] Standing Committee, see n 13 above, col 27 *per* the Under-Secretary of State for the Home Office, P Goggins.
[15] [1991] Fam 121, CA.

If the order prohibits behaviour which is a criminal offence, such as assault, **2.12** and uses that technical term, presumably it imports the technicalities of the offence in deciding whether the respondent has done something which he is prohibited from doing by the order. For example, if the respondent was acting in self-defence, he would be entitled to be acquitted because he was not guilty of assault, the conduct prohibited by the non-molestation order. Similarly, the respondent who threatens to hit his wife 'if I ever see you with another man' is not making a threat of immediate personal violence to her. He has not therefore committed an assault, although he may be in breach of other parts of the order.

On the face of it, the offence is committed only if the person *does* something **2.13** that he is prohibited from doing by the non-molestation order. Because the offence is triable on indictment, however, the Criminal Attempts Act 1981 applies to the offence. If the respondent with intent to commit the offence, does an act which is more than merely preparatory to the commission of the offence, he is guilty of attempting to commit the offence, and liable to the same punishment. If the non-molestation order restrains the respondent in terms from 'doing or attempting to do' specific acts, then the respondent who made an attempt would be doing something prohibited by the order, and therefore would commit the full offence.

The expression 'is prohibited' implies that the respondent is prohibited by a **2.14** current order. If the respondent was prohibited for a fixed length of time, and that time has expired by the date of the act complained of, it is not a criminal offence, any more than it could be punished by committal.

The offence is only committed by breach of a non-molestation order. It does **2.15** not apply to the breach of an undertaking in similar terms.

C. THE NEW CRIMINAL OFFENCE: (2) THE NECESSARY MENTAL ELEMENT

There is nothing to suggest that this is intended to be an offence of strict **2.16** liability. The prosecution will need to show that the defendant intended to commit the act which was prohibited by the order, or that he was reckless whether he committed it or not, on general criminal principles. The difficult area is whether they also need to prove that he knew that what he was doing was in breach of a non-molestation order.

Under the existing law, the general rule is that before he can be punished for **2.17** contempt of court in respect of any breach of a non-molestation order, a respondent has to be served with a copy of the order, or have been present when it was made, so that he is aware of both the existence of the order and its terms. The High Court has inherent jurisdiction to make the order ex parte, ie without the respondent being given notice of the application, but the power is rarely exercised.[16] The County Court and the Family Proceedings Court have power to dispense with service of the order and the notice of application for committal, if the court thinks it is just to do so.[17] One such circumstance is if there is clear evidence that the respondent is deliberately avoiding service of the order. That position is significantly changed in relation to the new criminal offence. It is also different depending on whether the order was made without notice to the respondent, or at a hearing of which he has been given notice.

2.18   The new s 42A(2) of the Family Law Act 1996 provides that:

In the case of a non-molestation order made by virtue of section 45(1), a person can be guilty of an offence under this section only in respect of conduct engaged in at a time when he was aware of the existence of the order.

Section 45(1) deals with the court's power to make an ex parte non-molestation order, ie without the respondent being given notice of the application. There is no corresponding provision once there has been a hearing on notice.

2.19   In family proceedings, where the court makes an order under s 45(1), a copy of the order, together with a copy of the application and of the sworn statement in support, have to be served by the applicant on the respondent personally.[18] The criminal offence is committed not only by a respondent who has been served with a copy of the order, but by a person who is aware of the existence of the order, even though he has not been served with it. He has only to be aware of the existence of the order, not its terms.

2.20   There was much debate during the committee stages in both Houses of Parliament as to whether this should be amended so that the respondent was required to know not only of the existence of an order, but also its terms.[19] There was concern that a person could be convicted of doing something which he is prohibited from doing by an order when he did not know exactly what he was not meant to do. The reason why the amendment was not accepted was because of the problems posed by the respondent who evades service of the order made without notice. It was considered undesirable that a respondent, who was well aware that there was an order in existence, and acted in breach of it, should escape criminal liability by claiming that he did not know what the terms of it were.

2.21   That argument obviously has force where the breach alleged is already a criminal offence, such as an assault or threat of physical violence. Whether it is quite so compelling in relation to behaviour which is not, such as contacting the

---

[16] *Warwick Corporation v Russell* [1964] 1 WLR 613; *Re G (wardship) (jurisdiction: power of arrest)* (1983) 4 FLR 538, CA.

[17] CCR, r 29(1)(7) (which still applies in family proceedings) and FPC(MP)R 1991, r 20(8) and (12).

[18] Under r 3.9(2) of the Family Proceedings Rules 1991 or r 12A(2) of the FPC(MP)R 1991.

[19] HC Standing Committee E *Hansard*, cols 30 and 34 (22 June 2004); House of Lords in the Grand Committee on the Bill, *Hansard*, cols GC224 onwards (19 January 2004).

applicant other than through her solicitors, is more doubtful. The provision applies to the respondent who is not evading service, as well as the one who is.

On the face of it, the offence covers awareness of the existence of the order **2.22** from any source, not just by service or attempted service of the order. If an order has in fact been made, the fact that the respondent did not believe the person who told him of it, for example, his mother-in-law who disliked him, would not be a defence. Nor would the fact that the information came to the respondent at second or third hand, or in other circumstances which made the information appear unreliable.

Such awareness can give rise to criminal liability for a breach of the non- **2.23** molestation order, however misleading the information given about its contents. For example, a father who has recently left the home, and has not been served with an order made without notice, telephones his partner to make arrangements to see the children. During the conversation, she tells him that she has been to court that morning and got an order to stop him hitting her. She says that her solicitor has advised her not to let him see the children until the matter has gone back to court. In fact the non-molestation order also prohibits him from abusing or threatening her. He calls her a 'bitch' and says that if she tries to stop him seeing the children, he will make her sorry. Subject to any argument about whether he has a reasonable excuse (see below), the father has committed the offence.

Where the court makes an order under s 45(1) of the Family Law Act 1996, it **2.24** must afford the respondent an opportunity to make representations relating to the order as soon as just and convenient at a full hearing: s 45(3). Usually the respondent will be served with notice of that hearing at the same time as he is served with the order made without notice. If the respondent has been served with notice of the full hearing, he has the opportunity to attend it. Obviously, if the respondent attends that hearing, and a fresh order is made, he will know of the existence of the order and what its terms are. If he does not attend, because he is deliberately evading service, the court can make a fresh ex parte order for a limited period: s 45(2)(c). That order will also have to be served or its existence brought to the respondent's attention before he can be guilty of the offence under s 42A, as discussed above.

Not all non-molestation orders are made following an ex parte order. The **2.25** applicant can simply issue an application for the order, giving the respondent not less than two days' notice of the hearing. The application for a non-molestation order has to be served personally.[20] If the respondent has been served with notice of the full hearing, but chooses not to attend, or is unable to do so, an order may be made in his absence. The notice of the hearing tells him that.

A non-molestation order made following the giving of notice, will be an order **2.26**

---

[20] FPR 1991, r 3.8(6) and FPC(MP)R 1991, r 3A(2).

made under s 42 of the Family Law Act 1996, not s 45(1). Accordingly, s 42A(2) does not apply, and the respondent will commit the offence if he does anything which he is prohibited by the order from doing, even though he is unaware of the existence of the order or of its terms. The rules in family proceedings require the respondent to be served personally with an order made at the full hearing.[21] Unless the court dispensed with service, the order could not be enforced by committal (see para 2.17 above). The effect of this provision is that even if he is never served with the order made at the full hearing, a respondent can commit the criminal offence.

2.27 For the respondent in this example, this may not be too unfair. Because he has been served with notice of the order that the applicant was asking the court to make, the respondent will have a general idea of the contents of the order made at the full hearing. There will be a problem if the order made is in different terms from the notice of application, or includes a provision in respect of which no notice was given. Subject to the argument that he had a reasonable excuse (see below), the respondent can be found guilty even though he did not know that he had been prohibited from behaving in the way he did.

2.28 When the proceedings are begun by application, it will generally be clear whether the order was made under s 42 or s 45(1) of the Family Law Act 1996. In future, it may be that the order should state on its face whether it is made under s 45(1) or s 42, so that the police arresting someone can be clear whether or not s 42A(2) applies.

2.29 It may not be so clear if the court exercises the power it has under s 42(2)(b) to make a non-molestation order in any family proceedings to which the respondent is a party, even though no application has been made. It may do so if it considers that the order should be made for the benefit of any other party to the proceedings or any relevant child. The respondent only has to be a party to the proceedings, for example, a residence or contact application, he does not have to be actually present for the court to exercise this power.

2.30 This provision sits uneasily with s 45(1), which states:

> The court may in any case where it considers it just and convenient to do so, make an occupation order or a non-molestation order even though the respondent has not been given such notice of the proceedings as would be required by rules of court.

That presupposes the issue of proceedings in respect of which notice is required to be given. Under s 42(2)(b), the court may make the order without an application being issued. It may therefore be arguable that there are no proceedings in respect of which the respondent should have been given notice, and therefore an order made under s 42(2)(b) in the absence of the respondent is not made under s 45(1), but under a free-standing power, arising in the specific circumstances described. The Act provides that the definition of 'the applicant'

---

[21] FPR 1991, r 3.8(4) and FPC(MP)R 1991, r 12A(5).

includes a person for whose benefit such an order is made,[22] but it does not deem an application to have been made. At present, the point has no significance, since the respondent would usually have to be served with either order before he could be committed to prison for any breach. The difficulty is that the new s 42A(2) defence refers specifically to an order made under s 45(1), and not simply to an ex parte order. This gives rise to the possibility that a person may break the order, without being aware of its existence, and commit the offence.

Where an order is made under s 42(2)(b) there may also be a real evidential **2.31** difficulty in deciding whether the respondent was or was not aware of the making of the order or whether it was in effect an ex parte order. It will not necessarily be clear on the face of the order. Suppose in a contested application for contact, the judge towards the end of his judgment, indicates that he intends to make an order only for very limited contact. The father angrily threatens the mother and storms out of court. Because of that, the judge makes a non-molestation order under s 42(2)(b). Alternatively, suppose that at the same point in the judgment the judge had said he was concerned about the evidence he had heard of arguments at the contact handovers and intended to make orders to put a stop to it. The father is distressed by not getting more contact, leaves the court in tears, and goes home without waiting for the outcome. In each case the orders made include an order under s 42(2)(b). In each example, are those ex parte orders or not? Does it make a difference to the nature of either order if the respondent was legally represented and his representative remained in court after he left? Suppose the representative made it clear that he was without instructions to argue the point?

A further difficulty is that none of this is going to be apparent to the police **2.32** officer arresting the respondent for breach of the order. Moreover, if similar problems arose in committal proceedings in the same court, the judge would accept an account of what happened from the legal representatives. The fact that the offence is being dealt with as a crime means that they may well have to give witness statements and attend the hearing to give evidence.

D. THE NEW CRIMINAL OFFENCE: (3) 'WITHOUT REASONABLE EXCUSE'

The person has to act 'without reasonable excuse'. It remains to be seen how **2.33** that will be interpreted, and the following paragraphs give no more than tentative suggestions. The phrase appears in other criminal offences, where it is distinct from the mental element of the offence. But for the reasonable excuse, the person has committed both the act required for the offence, and has the necessary intent. For example, it is an offence under s 1(1) of the Prevention of Crime

---

[22] FLA 1996, para 42(4B) inserted by Sch 10, para 36 to the Act.

Act 1953 for someone to have in his possession an offensive weapon in a public place without lawful authority or reasonable excuse. The prosecution have to show that the defendant knowingly had an offensive weapon in his possession in a public place. The defendant has the evidential burden of establishing that he had a reasonable excuse, for example, that he was carrying it because he was in fear of an imminent attack or was going to a fancy dress party as a policeman, carrying a truncheon. The prosecution then have to disprove it to the required criminal standard.

2.34   In the debate on the proposal to amend the offence from 'does anything' to 'commits an act of domestic violence' (see para 2.07 above) the Government further objected to the amendment because it implied that there could be a reasonable excuse for an act of domestic violence, and the Government wished to send a clear message that there was none.[23]

2.35   If that approach is followed through, it is unlikely that any of the classic excuses or justifications for domestic violence, and particularly physical violence, will be accepted as reasonable excuse. 'Finding her with another man' or 'believing she has another man'; other 'provocation' such as taunts, or 'not letting him see the children'; or 'slapping her face when she became hysterical' will pass into history. Whether, and to what extent, any of them will be accepted as mitigation of the penalty, remains to be seen.

2.36   More difficult is the issue of self-defence. As suggested above (para 2.12), if the order forbids the respondent from assaulting the applicant, the respondent would have a defence if he acted in self-defence. If, instead of using the word assault, the order says that the respondent is forbidden to 'to use or threaten violence' against the applicant, which is substantially the same behaviour, does he have a reasonable excuse? In those cases where the evidence would support self-defence as a defence to assault, it is suggested that it would be anomalous if the defence were not also available in these circumstances, albeit by a different route.

2.37   During the debates on the bill, there was some discussion about what might be a reasonable excuse. In particular, during the debate about whether the respondent should know of the terms or existence of the order, it was clearly envisaged that some respondents who were not aware that what they had done was prohibited by a non-molestation order, would be able to claim that they had a reasonable excuse for being in breach of it. If the respondent was unable to find out the terms of the order for good reason, for example because he was blind or had other disability or literacy problems, it was suggested that this would be a reasonable excuse.[24] Whether the respondent who is misled about the contents of an order (para 2.23 above) or who does not attend the full hearing for good reason and is unaware of changes made to the terms of the application

---

[23] HC Standing Committee E *Hansard*, col 20 (22 June 2004).
[24] ibid, col 36 *per* P Goggins.

(para 2.27 above) would be included within the ambit of that exception remains to be seen.

It was also suggested that a parent who was ordered not to telephone, but **2.38** heard that his child had been injured at school and rang up to enquire about it would have a reasonable excuse.[25] This presumably would apply to telephoning in other emergency situations as well.

Another area which may prove fertile is the fairly common situation where the **2.39** applicant herself permits conduct which the non-molestation order prohibits. For example, suppose the order prevents the respondent from telephoning the applicant. He does so, to make arrangements for contact. It suits her to do this, and she makes no complaint. This continues for some weeks, during which he is not abusive or threatening and does not try to put pressure on her in relation to the contact arrangements. Then, during one such call, he takes exception to something in a letter he has received that morning from her solicitors and there is an angry exchange of words. He does not threaten her. She decides to report him to the police. Does he have a reasonable excuse for telephoning, or does it only go to mitigation?

E. THE NEW CRIMINAL OFFENCE: (4) WHO CAN COMMIT THE OFFENCE?

The Act provides that the offence is committed by a person who does any- **2.40** thing that he is prohibited from doing by a non-molestation order. On the face of it, that is the person against whom the order is made. This will include some relatives who are 'associated persons' within the Act.[26] Non-molestation orders may be made, exceptionally, against other third parties, provided that they have had the opportunity to be joined in the proceedings and to make representations.[27]

Non-molestation orders are commonly drawn to prevent the respondent from **2.41** doing any of the prohibited acts himself or from instructing, encouraging, or in any way suggesting that any other person should do so. Such third parties are not directly prohibited from doing any of the acts that the non-molestation order prohibits. If, however, a third party is served with a copy of the order, and assists the respondent in breaking the order, he too is liable for contempt of court.[28]

On general criminal principles, there is no reason why someone who aids or **2.42** abets the respondent in breaking the non-molestation order should not also be

---

[25] ibid, col 20 *per* V Baird.
[26] FLA 1996, s 62(3)–(6).
[27] *Kalsi v Kalsi* [1992] 1 FLR 511, CA and RSC Ord 45, r 9 which still applies in family proceedings.
[28] *Elliott v Klinger* [1967] 1 WLR 1165; *Thorne RDC v Bunting (No 2)* [1972] 3 All ER 1084, CA.

guilty of the offence as a secondary party. The question of whether that person needs to know that the respondent's conduct is in breach of a non-molestation order may depend upon whether or not the conduct itself is a criminal offence. A person who helps his friend beat up that friend's former partner, may not be able to defend his conduct by saying he did not know it was in breach of a court order. In all probability a third party in those circumstances would be charged as a principal with assault. If, on the other hand, he lends his mobile phone to his friend, who then makes an abusive telephone call to his former partner, it could be argued that he ought not to be guilty of the offence unless he knew that that action was prohibited by the non-molestation order.

F. THE NEW CRIMINAL OFFENCE: (5) DOUBLE JEOPARDY

2.43 The new s 42A(3) and (4) provide that where a person is convicted of an offence under this section in respect of any conduct, that conduct is not punishable as a contempt of court. Similarly, a person cannot be convicted of an offence under this section in respect of any conduct which has been punished as a contempt of court.

2.44 These subsections provide a defence only where there has been a conviction or the defendant has been punished for contempt. Thus, if the defendant has been prosecuted but acquitted, an application may still be made for his committal, particularly if some evidence was excluded from the criminal trial which is admissible in the civil proceedings. More difficult is the case where the judge considered the application for contempt but decided it was not proved, or decided not to punish for the contempt but to redraw the injunction in stricter terms. If the defendant were then to be prosecuted on the same facts, these provisions would not provide a defence. This is likely to happen if the order does not make clear on its face the facts on which the application for committal was based.

G. THE NEW CRIMINAL OFFENCE: (6) SOME PRACTICALITIES

1. Using Evidence from the Family Proceedings

2.45 Evidence in support of an application for a non-molestation order takes the form of an affidavit or affirmation. The maker swears or affirms that the contents of the document are true. It is perjury if it is untrue. The maker may give evidence at an oral hearing. If so, the affidavit or affirmation will usually stand as the evidence in chief, and the oral evidence will be cross-examination on it. Most County Courts now have provision for mechanical recording of oral evidence, as does the High Court. Otherwise, the record is the judge's note, supplemented by any record kept by the parties' representatives. In the Family

Proceedings Court a note of the evidence is kept by the justices' clerk[29] and a record of the proceedings as well as the order itself is maintained.[30]

Applications for non-molestation injunctions are heard in chambers, unless 2.46 the court directs otherwise.[31] Copies of documents, including affidavits, on the court file can be obtained by those who are not parties to the proceedings only with leave of the district judge in the High Court or county court or the justices' clerk in the Family Proceedings Court.[32] Despite this, the disclosure to a third party of the evidence, by a party to the family proceedings is not contempt of court.[33] This means that it is permissible for either the victim or the accused to disclose this material to the police. The position is different if the injunction is made in proceedings related to a child. Then it is a contempt of court for anyone, including the parties, to publish information relating to the proceedings, other than details of the order.[34] Details of the evidence may only be disclosed to a third party, including the police, with the permission of the court.

The application for disclosure is made in the family proceedings to the court 2.47 dealing with those proceedings. The application should be made in writing and served on the parties to the non-molestation application. The principles, which have been applied in cases involving children, require a balance to be struck between the need to encourage frankness and the maintenance of confidentiality on the one hand and the need to ensure a fair trial for a person accused of a criminal offence on the other.

As this clearly creates a more onerous procedure than the present position, it 2.48 may be that the rules, which are not available at the time of writing, will be amended to allow the use of the parties' affidavits in criminal proceedings for breach of the order, without the need for leave.

2. Conflicts of Interest

Where the defendant is already legally represented, his solicitor in the family 2.49 proceedings may or may not be willing to act for him in the criminal case. If he needs a duty solicitor and that person is from a firm with a family department, there will need to be a system in place for checking out of hours whether the firm is already acting for the applicant.

---

[29] FPC(MP)R 1991, r 11.
[30] FPC(MP)R 1991, r 12A.
[31] FPR 1991, r 3.9(1). In the Family Proceedings Court, s 69(2) of the MCA1980 limits those who may be present at a hearing.
[32] FPR 1991, r 10.20(3); FPC(MP)R 1991, r 14.
[33] *Clibbery v Allen* [2002] Fam 261, CA.
[34] Administration of Justice Act 1960, s 12.

H. CHANGES TO FAMILY PROCEEDINGS

2.50 The Act makes no changes to the substantive law as to what is or is not domestic violence. Section 1 of the Act inserts a new s 42A into the Family Law Act 1996 which makes the breach of a non-molestation order, without reasonable excuse, a criminal offence. It is an arrestable offence, carrying a sentence of up to five years' imprisonment. It will no longer be possible to attach a power of arrest to a non-molestation order.[35] It will still be possible to enforce such an order by an application for committal, but the present alternative procedure whereby someone arrested under a power of arrest is brought to a family court by the police to be dealt with, will cease to be available.

1. Points to Note when Applying for or Opposing a Non-molestation Injunction

2.51 The new offence is breach of a non-molestation order. It will not be a criminal offence to breach an undertaking. Section 46 of the Family Law Act 1996 is amended[36] by inserting a new s 46(3A) which provides:

The court shall not accept an undertaking under subsection (1) instead of making a non-molestation order in any case where it appears to the court that—

(a) the respondent has used or threatened violence against the applicant or relevant child; and

(b) for the protection of the applicant or child it is necessary to make a non-molestation order so that any breach may be punishable under section 42A.

There are consequential amendments to s 46(4) which deals with the enforcement of undertakings. These will continue to be enforceable by committal.

2.52 This goes further than the similar requirement which currently exists in relation to a power of arrest.[37] The power of arrest is an infringement of liberty, but it is only an alternative means of bringing the respondent before a court so that the alleged breach may be dealt with. Now the decision whether or not to accept an undertaking is about whether the respondent's future behaviour is to be a serious criminal offence or not. It is suggested that in those circumstances, if the application alleges the use or threat of violence, it is not acceptable for public funding to be refused on the basis that the respondent does not need legal representation, as he can go along and give an undertaking. The judge may refuse to accept his offer. If the respondent disputes the allegations, there can only properly be a non-molestation order if the judge, following a hearing, makes the findings to justify it, or if the parties agree the facts which justify the making of an order. For an unrepresented party to be pressured into agreeing to

---

[35] Schedule 10 to the Act, para 38.
[36] Schedule 10 to the Act, para 37(3).
[37] FLA 1996, s 46(3).

an order which puts him at risk of a criminal conviction and up to five years' imprisonment without fully appreciating the implications of doing so, is simply unacceptable.

It will not be a criminal offence to breach an occupation order, which includes **2.53** an order that the respondent is not to return to the home. It will continue to be possible to attach a power of arrest to an occupation order on the same basis as at present,[38] and such an order will continue to be enforceable by committal. The court, in considering whether to make an occupation order shall also consider whether to make a non-molestation order under s 42(2)(b) of the Family Law Act 1996,[39] if no application for such an order has been made.

There are currently pilot schemes in a few magistrates' courts to have a single **2.54** court dealing with both the criminal and family aspects of breach of an injunction. Whether or not they are successful remains to be seen. What seems probable is that as a result of the changes to enforcement, there will be cases that leave the victim of domestic violence either having to deal with different aspects of the problem in two different courts, or falling between the two systems. Part of the task of the family practitioner will be to minimize the risk of this happening by ensuring that the order is soundly based and properly drawn up.

Because it will give rise to a criminal sanction, and may be dealt with by those **2.55** who are not familiar with the way in which non-molestation orders are granted, it will be more important than it is now to ensure that it is clear on the face of the order:

- whether it was granted without notice under s 45(1) of the Family Law Act 1996 or not;
- whether the respondent was present when it was made;
- precisely what behaviour is prohibited by the order; and
- what affidavits or oral evidence were relied upon to grant it.

During the course of the debates on the bill, the Government made it clear **2.56** that it was not its intention, in creating a criminal sanction for breach of a non-molestation order, to raise the standard of proof required for the making of a non-molestation order to the criminal one.[40] But it is suggested that it will be important to ensure that the evidence justifies the making of the prohibitions in the order. The practice in some courts of drafting non-molestation orders so that the prohibited acts of molestation include returning to the home, is probably unsustainable. It will now have the effect of making criminal that which Parliament has clearly decided should not be a criminal offence.

As suggested in para 2.11 above, there may be another consequence of **2.57**

---

[38] FLA 1996, s 47.
[39] FLA 1996, s 42(4A) inserted by Sch 10 to the Act, para 36.
[40] HC Standing Committee E (22 June 2004) *Hansard*, col 27 *per* Under-Secretary of State for the Home Office, P Goggins.

creating the criminal offence. In *Wookey v Wookey, Re S (a minor)*,[41] the Court of Appeal considered whether or not an order should be made either against a minor or where the respondent was incapable within the *M'Naughten* rules of understanding what he was doing or that it was wrong. The court held that an order should not be made in those circumstances. Similarly, the court considered that an injunction should not have been made against a boy of 16. Under the restrictions on custody then in force for juveniles, a court could only commit to prison a juvenile who had attained the age of 17. Since the court could not enforce the order against a 15-year-old by committing him to prison, the court held that the order should not have been made. The effect of criminalizing the behaviour is that the court now has a much greater range of sanctions open to it than imprisonment. The rationale for not making an order against a 15-year-old can no longer stand. The position is different in relation to a patient. There a balance has to be struck between laying open to criminal sanction someone who is incapable of regulating his conduct in accordance with the order, and the wider powers which the criminal courts have to deal with those who are unfit to plead or have a defence of insanity (see s 24 of the Domestic Violence, Crime and Victims Act 2004 and Chapter 9).

2.58 Service of the order remains important. It will be a defence to a charge of breaching a non-molestation order that it was made ex parte under s 45(1) of the Act and the respondent was unaware of its existence.[42] It will also be important to ensure that the application for the injunction to be heard on the return date accurately sets out all the orders that the applicant is asking for. If the respondent does not attend the full hearing, he may be found guilty of breach of an order even though he did not know that he had been prohibited from behaving in the way he did. It is suggested that there may be a problem if the order made is in different terms from the notice of application, or includes a provision in respect of which no notice was given. The respondent may be able to argue that he had a reasonable excuse for being in breach of the order, if it is substantially different from the one he was informed would be made.

2.59 As discussed above,[43] there may be particular problems in determining whether an order has been made ex parte under s 45(1) where the court makes its order under s 42(2)(b) of the Family Law Act 1996. This gives the court the power to make a non-molestation order in family proceedings to which the respondent is a party where it considers that the order should be made for the benefit of any other party or a relevant child, even though no application has been made. With this type of order there may also be a real evidential difficulty in deciding whether the respondent was or was not aware of the making of it. It will be important for it to be clearly stated on the face of the order whether or not the respondent or his legal representative was present when it was made.

---

[41] [1991] Fam 121.
[42] FLA 1996, s 42A(2).
[43] See para 2.31 above.

2. Points on Enforcement

The effect of the statutory provisions is that the decision how to enforce the **2.60** non-molestation order will in most cases be taken out of the hands of the victim and placed in the hands of the police. The respondent will be arrested and charged. He may or may not be bailed subject to conditions. If he disputes the breaches, she will have to give oral evidence in a criminal court, without the support of her legal representative's presence. The defendant may make allegations about what happened in the injunction proceedings, which her legal representative would know were untrue, but she is unable to refute.

Although it is clearly intended that the power to apply for committal in **2.61** respect of a breach of a non-molestation order will continue alongside the new offence, it seems likely that it will only be used where the police have decided not to charge. The applicant is unlikely to have the requisite knowledge to assert that, in her case, it would be sensible for all the matters to be dealt with in the family court. Take the case where, in addition to the non-molestation order, the respondent is ordered not to return to the home, except for the purpose of collecting the children for agreed contact and returning them afterwards. The applicant cancels contact twice, saying the children are unwell. On the third occasion, she says the children do not want to see him. He goes to the house and sees the children at an upstairs window. They wave to him. He knocks on the door and when the applicant opens it, there is a heated argument about why the children are not coming for contact. He is abusive, but not threatening.

Before the 2004 Act, all the breaches would be dealt with in a single committal **2.62** application. The court could, in addition, tighten up or extend the terms of the injunction and deal with the problems over contact. They would all be dealt with in the same court, on the same evidence, probably by the same judge who made the injunction, with the history readily available, and with the power to deal with all aspects of the problem, even if no applications had been made. In future, the applicant is unlikely to be in a position to choose to go down that route. Unless there is a unified court, the court dealing with the criminal offence will not be able to modify the terms of the non-molestation order. The applicant will have to deal separately with enforcement proceedings in the appropriate family court for breach of the occupation order and to vary the contact order.

The fact that these cases are dealt with in different courts will have other **2.63** consequences. Where the respondent is arrested and charged with breach of the non-molestation order and is also arrested under a power of arrest for being in breach of an occupation order, the police may be trying to bring the respondent before two different courts within twenty-four hours to be dealt with. If they are near one another that may be feasible. If they are in different parts of the country, it may not be. Proceedings in respect of the offence under s 42A are criminal, not family, proceedings.[44] If the respondent has a public funding

---

[44] FLA 1996, s 42A(6).

certificate for the injunction, this will not cover the criminal proceedings for breach.

2.64   A party to injunction proceedings which do not relate to children is not prevented from disclosing the evidence to a third party.[45] Unless the rules are changed, copies of documents, including affidavits, on the court file can only be obtained by someone who is not a party with leave of the district judge in the High Court or County Court.[46] Where the application relates to children, the disclosure to a third party, including a police officer, of such material, without leave, is contempt of court. This is the case even if the disclosure is made by a party to the family proceedings who is entitled to have possession of the document.

2.65   The new s 42A(3) and (4) provide that where a person is convicted of an offence under this section in respect of any conduct, that conduct is not punishable as a contempt of court. Similarly, a person cannot be convicted of an offence under this section in respect of any conduct which has been punished as a contempt of court. These subsections provide a defence only where there has been a conviction or the respondent has been punished for contempt. It will be important for the order to make clear on its face the facts on which the order for committal was based. If the defendant has been prosecuted but acquitted, an application may still be made for his committal, particularly if some evidence was excluded from the criminal trial which is admissible in the family proceedings.

3. Other Substantive Changes Made to Part IV of the Family Law Act 1996

2.66 There is no change in this Act to the statutory provisions regarding the way in which issues of domestic violence are to be dealt with in relation to residence and contact disputes.[47] The Act does not have any impact on the power given to a local authority under s 44A of the Children Act 1989 to apply for an exclusion requirement in an emergency protection order. Nor is there any change to the basic framework of occupation rights and the making of occupation orders.

2.67   The other main change is to extend the categories of those who have or can be given occupation rights in their home, so that they can apply to the court for an occupation order. The most publicized is the change to the definition of 'cohabitants' in s 62(1)A of the Family Law Act 1996 that gives those rights to same-sex couples. Cohabitation ceases to be 'living together as husband and wife'. Instead cohabitants are 'two persons who, although not married to each other, are living together as husband and wife or (if of the same sex) in an

---

[45] *Clibbery v Allan* [2002] Fam 261, CA.
[46] FPR 1991, r 10.20(3).
[47] The Adoption and Children Act 2002, s 120 modifies the definition of harm in s 31(9) of the Children Act 1989 by adding to the definition of 'impairment' 'including, for example, impairment suffered from seeing or hearing the ill-treatment of another.'

equivalent relationship'. There are consequential amendments to ss 36 and 38 and Sch 7 which substitute 'cohabit' for 'living together as husband and wife'.

Section 41 of the Family Law Act, which provided that where the court was **2.68** required to consider the nature of the parties' relationship, it was to have regard to the fact that they had not given each other the commitment involved in marriage is repealed.[48] Instead the court has to consider the nature of the relationship 'and in particular the level of commitment involved in it'.

The Act also changes the definition of 'associated persons' to include first **2.69** cousins and those who 'have or have had an intimate personal relationship with each other which is or was of significant duration'.[49] This brings within the definition those whose relationship, whilst intimate and of significant duration, has not led to cohabitation. The effect is to bring them within the scope of the Family Law Act rather than having to bring a civil action for assault. What duration will be regarded as significant remains to be seen.

---

[48] Section 2(1) of the Act.
[49] Schedule 10, para 41(3) and s 4.

3

CAUSING OR ALLOWING THE DEATH
OF A CHILD OR VULNERABLE ADULT

A. INTRODUCTION

This new offence hopes to be an answer, in part at least, to those situations **3.01** where a child or vulnerable adult has died as a result of an unlawful act in the care and protection of more than one person, but it is impossible despite sophisticated investigatory techniques to determine which of those carers was responsible for causing the death. Such situations have for many years caused widespread concern and are not, sadly, properly described as isolated cases.

According to research conducted by the National Society for the Prevention **3.02** of Cruelty to Children (NSPCC) Working Group who sought information from forty-three police forces throughout England and Wales, during the three-year period of the survey 'no less than 3 children under 10 years old a week were killed or suffered serious injury'. Of these children, just over half were under six months and 83% were under 2 years old. Of those investigations which reached a conclusion, 61% resulted in no prosecution at all.[1] The research of the NSPCC and the work of the Law Commission[2] were confined to reforms that would afford children greater protection but, as is apparent, the Government have extended the ambit of the offence to cover deaths of vulnerable adults.

---

[1] Findings of working group summarized by HH Judge Plumstead in papers for the NSPCC 'Which of you did it?' Conference in Cambridge, 12 November 2002.
[2] *Children: Their Non-accidental Death or Serious Injury (Criminal Trials), A Consultative Report* (Law Com No 279).

3.03   Currently where one person with the requisite *mens rea* kills a child or vulnerable adult that person, in the absence of any valid defence, is guilty of either murder or manslaughter. Anyone who assists or encourages such actions will be guilty as an accessory. Where it cannot be shown which of two suspects was directly responsible for causing the death and it cannot be shown that whoever was not directly responsible must have been guilty as an accomplice, then the law to date is such that there is no prima facie case against either, and both would have to be acquitted at the close of the prosecution case.

3.04   This was precisely the situation that arose in the case of *R v Lane and Lane*,[3] and the facts of that case provide a good illustration of why it has been felt necessary to create a new substantive offence where it is difficult if not impossible for the prosecution to prove either sole or joint responsibility for the death. A 22-month-old child died soon after admission to hospital from a fractured skull, sustained as a result of a violent blow the day before between 12:00pm and 8:00pm. The suspects were the child's mother and stepfather. During the relevant period both had been absent from home, leaving the child in the care of the other, and there had been periods when they were both in the house together. Both denied responsibility and both told lies to the police in interview. They were both charged with manslaughter and, following an unsuccessful submission of no case to answer, both were convicted. Their appeals were allowed and convictions quashed. The prosecution had been unable to show when exactly the injury was inflicted, by whom, or how many people were present. Neither parent had offered any explanation. After reviewing the evidence the Court of Appeal said:

> The evidence against each appellant taken separately, at the end of the prosecution case did not establish his or her presence at the time when the child was injured, whenever that was, or any participation. Neither had made any admission; both had denied taking part in any injury; both had told lies but lies which did not lead to the inference of that defendant's presence.

3.05   As a result of this and other similar cases the Law Commission[4] in its process of consultation soon discovered that there was a near universal consensus that this problem needed to be resolved although the offence as drafted departs significantly from the proposal of the Commission as detailed in their final report.[5] The offence is aimed at those situations where a death has occurred as a result of an unlawful act in a domestic setting and it is impossible for the authorities to assert with any certainty who is culpable in the traditional way. Culpability will now extend to those who were members of the same household and had frequent contact with the victim and at the time of the act which caused the

---

[3] (1985) 82 Cr App R 5.

[4] Law Commission, *Children: Their Non-accidental Death or Serious Injury (Criminal Trials), A Consultative Report* (Law Com No 279, April 2003).

[5] Law Com No 282 published in September 2003.

death there was a significant risk of physical harm being caused to the victim of which they knew or ought to have known.

An isolated act of violence with no background of like behaviour is not covered by this provision. Where, however, the prosecution are able to show that death resulted from an unlawful act in circumstances where there was a significant risk of serious physical harm being caused, then any member of the victim's household (who had frequent contact) is guilty of an offence if either they caused the death or they knew or ought to have known of the risk, failed to take reasonable steps to protect the victim, and the act which caused the death occurred in circumstances that were or ought to have been foreseen. Under this provision it is not necessary to prove whether a particular defendant caused the death or was guilty of failing to protect as fully defined. As the name of the offence makes clear, culpability attaches to someone who causes or allows the death of a child or vulnerable adult. **3.06**

Using the facts of *R v Lane and Lane* (above) as a backdrop, then, assuming there was at the time of death a background of violence and both parties had failed to protect as fully defined, both could be guilty of this new offence without it ever being established who caused the death. Although this situation is precisely the one the offence is designed to cover, it will give rise to difficulties and concerns over, for example, sentence where it is difficult to identify with any precision the extent of a particular defendant's culpability. A potential benefit, however, of this offence being added to the prosecutor's armoury is that when confronted with the threat of conviction on such a charge, carrying with it, as it does, a maximum penalty of fourteen years' imprisonment, a suspect is likely to be more willing to cooperate with investigators and give an account as to how the death occurred, thereby negating, to an extent at least, the unsavoury aspect of many cases where the interests of suspects and defendants alike are best served on occasion by giving the investigation team or court little or no help as to what has occurred. **3.07**

It is important to note that the offence is not limited to the *R v Lane and Lane* situation. It commonly happens at present that where a couple are charged in relation to the death of a child and the evidence does point to one rather than the other parent as the perpetrator, the other parent is charged with cruelty to a child under s 1 of the Children and Young Persons Act 1933. Such a parent could in future be charged with this offence. Indeed there is no need for more than one person to be charged. The offence can be committed by an adult acting alone. **3.08**

B. THE OFFENCE

For the purposes of this commentary it is useful to look at s 5 in two parts. The first, encompassing s 5(1)(a)–(c) inclusive, defines the circumstances in which and by whom an offence may be committed, whilst s 5(1)(d) concentrates **3.09** on the particular acts or omissions necessary to incur liability. The remaining subsections will be referred to as they arise in looking at s 5(1).

1. Circumstances in Which and by Whom an Offence may be Committed

3.10 Section 5(1) provides that a person ('D') is guilty of an offence if:

(a) a child or vulnerable adult (V) dies as a result of the unlawful act of a person who—
    (i) was a member of the same household as V, and
    (ii) had frequent contact with him,
(b) D was such a person at the time of the act,
(c) At that time there was a significant risk of serious physical harm being caused to V by the unlawful act of such a person, and
(d) Either D was the person whose act caused V's death or—
    (i) D was, or ought to have been, aware of the risk mentioned in paragraph (c),
    (ii) D failed to take such steps as he could reasonably have been expected to take to protect V from the risk, and
    (iii) The act occurred in circumstances of the kind that D foresaw or ought to have foreseen.

(a) *'A Child or Vulnerable Adult'*

3.11 The offence is victim specific and applies only to children, ie a person under the age of 16 (see s 5(6)), and, contrary to the recommendations of the Law Commission, vulnerable adults who have died as a result of an unlawful act. 'Vulnerable adult' means a person aged 16 or over whose ability to protect himself from violence, abuse, or neglect is significantly impaired through physical or mental disability or illness, through old age or otherwise: s 5(6). The Law Commission were reticent about including vulnerable adults in their proposed offence as there had been no consultation equivalent to that conducted in respect of children. In extending protection to 'vulnerable adults' Baroness Scotland of Asthal said:[6]

> The Government knew of at least one case where a vulnerable adult had died in domestic circumstances and the prosecution had been unable to prove which close family member had been responsible. The Government would be failing in its duty when faced with such cases if it did not take the opportunity to amend the law. As to the definition of vulnerable adult . . . This was a matter of common sense properly and safely left to the courts.

3.12 The definition is potentially far-reaching, protecting, it seems, any adult whose ability to protect himself is significantly impaired for whatever reason. It could include, it is submitted, a person who through years of abuse, both mental and physical, has lost the ability to protect himself without there being any obvious or outward signs of disability. It will be necessary, however, for the prosecution to prove the required degree of vulnerability to the satisfaction of a

---

[6] *Hansard*, HL Vol 656, col GC334 (21 January 2004).

jury. This may prove to be problematical, as perhaps in the above example, and will no doubt limit the scope of those who are afforded protection as a result.

(b) *'Dies as a Result of an Unlawful Act'*

Limiting the offence only to those cases where death has resulted signifies, **3.13** unusually, a more conservative approach by the Government than that proposed by the Law Commission. The latter recommended that the new offence should extend to cover cases resulting in 'serious injury' as well as death.

Death must result from an *'unlawful act'*. Section 5(6) provides as follows: **3.14**

For the purposes of this section an 'unlawful act' is one that:
(a) constitutes an offence, or
(b) would constitute an offence but for being the act of—
    (i) a person under the age of 10, or
    (ii) a person entitled to rely on the defence of insanity.

Paragraph (b) does not apply to an act of D.

The unlawful act must constitute an offence and by virtue of s 5(6) 'act' **3.15** includes a course of conduct and also includes omission. The Law Commission's proposed offence only applied where specified offences were committed. The new offence is not so limited and will apply where any unlawful act (or omission) results in death. Clearly no liability arises where death results because of an accident or for example as a result of cot death. Liability can also arise where the unlawful act is committed by a person under the age of criminal responsibility or someone who is legally insane at the relevant time although such person is not himself liable.

(c) *'Member of the Same Household'*

Both the defendant (D) and the person who committed the unlawful act **3.16** resulting in death (where they are not one and the same) are, under the terms of the new offence, to share a 'domestic connection' with the victim. Both have to have been 'members of the same household' as V and both are to have had 'frequent contact with him' in order for D to be found liable. An unlawful act committed by someone outside these definitions, for example a childminder, would not give rise to any prosecution for this offence. It is this requirement that gives the offence its domestic context. Where the prosecution are unable to prove that either D or the person whose unlawful act resulted in death falls within that definition then no liability can arise.

Section 5(4) provides that: **3.17**

(a) a person is to be regarded as a 'member' of a particular household, even if he does not live in that household, if he visits so often and for such periods of time that it is reasonable to regard him as a member of it;
(b) where V lived in different households at different times, 'the same household as V' refers to the household in which V was living at the time of the act that caused V's death.

The Law Commission did not envisage any problems with the concept of 'living in the same household'. It is used in Pt IV of the Family Law Act 1996, although there it is qualified by the proviso that it is 'otherwise than merely by reason of one of them being the other's employee, tenant, lodger or boarder': s 62(3)(c) of the Family Law Act 1996.

3.18 The Law Commission in their proposals rejected the need for a similar restriction on the basis that their draft bill included an additional requirement that a person must in any event have been 'responsible' for the child. They recommended that there should be a single concept of responsibility and it should have the same meaning as for the offence of child cruelty or neglect under s 1 of the Children and Young Persons Act 1933. The Government felt[7] the Law Commission's definition of who could commit the offence was too narrow, as it might exclude cases which should be caught, such as a violent boyfriend who was a frequent visitor.

3.19 Section 5 therefore does not restrict the offence by importing the concept of 'responsibility' for the victim as a determining factor in culpability. Consequently, the offence is potentially far-reaching in terms of who may be guilty, bringing within its ambit 'non family' members such as nannies and au pairs, and lodgers, assuming they have frequent contact with the victim, and therefore can reasonably be expected to be aware of any risk of harm. It is not even confined to those who sleep under the same roof as V.

3.20 Section 5(4)(a) is wide enough to allow the prosecution of a person who is not normally resident at the household concerned, assuming such person visits it so often and for such time that it is reasonable to regard him as a member of it. For example, a parent who works abroad on a regular basis or a sibling of the victim away at college. Indeed, because the definition contemplates that a person who has no legal responsibility for the child and who maintains another household may be considered part of V's household on the basis of the frequency of his visiting, it could include grandparents and other relatives, or even neighbours or friends of the family, if they visit often enough.

3.21 Section 5(4)(b) intends to deal with the not uncommon situation where V lived in different households at different times, for example, the not uncommon situation where a child V lives part of the time with mother and the remainder of time with the father. Section 5(4)(b), in assigning potential liability, invites focus on the 'household' in which V was living at the time of the act that caused death. Let us assume in our example that V died, as a result of an unlawful act, whilst he was living at the maternal home. Let us assume further that the father never visited that home and could not therefore be regarded as a member of that household. It may well be that the father was aware of a significant risk to V and failed to take any steps to protect him. It seems, however, that despite his failure he would not be liable under this section as he could not be regarded as 'a

---

[7] HL Vol 656, col GC347 (21 January 2004).

member of the same household' in which V was living at the time of his death. It may be that liability could be founded under the Children and Young Persons Act 1933 where culpability is ascribed to those 'responsible' for the child.

It is to be hoped that the concept of 'a member of the same household' will **3.22** not cause too many problems in practice. In most cases such a person will be easy to identify. Whether the phrase generates much litigation will depend in large part on the approach to the offence taken by the police and prosecuting authorities, and whom they investigate and prosecute. Where an issue arises as to whether a person is properly described as a 'member of the same household' this will be a question of fact for the jury to determine.

(d) 'Frequent Contact'

Not only must D be a member of the same household as V, he must also have **3.23** had frequent contact with him. The Act does not seek to define what is meant by 'frequent contact' with the victim. It was argued in Grand Committee in the House of Lords[8] that the absence of any definition meant the clause was 'fraught with difficulty'. Baroness Scotland indicated[9] that 'frequent contact and proximity to a child or vulnerable adult should lead to responsibility, whether or not the person wished to have that responsibility'. In the absence of any definition it is difficult to determine how the courts will interpret 'frequent' or indeed the nature of the contact required. A lodger properly described as a member of the household who has contact in the sense of daily sightings, saying hello and goodbye, for example, but without spending significant time with the victim, is potentially liable. Again it will be a question of fact and degree for the jury to determine and of course it will be necessary to show by virtue of s 5(1)(d)(i) that a defendant was or ought to have been aware of the risk of harm which cannot be divorced from the nature and degree of contact required.

The extent to which this phrase is litigated will, it is submitted, depend on the **3.24** approach taken to the offence by the prosecuting authorities. In dealing with concerns over the phrase and a lack of statutory definition, Baroness Scotland indicated[10] that the phrase 'was intended to encapsulate the responsibility of the close members of the household without being too limiting. It was necessary to be very wary that family relationships in modern times were much more fluid and flexible than they had been in the past and might become more so in the future'. Perhaps our hypothetical lodger can breathe a sigh of relief.

(e) 'Significant Risk of Serious Physical Harm'

Section 5(1)(c) provides that 'at that time [of V's death] there was a significant **3.25** risk of serious physical harm being caused to V by the unlawful act of such a person'. In s 5(6) 'serious' harm means harm that amounts to grievous

---

[8] ibid, col GC344.
[9] ibid, col GC347.
[10] ibid, col GC348.

bodily harm for the purposes of the Offences against the Person Act 1861. The prosecution will have to demonstrate that at the time of the unlawful act resulting in death, there was a significant risk of serious harm to him. A background of regular but minor chastisement would not create the 'significant risk of serious harm' required. It is not confined to assaults but would include gross neglect.

3.26   The risk must come from a 'member of the household'. So in the case of an outsider conducting a campaign of violence against a particular family, the offence would not be committed even though, on any view, there was at the relevant time a significant risk of physical harm to the child, and even though there was a demonstrable failure to protect.

3.27   The prosecution has to prove that there was at the time of V's death a significant risk of serious harm. That can not simply be inferred from the fact that V has died. The offence will not apply if the victim died of a blow where there was no previous history of abuse nor any reason to suspect a risk. The risk is likely to be demonstrated by a history of violence towards either the victim or towards others in the household. This no doubt will create difficulties in practice in terms of presenting cogent evidence of risk. In some cases there will be evidence of previous injury on post-mortem examination. Where there is not, in the absence of cooperation from other household members, this may well prove to be a difficult task, unless the history was apparent to others, for example, doctors, teachers, neighbours, social workers, etc. In an ideal world if a child or vulnerable adult is at significant risk and this is known to outside agencies, intervention will, or at least should, occur, thereby avoiding the tragic final consequence. More often than not, however, domestic violence is conducted behind closed doors—the outside world oblivious to what is happening until it is too late. It has to be doubted whether investigators will get much help from the household members in such a situation. If they speak of the history and the fact of significant risk, they lay themselves open to the possibility of prosecution, the very mischief the offence was designed to address and overcome.

2. Acts or Omissions Necessary to Incur Liability

(a) *'Causing or Allowing the Death of a Child or Vulnerable Adult'*

3.28 As the name of the new offence makes clear, a person can be guilty if either they caused the death or 'allowed' it in the sense defined. Section 5(1)(d) provides that:

either D was the person whose act caused V's death or—
(i)   D was, or ought to have been, aware of the risk mentioned in paragraph (c),
(ii) D failed to take such steps as he could reasonably have been expected to take to protect V from the risk, and
(iii) The act occurred in circumstances of the kind that D foresaw or ought to have foreseen.

Section 5(2) provides: 'The prosecution does not have to prove whether it is the first alternative in subsection (1)(d) or the second (sub-paragraphs (i) to (iii)) that applies.'

It is not necessary for the prosecution to prove whether a particular defendant **3.29** caused the death or 'allowed' it. This provision has generated some criticism. The Criminal Bar Association thought that the offence should allow for each defendant's culpability to be identified. This is important not least for the purposes of sentence.[11] Justice (Response to the Domestic Violence, Crime and Victims Bill: sections 4 and 5 (January 2004)) considered that not requiring the prosecution to prove which defendant committed the unlawful act and which defendant failed to protect, removed or diminished responsibility from the Crown to discharge the burden of proof in respect of an essential ingredient of the offence, namely the *actus reus*, by reference to the defendant.

Such a situation is not, however, without precedent. In *R v S and M*,[12] a child **3.30** was found to have bruising. The mother and her boyfriend were charged with an offence of cruelty under s 1 of the Children and Young Persons Act 1933. There was no evidence as to which adult had assaulted the child and the prosecution did not seek to argue that there was a joint enterprise between them. The Crown's case was that one had assaulted the child and the other had been guilty of wilful neglect, by failing to seek medical attention after the injuries had been inflicted. Their appeals against conviction were dismissed. Professor Sir JC Smith QC in his commentary upon the case observed:

That both were guilty of neglect seems acceptable; but that both are guilty of the offence because one (we do not know which) was guilty of assault under the section and the other (we do not know which) of neglect under the section is difficult to reconcile with the principles of burden of proof.

Where, it is submitted, the prosecution have cogent evidence to prove who **3.31** caused the death, such person would no doubt be prosecuted for murder or manslaughter. Where there is no such evidence (save for the safe inference that it was caused by a 'member of the same household') and there is evidence of there having been a 'significant risk' and a 'failure to protect', a prosecution under s 5 of the Act will no doubt follow. It can be anticipated that the new offence will accompany allegations of murder or manslaughter on an indictment. It is to be hoped that in most of these cases the verdicts on such an indictment looked at together and the evidence upon which they are based would allow a court to satisfactorily determine the degree of culpability to be ascribed to a particular defendant and thereby sentence accordingly.

---

[11] CBA, *Domestic Violence, Crime and Victims Bill—CBA Responses* (February 2004) available at http://www.criminalbar.com/reports/feb04.cfm.
[12] [1995] Crim LR 486.

(b) *'D Was or Ought to Have Been, Aware of the Risk'*

3.32 The significant risk (of serious physical harm) must be one of which the person is either aware or ought to have been aware. This is not a purely subjective requirement. As the Law Commission pointed out,[13]

> it would be odd and wrong if a person, on the one hand could be criminally liable where they were sufficiently concerned for the welfare of the child to be aware of a significant risk but were careless about doing anything to prevent it, but, on the other hand, could not be liable if they were so careless of the child's safety that they did not even think there was a risk when they ought to.

3.33 The test does not refer to a risk of which a 'reasonable person' would be aware. It is what the person himself ought to have been aware of which will determine whether he is potentially liable. Clearly, the defendant's intelligence and mental capacity, as well as the nature and degree of contact with the victim and the relationship with him, will all have a bearing on this.

3.34 Most people, other than those concerned with child protection, if they see a child with a bruise or a cut do not normally think that it is a non-accidental injury. Many babies who die, do so as the result of alleged shaking/impact injuries. There is often no previous history of injury. Sometimes old fractures are found, commonly metaphyseal fractures of the long bones. Paediatricians usually agree that unless a person who did not cause the injuries was present when they were caused, he would not necessarily realize if the baby was fractious that this was due to injury. Similarly, a person who is out at work all day may not appreciate that the deterioration in an elderly relative's condition is due to them being deliberately starved or mishandled. It is only to easy to infer with hindsight that a person 'must have known'. In practice that is very far from the case.

(c) *'D Failed to Take Such Steps as He Could Reasonably Have Been Expected to Take . . .'*

3.35 It will be necessary for the prosecution to show, to the required standard, the steps that D failed to take and the circumstances in which he could reasonably have been expected to take them. Not an easy task in every situation. The Act does not place any evidential burden on the defendant to show that he took all reasonable steps. A defendant will be convicted only where the jury is sure that any reasonable person in the defendant's position would have taken action and that he has not, and this will be for the prosecution to prove.

3.36 Concerns were raised during the consultation process by a number of interested bodies including Justice and Refuge who argued that women (and older children) who were themselves subject to domestic violence, might be fearful or unable to leave or complain about a violent partner (or parent), which would necessarily have a bearing on what steps they were able to take. It was argued

---

[13] *Children: Their Non-accidental Death or Serious Injury (Criminal Trials)* (Law Com No 282) 6.23.

that their position should be specifically recognized in the legislation. In rejecting the suggestion of special recognition, within the Act, for victims of domestic violence, Baroness Scotland of Asthal said:[14]

The question of what steps were reasonable for a victim of domestic violence is, of course, ultimately an issue for the jury, albeit that the prosecution will have to identify the steps that the defendant could have reasonably taken as part of the Crown's case.

(d) *'The Act Occurred in Circumstances of the Kind that D Foresaw or Ought to Have Foreseen'*

This will provide protection in cases in which the person responsible ought to have anticipated, for example, a serious assault by an abusive separated parent to whom the child is sent but, where in fact, the child is killed in the street by a stranger on the way. In this instance no liability will arise as the specific incident resulting in death was not foreseeable even though the category of offence was.   3.37

More difficult is the case where the mental condition of the other parent is deteriorating, for example, through depression, or the abuse of drink or drugs. D may have concerns about whether or not she is able to cope with the child, but not that she may kill the child in the belief that he is better off without her, or in a psychotic outburst. On the other hand, if she is becoming more aggressive or volatile, and the child is subsequently injured and dies, at what point should D, a lay person, realize that the child might die?   3.38

C. AGE FOR PROSECUTION

Section 5(3) provides: 3.39

If D was not the mother or father of V—
(a) D may not be charged with an offence under this section if he was under the age of 16 at the time of the act that caused V's death;
(b) for the purposes of subsection (1)(d)(ii) D could not have been expected to take any such step as is referred to there before attaining that age.

Members of the household under 16 will not have a duty of care or be expected to take steps to prevent a victim from coming to harm, so for example, a child (a person under the age of 16) will have no duty to prevent his parents from harming a sibling.

The parents of a child will be expected, however, to take reasonable steps to protect even where they are themselves under the age of 16. This represents a departure from the Law Commission's proposals which aimed for consistency with other relevant legislation, in particular the Children and Young Persons Act 1933, where 16 represents the minimum age for prosecution, regardless of   3.40

---

[14] HL Vol 658, col 1163 (9 March 2004).

the 'relationship' to the victim. Although the prospect of prosecuting children for a failure to protect is seen by many as unpalatable (the Criminal Bar Association thought that the minimum age for prosecution should be 18), the Government clearly feel that the special relationship of the biological parents carries with it a special responsibility to protect.

3.41   By virtue of s 5(3)(b), D could not be expected to take any steps to protect V from any risk before attaining the age of 16. So where, for example, at the time of the unlawful act D had attained the age of 16, the prosecution would not be able to rely on any failures to take steps before D attained that age in attempting to prove their case.

D. SENTENCE

3.42   Section 5(7) provides: 'A person guilty of an offence under this section is liable on conviction on indictment to imprisonment for a term not exceeding 14 years or to a fine, or to both.' The level of sentence exceeds that proposed by the Law Commission who suggested a maximum of seven years. As indicated earlier, in cases involving more than one defendant, a sentencing judge may well encounter difficulties in assessing the correct level of culpability.

E. CONCLUSION

3.43   As stated in the introduction, the mischief the new offence is designed to address is one that has caused concern for many years. One cannot criticize the intention behind the legislation. Whether s 5 of the Act will achieve what it is designed to do remains to be seen. Only time will tell. The Government have seen fit to depart in many important respects from the recommendations and proposals of the Law Commission. Perhaps the most significant of these is that the section 5 offence can be committed by the defendant doing the fatal act himself *or* by his failure to take reasonable steps to protect.

3.44   The offence will be classified as an offence of homicide for certain purposes, although a defendant who does not actively cause a death could, and no doubt will, be convicted of the offence. In cases where defendants are themselves victims of domestic violence (albeit not to the extent they are afforded a defence), this will, it is submitted, cause a devastating and debilitating stigma that will be extremely difficult to overcome and not altogether, in some cases at least, deserved. One only has to look at the experience of Maxine Carr to see the implications of any association with a child's death, however remote, and, of course, s 5 contemplates the prosecution of children themselves where they are the natural parent of the victim. It is, however, to the new rules of evidence and procedure, detailed in s 6 (see chapter 4), that we must look to see the full impact of this legislation as it relates to domestic homicides.

4

EVIDENCE AND PROCEDURE: ENGLAND AND WALES

A. INTRODUCTION

Section 6 represents a significant change to well-established principles of evi- **4.01** dence and procedure in respect of a particular category of defendant charged with offences of homicide. The provisions are seen by the Government as a necessary corollary to the new offence created by s 5, 'enabling the appropriate conviction to be secured against the more culpable party'.[1] It is these provisions that have caused the most controversy and were removed at third reading in the House of Lords. Justice, Response to the Domestic Violence, Crime and Victims Bill, described the proposal as 'a disturbing provision that drives a coach and horses through the burden of proof and the right to silence'.

The significant provisions apply where the prosecution establish a case to **4.02** answer in respect of the new offence. In such circumstances where the defendant is also charged with an offence of murder or manslaughter[2] in respect of the same death, the court will not consider the question of whether there is a case to

---

[1] HL Vol 657, col GC164 (28 January 2004) *per* Baroness Scotland.
[2] But not infanticide.

answer on the charge of murder or manslaughter until the conclusion of the defence case. The section also makes provision for inferences from the defendant's silence in respect of the murder or manslaughter charges.

B. WHEN THE PROVISIONS APPLY

4.03   Section 6(1) reads: 'Subsections (2) to (4) apply where a person ("the defend-ant") is charged in the same proceedings with an offence of murder or man-slaughter and with an offence under section 5 in respect of the same death ("the section 5 offence").' Suspects to offences of homicide involving children or vulnerable adults committed in a 'domestic context' can expect, where the evi-dence allows, to be indicted with both charges of murder or manslaughter and the new offence. It is in this situation that the new provisions apply. Where the prosecution proceed in respect of the new offence alone, this section has no application. Similarly where murder alone is charged the provisions do not apply.

4.04   The justification for these controversial changes, in part at least, is that because the defendant to which these provisions apply is by definition someone who was 'responsible' for the victim, it is not unreasonable to postpone con-sideration of a submission of no case until such person has had an opportunity to provide an account. The section 5 offence itself is unaffected by these changes. The existing laws of evidence and procedure apply to it. The defence retain the right to apply to dismiss the charge pursuant to the Crime and Dis-order Act 1998 and the option of making a submission of no case to answer at the close of the prosecution case. If either application were successful the new provisions would not apply to any remaining offence of homicide.

C. THE NEW RULES

4.05   Section 6(2) to (4) read as follows:

(2) Where by virtue of section 35(3) of the Criminal Justice and Public Order Act 1994 (c.33) a court or jury is permitted, in relation to the section 5 offence, to draw such inferences as appear proper from the defendant's failure to give evidence or refusal to answer a question, the court or jury may also draw such inferences in determining whether he is guilty—
   (a) of murder or manslaughter, or
   (b) of any other offence of which he could lawfully be convicted on the charge of murder or manslaughter,
   even if there would otherwise be no case for him to answer in relation to that offence.
(3) The charge of murder or manslaughter is not to be dismissed under paragraph 2 of Schedule 3 to the Crime and Disorder Act 1998 (c.37) (unless the section 5 offence is dismissed).

(4) At the defendant's trial the question whether there is a case to answer on the charge of murder or manslaughter is not to be considered before the close of all the evidence (or, if at some earlier time he ceases to be charged with the section 5 offence, before that earlier time).

D. APPLICATION TO DISMISS

It is worth restating that these new provisions as to procedure and evidence 4.06 only apply to situations where a defendant is charged with the new section 5 offence together with an offence of murder or manslaughter in respect of the same death. As soon as the section 5 offence, for whatever reason, ceases to be a live issue one, the trial of the murder or manslaughter charge reverts to the 'old' rules of procedure and evidence.

By virtue of s 6(3) a person charged with murder or manslaughter (together 4.07 with the new offence) loses the right to seek dismissal of the murder or man- slaughter charge under the Crime and Disorder Act 1998, unless the section 5 offence is dismissed. Paragraph 2 of Sch 3 to the Crime and Disorder Act 1998 applies where a person is sent for trial under s 51 of the 1998 Act (no commit- tal proceedings for indictable only offences). A person is, prior to arraignment, entitled to apply to dismiss the charges on the basis that the evidence against the applicant would not be sufficient for a jury properly to convict. Whilst it is possible for the defendant to seek dismissal of the section 5 offence at this stage, no such right exists in relation to a murder or manslaughter charge in respect of the same death unless the application on the section 5 offence is successful.

E. POSTPONEMENT OF SUBMISSION OF NO CASE

A person charged with the new offence and a charge of murder or man- 4.08 slaughter in respect of the same death, by virtue of s 6(4), is not entitled to make a submission of no case until the close of all the evidence, or such earlier time as he ceases to be charged with the section 5 offence. At the conclusion of the prosecution case a defendant is entitled to submit that there is no case to answer in respect of the section 5 offence but not in respect of the accompanying murder or manslaughter charge, unless the submission on the section 5 offence is successful.

It is hard to envisage many circumstances where there is no case to answer on 4.09 the section 5 offence but sufficient evidence to continue on the murder or man- slaughter charge. Presumably it might arise if the prosecution could not prove that the defendant was part of the same household, but the child had died during one of his visits to the home. The real purpose of the legislation is to prevent a successful submission in respect of the more serious charge at this stage, as should have been allowed in *R v Lane and Lane*.[3] Now a defendant will have to wait until the conclusion of all the evidence before making any submissions on the strength of the prosecution case as it relates to a murder or manslaughter charge. The court, at this later stage, will have the benefit of evidence from the defence or the potential of adverse inferences to be drawn from a failure to testify or answer a question in assessing whether there is a case to answer.

F. INFERENCES

4.10 It is arguably s 6(2) of the Act that represents the most significant and controversial of the new provisions. The subsection in its terms ('even if there would otherwise be no case to answer in relation to that offence') contemplates a situation where a person charged with murder (together with the new offence) can be convicted of murder where, under the previous law, there would have been no case to answer. A judge would be entitled to take into account a defendant's failure to give evidence or refusal to answer a question in determining whether a case to answer exists. This sits uneasily with s 38(3) of the Criminal Justice and Public Order Act 1994. A decision to leave a case to the jury could not be based entirely on an inference drawn under the terms of s 35 of the 1994 Act, a conviction could be founded on the basis of an inference taken together with 'less' evidence than would have formerly been necessary to obtain a conviction for murder or manslaughter.

4.11 The phrase 'even if there would otherwise be no case to answer in relation to that offence' is designed to ensure that the decision of the Court of Appeal in *R v Cowan*[4] would not apply in circumstances where a person is charged with murder or manslaughter and the new offence. In *Cowan*, the court held (in relation to the drawing of an adverse inference from silence under s 35 of the Criminal Justice and Public Order Act 1994) that the prosecution must have established a case for the defendant to answer, in the sense of a strong enough case to justify the judge leaving it to the jury, before the defendant has any need to consider giving evidence, and so before it can be proper to draw an inference of guilt from a defendant's failure to give evidence.

4.12 In a case where a person is charged with the new offence and a charge of murder or manslaughter the prosecution need not, any more, establish a case for the defendant to answer in relation to the charge of murder or manslaughter before an inference of guilt can be drawn from a defendant's silence.

---

[3] (1986) 82 Cr App R 5.
[4] [1996] 1 Cr App R 1, CA.

G. SCENARIOS

It is instructive to look at a hypothetical case, similar on the facts to that   **4.13**
found in *R v Lane and Lane*[5] (for the facts see para 3.04 above).

R v A and B—a hypothetical case:

- The case involves the death of a child in a domestic context.
- Mother and father (A and B respectively) are charged with the new offence and an offence of manslaughter.
- Prosecution is unable to establish the presence of both at the relevant time. One or other of them is present at all relevant times but cannot say which.
- Prosecution is unable to establish that A and B acted in concert.
- One or other is responsible for inflicting injuries that caused death; cannot say who.

Prior to this Act a prosecution against A and B for manslaughter would fail at   **4.14**
the close of the prosecution case (if not earlier, on an application to dismiss): see
Lane and Lane. In our case, A and B are also charged with a section 5 offence of
causing or allowing the death of their child. As a result they are prevented from
either applying to dismiss the charge of manslaughter pursuant to the Crime
and Disorder Act 1998 (see s 6(3)), or making a submission of no case on the
manslaughter charge, until the conclusion of all the evidence (see s 6(4) of the
Act).

The court have found a case to answer on the section 5 offence in respect of   **4.15**
both A and B. A and B now have to decide whether to give evidence in their own
defence. This will not be an easy decision. On the one hand there is a case to
answer on the new offence (maximum sentence fourteen years). Failure to testify
in relation to this may result in adverse inferences and consequent conviction.
The more serious manslaughter charge remains. Consideration will have to be
given to the impact that the defendant's evidence will have on this charge.

Let us look at three scenarios with these basic facts in mind.   **4.16**

(a) *Both A and B Refuse to Testify*
Both are in danger of being convicted of the section 5 offence. There is a case
to answer on the prosecution evidence and inferences may be drawn from their
silence. Remember it is not necessary for the prosecution to show which defendant caused the death (s 5(2)) to found convictions under s 5. It is a moot point as
to whether the defendant's failure to testify, in these circumstances, would be
sufficient to allow a jury to consider the guilt or otherwise of A and B on the
manslaughter charge. No doubt a submission of no case would be made on their

---

[5] (1985) 82 Cr App R 5.

behalf at the conclusion of all the evidence. Remember, however, the words in s 6(2): 'even if there would otherwise be no case for him to answer in relation to that offence'. As indicated earlier, the Act contemplates the situation of a case going before a jury, in circumstances where there would normally be no case to answer. In our hypothetical example, would inferences from silence together with the other evidence be sufficient to found a conviction for manslaughter? It is submitted that on these facts, a judge is likely to withdraw the case from the jury at the close of evidence. Assuming only one is guilty, a jury cannot choose which defendant to convict of the manslaughter charge or use an inference against one and not the other. In the absence of cogent evidence that suggests the guilt of one and not the other, it is hard to see how any reasonable jury, properly directed, could convict either. One wonders whether the Government have succeeded in fully addressing the problem found in *R v Lane and Lane* if that is right. If both are convicted of the new offence, how is a judge to address the question of sentence? One of the defendants caused the death, the other allowed it. The judge has no evidential basis to say which.

(b) *A Fails to Testify, B Gives Evidence*

4.17   A refuses to give evidence out of loyalty to B or an unwillingness to incriminate him. B, in evidence, gives an exculpatory account as far as he is concerned and blames A. It would now be open for B to submit that there is no case to answer against him on the manslaughter charge assuming he has not incriminated himself. A is convicted of the manslaughter charge on the basis of the prosecution evidence (albeit that it does not disclose a case to answer), the evidence of B, and an inference from A's silence. One can see from this example the importance of the order in which the defendants appear on the indictment. B clearly has a tactical advantage in coming second, that in this instance, he has exploited to the full. The importance of the order on the indictment, the evidence of co-defendants, and the prospect of adverse inferences have all been features of criminal trials for many years. The difference now, however, under the terms of this Act, is that A, in our example, has, on the prosecution case, no case to answer in respect of the more serious offence, and yet remains at risk of conviction of it. One can see from this example, the potential, at least, for injustice.

(c) *A Gives Evidence Blaming B*

4.18   In such circumstances B would be unwise not to give evidence bearing in mind the evidence of A and the potential for inferences to be drawn from his silence. Let us assume he gives evidence and blames A. On the manslaughter charge there is now the evidence of the defendants to take into account and any other evidence called on their behalf. It may well be that there is now a case to answer, on the manslaughter charge, in respect of both defendants, because of incriminating evidence adduced in cross-examination. Are the jury to choose which account they prefer, and return verdicts accordingly, even though on the face of the prosecution case there was no case to answer against either defendant? One can see the dangers. It is to be hoped, by the authors at least, that in a situation like this, a judge would withdraw the case from the jury in respect of both defendants.

H. HUMAN RIGHTS CONSIDERATIONS

4.19 The Joint Committee on Human Rights[6] felt, initially at least, that the Domestic Violence, Crime and Victims Bill ran the risk of being incompatible with the right to a fair hearing under Art 6.1 of the European Convention on Human Rights (ECHR). When they reported further, having listened to the Government's response, they concluded that there was not a significant risk of incompatibility. Given the amount of criticism the provisions have already attracted, one can be fairly certain that these new rules of evidence and procedure will be challenged as representing an attack on convention rights enshrined in Arts 6.1 and 6.2 (presumption of innocence). The Criminal Bar Association's Working Party set up to respond to the Law Commission's consultation paper, considered that the postponement of a submission of no case to answer was inherently incompatible with the presumption of innocence. It attacked the fundamental principle that it is not for the defendant to tell the court what happened but for the prosecution to prove what happened.

4.20 They regarded the proposals as being based on a misconception as to the proper role of a criminal trial. It is not an investigation into the circumstances of a death but a determination of whether the prosecution can prove guilt. Justice[7] felt the provisions did not involve simply a postponement of the submission of no case but an alteration to the *R v Galbraith*[8] analysis. The judge is now able to take into account the defence case to see if it cures any defects in that of the prosecution.

4.21 Much will depend on the interpretation of the legislation. If it is the intention of Parliament for persons to be convicted on the basis of an inference alone, such an analysis would result in incompatibility, it is submitted, and conflict with *Murray v UK*,[9] which said that an important protection was that an adverse inference from a failure to give evidence could only be drawn if the prosecution case clearly called for an explanation. The Government will no doubt argue that these new provisions are justified because of the exceptional and serious nature of the offences with which they are concerned. The new rules only apply, they might argue, where there is a case to answer on the new section 5 offence, a

---

[6] Joint Committee on Human Rights, Third Report of session 2003–4, Scrutiny of Bills: Progress Report (HL 23/HC 252) (January 2004).

[7] Justice, Response to the Domestic Violence, Crime and Victims Bill.

[8] (1981) 73 Cr App R 124.

[9] (1996) 19 EHRR 193.

serious offence in itself. The prosecution would have established that a crime had been committed and that the defendant comes from a small defined group who may be responsible and who can give material evidence as to what has happened. The court would not draw any inference from silence if it appears to the court that the physical or mental condition of the accused makes it undesirable for him to give evidence (see s 35(1)(b) of the Criminal Justice and Public Order Act 1994). The court would be required to direct an acquittal of a defendant, if satisfied at the end of all the evidence, that no jury could properly convict him. A judge would have to direct a jury that if silence is or may be for reasons other than guilt, they should acquit if the evidence, without any inference from silence, would not support a conviction.

I. SECTION 5 OFFENCE IS AN OFFENCE OF 'HOMICIDE'

4.22 By virtue of s 6(5) of the Act an offence of causing or allowing the death of a child or vulnerable adult is an offence of homicide for the purposes of the following enactments:

- Sections 24 and 25 of the Magistrates' Courts Act 1980 (mode of trial of child or young person for indictable offence).
- Section 51A of the Crime and Disorder Act 1998 (sending cases to the Crown Court: children and young persons).
- Section 8 of the Powers of Criminal Courts (Sentencing) Act 2000 (power and duty to remit young offenders to youth courts for sentence).

4.23 Treating the new offence as an offence of homicide for ss 24 and 25 of the Magistrates' Courts Act 1980 and s 51 of the Crime and Disorder Act 1998 means that the offence will always be tried in the Crown Court even where the defendant is a juvenile. Including the offence as a homicide for the purposes of s 8 of the Powers of Criminal Courts (Sentencing) Act 2000 means the offender can be sentenced in the Crown Court even if they are under 18. The provisions are justified on the basis of the seriousness of the new offence.

5

DOMESTIC HOMICIDE REVIEWS

A. WHAT ARE DOMESTIC HOMICIDE REVIEWS?

Section 9 of the Act makes provision for the establishment and conduct of **5.01** 'domestic homicide reviews'. Section 9(1) defines such a review as:

(1) In this section domestic homicide review means a review of the circumstances in which the death of a person aged 16 or over has, or appears to have, resulted from violence, abuse or neglect by,
   (a) a person to whom he was related or with whom he was or had been in an intimate personal relationship, or
   (b) a member of the same household as himself
held with a view to identifying the lessons to be learnt from the death.

There has been, to date, in relation to deaths of adults, no coherent national **5.02** system for investigating lessons that can be learned from domestic homicides. When a child under the age of 18 is killed, and abuse or neglect is a factor, then a serious case review will be conducted by relevant professionals to determine what, if any, lessons can be learned.[1] In Grand Committee in the House of Lords, Baroness Walmsley argued that section 9 reviews should be extended to any adult or child covered by the section.[2] It is perhaps unfortunate that the Government did not avail themselves of the opportunity to create a review system whereby the death of any person, whether a child or an adult, in a domestic context, involving violence, abuse, or neglect, could be brought under the same umbrella. It is by no means uncommon to hear of cases involving the

---

[1] Department of Health, *Working Together to Safeguard Children* (1999).
[2] HL Vol 657, col GC223 (2 February 2004).

deaths of children and adults from the same household. Are we to have differently constituted reviews dealing with, on the one hand, the death of a child, and on the other, the death of an adult, even when they arise out of the same circumstances? This would, on the face of it at least, result in an unnecessary duplication of work.

B. ESTABLISHMENT AND PARTICIPATION

5.03 Section 9(2) of the Act states that the Secretary of State may in a particular case direct a specified person or body within s 9(4) to establish, or to participate in, domestic homicide review. By s 9(4)(a), the persons and bodies within this subsection are, in relation to England and Wales:

- chief officers of police for police areas in England and Wales;
- local authorities;
- local probation boards established under s 4 of the Criminal Justice and Court Services Act 2000;
- Strategic Health Authorities established under s 8 of the National Health Service Act 1997;
- Primary Care Trusts established under s 16A of that Act;
- Local Health Boards established under s 16BA of that Act;
- NHS trusts established under s 5 of the National Health Service and Community Care Act 1990.

5.04 Section 9(4)(b) specifies relevant persons and bodies in relation to Northern Ireland outside the scope of this work, whilst s 9(5) defines what is meant by 'local authority' for the purposes of s 9(4) (b). Section 9(6) permits amendment to s 9(5) and (6) by the Secretary of State by order.

C. AIM OF REVIEWS

5.05 Put simply, the aims of a particular review are to determine whether any lessons can be learned from a particular homicide and hopefully allow for measures to be put in place to prevent a similar tragic consequence in the future. The aim is to address a problem identified by Safety and Justice,[3] and described as follows:

A domestic attack that results in the death of the victim is often not the first attack. Many people and agencies may have known of these attacks—neighbours for example, may have heard of violence, a GP may have examined injuries, the child's teacher may have suspected abuse, the police may have been called, there may have been previous

---

[3] Home Office, *Safety and Justice: The Government's Proposals on Domestic Violence* (Cm 5847, June 2003) available at http://www.homeoffice.gov.uk/docs2/domesticviolence.pdf, pp 37–8.

prosecutions, and so on. It is important to learn as much as possible from domestic violence homicides, to understand where systems failed, why the involvement of agencies or professionals did not lead to effective intervention and what can be done to put the system right and avoid future deaths.

D. CONDUCT OF REVIEWS

The Act says nothing about how the reviews will be conducted. The Govern- **5.06** ment's intention is to publish guidance on their establishment and conduct. The guidance, it is anticipated, will encourage multi-agency reviews and provide details as to leadership, format, timing, and participants depending on the individual circumstances of a case. Until the guidance is published it is not clear what the likely timetable will be. One can assume that the review itself would not take place until the conclusion of any criminal or civil proceedings arising from the relevant death. The success or otherwise of the reviews will depend, it is submitted, on the willingness of the various agencies to participate fully and candidly, their ability to communicate a review's findings nationwide, and their ability to instigate changes if they are felt to be necessary.

6

ASSAULT AND RESTRAINING ORDERS

A. COMMON ASSAULT TO BE AN ARRESTABLE OFFENCE

6.01 Schedule 1A to the Police and Criminal Evidence Act 1984 sets out specific offences, the penalties for which are less than five years' imprisonment, and makes them arrestable offences. Section 10(1) of the Domestic Violence, Crime and Victims Act amends that Schedule to include common assault. There is a similar provision applying to Northern Ireland.[1]

6.02 An 'arrestable offence' is defined by s 24 of the Police and Criminal Evidence Act 1984 as offences for which the sentence is fixed by law, those which carry a sentence of five years' imprisonment or more, and those set out in Sch 1A.[2] It includes attempts to commit those offences and acting as a secondary party: s 24(3). So a man who incites his friend to assault his (the first man's) wife, can be arrested for assault, as can the brother who advises a man to hit his wife to teach her a lesson.

---

[1] Section 10(2) amends the Police and Criminal Evidence (Northern Ireland) Order 1989, art 26(2) by inserting 'an offence under section 42 of the Offences Against the Person Act 1861 (common assault etc.)'.

[2] This replaced the original list in s 24(2) of that Act by virtue of s 48(1) and Sch 6 of the Police Reform Act 2002 with effect from 1 October 2002 (Police Reform Act 2002 (Commencement No 1) Order 2002).

6.03   In 2003/4, the police recorded 1,109,017 violent crimes (ie violence against the person, sexual offences, and robberies).[3] Common assault constituted 24% of police recorded violent crime (266,164 incidents). The 2003/4 British Crime Survey (BCS) estimated that there were 2,708,000 violent incidents against adults in England and Wales, and that 39% of all violent incidents reported were common assault with no injury. Of the incidents of domestic violence reported to the BCS, 30% resulted in no injury. In view of this, the potential impact of this change is considerable. Historically, the victims of common assault have largely been left to pursue their own remedies against their attackers, either through the civil courts or by issuing a summons in the magistrates' court.

6.04   One consequence of the change will be that police who attend an incident of domestic violence will be able to arrest a person who has or whom they reasonably believe to have committed a common assault, thereby giving a protection to the victim which is currently lacking. Thus even before a non-molestation injunction is obtained, the police will now have the power to arrest those who are threatening immediate violence or using it. One consequence may be that in some situations the police will arrest both parties and sort out issues about who attacked whom at the police station.

6.05   The power to arrest without warrant for an arrestable offence, however, is not confined to the police. Section 24(4) provides that 'any person' may arrest anyone who is in the act of committing an arrestable offence or anyone whom he has reasonable grounds for suspecting to be committing such an offence. Similarly, where an arrestable offence has been committed, any person may arrest anyone who is guilty of the offence or anyone whom he has reasonable grounds for suspecting to be guilty of the offence. This would allow relatives or friends, passers by, or even the victim to arrest someone committing a common assault, or to go after an attacker who has fled the scene in order to arrest him.

6.06   Only the police have the power to arrest without warrant someone who is either about to commit an offence or whom they reasonably suspect is about to do so: s 24(7). Where the police are called to an escalating incident of domestic violence, they would be able to arrest someone about to commit an assault or whom they reasonably believe is about to assault someone else.

6.07   All the requirements for any lawful arrest will apply to an arrest for common assault, whether by the police or anyone else. The person must be informed of the true reason for his arrest at the time,[4] even if, in the case of arrest by a constable, the reason for the arrest is obvious. Only such force as is reasonable in all the circumstances may be used.[5] A person making an arrest is obliged to ensure that the person arrested is properly taken into custody. In the case of a civilian arrest this is achieved either by handing the arrested person over to a

---

[3] All the figures in this paragraph are taken from Home Office Statistical Bulletin, *Crime in England and Wales 2003/4* by T. Dodd, S. Nicholas, D. Povey, and A. Walker.
[4] PACE 1984, s 29.
[5] Criminal Law Act 1967, s 3; PACE 1984, s 117.

constable or taking him to the police station. The codes of conduct under the Police and Criminal Evidence Act 1984 apply.

The new power to arrest for common assault is obviously not limited to **6.08** situations of domestic violence. If used in circumstances of public disorder, for example, it would allow the police to avoid the restrictions on arrest imposed by some of the Public Order Acts, for example that the arrest may only be made by a constable in uniform or after a warning or direction has been given to stop the offending conduct.[6] Those safeguards were intended to strike a balance when new offences were being created between freedom of expression and the safe-guarding of the rights of others. The extent to which this new power will encroach upon the legitimate freedom to demonstrate in public places remains to be seen.

B. COMMON ASSAULT, ETC AS AN ALTERNATIVE VERDICT

Common assault and battery is now only a summary offence by virtue of s 39 **6.09** of the Criminal Justice Act 1988. It is already available as an alternative verdict where a more serious offence, which is founded on the same facts or evidence, or is part of a series of offences of a similar character, is tried on indictment, by virtue of s 40 of the same Act. But that section requires a count charging the offence to be included in the indictment, and the facts or evidence relating to it to have been disclosed at the time the person was sent for trial. That count is then dealt with as though it were an indictable offence, but the Crown Court is limited to the penalties the magistrates' court could have imposed.

Section 40(3) of the Criminal Justice Act 1988 sets out a list of summary **6.10** offences to which this provision applies. They are:

- common assault;
- assaulting a prison custody officer (s (90)(1) of the Criminal Justice Act 1991);
- assaulting a secure training centre custody officer (s 13(1) of the Criminal Justice and Public Order Act 1994);
- taking a motor vehicle or other conveyance without authority (s 12(1) of the Theft Act 1968);
- driving a motor vehicle whilst disqualified (s 103(1)(b) of the Road Traffic Act 1988);
- an offence mentioned in the first column of Sch 2 to the Magistrates' Courts Act 1980 which would otherwise be triable only summarily by virtue of s 22(2) of that Act;
- any summary offence specified by regulation made by the Secretary of State.

---

[6] See for example Public Order Act 1986, s 5(4) and Criminal Justice and Public Order Act 1994, s 61.

6.11   Section 11 of the Domestic Violence, Crime and Victims Act 2004 removes the onerous burden from prosecutors of always having to include the alternative count in the indictment. It does this by amending s 6 of the Criminal Law Act 1967. Section 6(3) of that Act provides that:

> Where, on a person's trial on indictment for any offence except treason or murder, the jury find him not guilty of the offence specifically charged in the indictment, but the allegations in the indictment amount to or include (expressly or by implication) an allegation of another offence falling within the jurisdiction of the court of trial, the jury may find him guilty of that other offence or of an offence of which he could be found guilty on an indictment specifically charging that other offence.

6.12   The 2004 Act inserts a new s 6(3A), which states:

> (3A) For the purposes of subsection (3) above an offence falls within the jurisdiction of the court of trial if it is an offence to which section 40 of the Criminal Justice Act 1988 applies [see above] . . . even if a count charging the offence is not included in the indictment.

It appears that the only change made is that there no longer needs to be a count on the indictment. The expression 'even if' in the new s 6(3A) suggests that the present practice of including such a count should continue to be the norm. The other requirements of s 40 continue, namely that the alternative offence to that being tried on indictment must be founded on the same facts or evidence, or be part of a series of offences of a similar character, and the facts or evidence relating to it to have been disclosed at the time the person was sent for trial. If that is correct, it is not open to the jury to convict of the alternative offence if the evidence in respect of it only emerges during the course of the trial, or it involves a different set of facts, not part of a series.

6.13   A person convicted under this section may only be dealt with for it in a manner in which a magistrates' court could have dealt with him.[7]

C. RESTRAINING ORDERS: (1) WHAT IS A RESTRAINING ORDER?

6.14 Restraining orders are made under s 5 of the Protection from Harassment Act 1997. Section 5(2) provides:

> The order may, for the purpose of protecting the victim of the offence, or any other person mentioned in the order, from further conduct which—
> (a) amounts to harassment, or
> (b) will cause a fear of violence,
> prohibit the defendant from doing anything described in the order. The purpose of a

---

[7] Criminal Law Act 1967, s 6(3B) inserted by s 11.

restraining order is to prohibit particular conduct which would amount to harassment or cause people to fear violence.[8]

Restraining orders often use the same form of words as non-molestation orders. For example, 'not to use or threaten violence against the named person and not to instruct encourage or in any way suggest that any other person should do so.' Restraining orders may prohibit the defendant from going to a certain place such as a person's home or place of work, and may prohibit the defendant from communicating with the person named in the order.

D. RESTRAINING ORDERS: (2) WHEN CAN THE COURT MAKE A RESTRAINING ORDER?

1. Restraining Orders following Conviction

The Act amends s 5 (1) of the Protection from Harassment Act 1997 to extend **6.15** the court's powers to make restraining orders within criminal proceedings. The amended s 5(1) provides: 'A court sentencing or otherwise dealing with a person ("the defendant") convicted of an offence may (as well as sentencing him or dealing with him in any other way) make an order under this section.' The court is able to make a restraining order where the defendant is convicted of *any* offence, not just an offence of harassment or putting people in fear of violence. For example, if the defendant is convicted of an assault, the court can make a restraining order. Previously the court was only able to make an order when the defendant had been convicted of an offence under either s 2 or s 4 of the Protection from Harassment Act 1997.[9]

If the court is making a restraining order under the amended s 5(1) when the **6.16** defendant has either been found guilty or pleaded guilty to an offence, the court will have heard or read evidence that leads it to consider it necessary to make a restraining order. If harassment was a feature in the case, however, one would expect either that the defendant would have been charged with an offence under the Protection from Harassment Act 1997 or the victim would have obtained a civil injunction. If neither of those has occurred, it is submitted that the court has to proceed carefully. In principle, there ought to be an evidential link between the offence and harassment. For example:

1. Husband and wife have separated. He sees her with another man, loses his

---

[8] Harassment is not defined in the Protection from Harassment Act 1997. The interpretation of ss 1 to 5 are contained in s 7.

[9] Section 2(1) provides: 'A person who pursues a course of conduct in breach of section 1 (that is a course of harassment) is guilty of an offence'. Section 4 is a more serious offence. Section 4(1) provides: 'A person whose course of conduct causes another to fear, on at least two occasions, that violence will be used against him is guilty of an offence if he knows or ought to know his conduct will cause the other so to fear on each of those occasions'.

temper, and punches her on the shoulder. It is a one-off incident following which he has not communicated with her. He then pleads guilty or is found guilty. In order to make a restraining order the victim would need to give evidence to the court or the court would need to be satisfied that because of that incident she feared further violence, otherwise it is difficult to see on what basis the court could make a restraining order.

2. Using the same factual basis as example 1, if the defendant said in evidence that he would not leave her alone if he saw her with another man, one can see the evidential link between the offence and the need for a restraining order.

2. Restraining Orders following Acquittal

6.17   The new s 5A(1) of the Protection from Harassment Act 1997 provides:

A court before which a person ('the defendant') is acquitted of an offence may, if it considers it necessary to do so to protect a person from harassment by the defendant, make an order prohibiting the defendant from doing anything described in the order.

The court is able to make a restraining order when a defendant has been acquitted of any offence. By virtue of s 5(2) (see para 6.14 above) the offence would have to relate to harassment or putting people in fear of violence or domestic violence. Examples of when the court may use this power are:

1. The defendant is acquitted on a technicality.

2. The defendant is charged with harassment; however, the evidence does not meet the criminal standard of proof. For example, the defendant has only once directly communicated with the victim, but she believes that he is responsible for sending unwanted taxi cabs, pizzas, and obscene publications to her.

Unlike a bind over to keep the peace, a defendant does not have to agree to the making of the order.

6.18   The position is more difficult if the defendant has been acquitted following a hearing on the merits. If the defendant has been acquitted because the court was not persuaded that the allegations were true, it is hard to see how it could justify the making of the order. But if, for example, the defendant was acquitted of assault on his girlfriend's brother, on the grounds of self-defence, but the court heard that the background to the fight had been that the defendant would not leave the girlfriend alone, an order might be appropriate.

6.19   The test for making an order under s 5A, is for the court to 'consider it necessary'. This mirrors the provisions in s 1 of the Crime and Disorder Act 1998. This allows an anti-social behaviour order to be made on application where the relevant authority alleges that a person has acted in a manner that caused or was likely to cause harassment, alarm, or distress to others not in the same household, where the court considers it is necessary to protect relevant persons from further anti-social behaviour. A similar power exists where the offender is convicted,[10] but there is no comparable power to make an order where the defendant is acquitted. In *C v Sunderland Youth Court*[11] the defendant had been convicted five months earlier of anti-social behaviour. There were other pending charges. The court declined to make an order under s 1C. A month later, following his conviction on one of the other charges, the same court made an anti-social behaviour order. The magistrates gave no reasons for their decision to do so. The Administrative Court stated that whilst the court was entitled to change its mind, particularly if there had been a change of circumstances, the defendant was entitled to know why they had done so. The only apparent change was that he had responded favourably to a probation order, so it was not apparent why the court below considered that an order was necessary.

Since a defendant who has been acquitted is not usually subjected to any **6.20** restraint on his activities, it is suggested that 'necessary' should be given its primary dictionary meaning of: 'Indispensable, requisite, needful; that cannot be done without'.[12] In *C v Sunderland*, the court considered that the discretion conferred by the statute had to be exercised 'fairly, reasonably, and with regard to all relevant circumstances'. By analogy with that case, there would have to be some evidence which justified the making of the order. In principle, that should be evidence to show that the victim is at risk of harassment and therefore an order is necessary. The effect of the legislation appears to be that if the court is not satisfied of the defendant's guilt beyond reasonable doubt, it can nevertheless make a restraining order on the basis of the same evidence, provided that it makes it clear why it considers it necessary.

The penalty for breaching a restraining order can be severe. A defendant in **6.21** breach of a restraining order may receive a custodial sentence. *R v Liddle; R v Hayes*[13] were appeals against sentence by two offenders. Both had pleaded guilty to two offences of breaching a restraining order. The first offender had been sentenced to total of eighteen months' imprisonment consecutive to a three-month sentence under s 116 of the Powers of the Criminal Court (Sentencing) Act 2000. This was reduced to a total of fifteen months (three plus twelve) where he had, within a short time of his release from prison for the offence which gave rise to the restraining order, sent two letters to his ex-wife and spoken to her on the street when they met accidentally, contrary to a prohibition on all contact. The second offender had his sentence reduced from two years to eleven months. He had rung the victim's doorbell at night and then disappeared; he was arrested and remanded in custody. He wrote to her from prison with such detail as to demonstrate that he had been watching her. He had been subject to a lifetime prohibition on all contact with her.

---

[10] CDA 1998, s 1C.
[11] [2004] 1 Cr App R (S) 76.
[12] *Shorter Oxford English Dictionary.*
[13] [1999] 3 All ER 816.

E. RESTRAINING ORDERS: (3) THE EVIDENCE REQUIRED

6.22 The new s 5(3)A of the Protection from Harassment Act 1997 provides: 'In proceedings under this section both the prosecution and the defence may lead, as further evidence, any evidence that would be admissible in proceedings for an injunction under section 3.' This subsection is intended to make clear that following either a conviction or an acquittal, the court can inform itself about whether to make a restraining order by considering additional evidence, for example hearsay evidence, that would be admissible in civil proceedings for an injunction. Section 3 of the Protection from Harassment Act 1997 is the section that provides the civil remedy.

6.23   Evidence not admissible in the criminal proceedings may be put before the court.[14] The prosecutor may have taken statements about the relationship as a whole and not just the conduct in relation to the charge. Whilst both the prosecution and the defence may lead further evidence, the difficulty for a defendant is that he may be unaware, especially if he has not been charged with an offence of harassment, that he may be subject to a restraining order, or of the evidence to be relied on. Before the Act a defendant would have been charged with harassment, and would know the case he had to meet. In civil proceedings, even if a without notice order was made, he would be served with a copy of the order, the statement in support, and would have the opportunity to make representations at a future hearing. When representing a defendant, charged with an offence of violence, practitioners will need to inform the defendant of the court's power to make a restraining order and to take instructions beforehand.

6.24   Both criminal and family practitioners will need to bear in mind that in civil proceedings some evidence, particularly hearsay, is only admissible if certain formalities are complied with.[15] An application for an injunction would normally have to be supported by an affidavit, that is, sworn evidence. Hearsay evidence may be included in such an affidavit, but the source has to be identified.[16] Since only evidence which would be admissible in proceedings for an injunction can be used, it must follow that evidence that fails to comply with the formalities would be inadmissible in injunction proceedings and therefore in hearings for restraining orders.

---

[14] This may become less important when the provisions of the Criminal Justice Act 2003, ss 114–126 widening the circumstances in which hearsay evidence is admissible in criminal proceedings, are brought into force.

[15] Civil Evidence Act 1995.

[16] Practice Direction—Written evidence under CPR Pt 32.

F. RESTRAINING ORDERS: (4) UNDERTAKINGS

In the civil courts the court has the jurisdiction to accept an undertaking. An **6.25** undertaking is a promise to the court to refrain from certain conduct. Undertakings usually adopt the same form of words as an order. The court also has the power to accept cross undertakings, whereby both parties are restrained from certain conduct. The provisions in this Act do not allow the court to accept undertakings.

G. RESTRAINING ORDERS: (5) APPEALS

The new s 5A(5) provides the person made subject to the restraining order **6.26** following an acquittal with the same rights of appeal as if he had been convicted of the offence and the order had been made under s 5 of the Protection from Harassment Act 1997.

The new s 5A(3) provides that 'where the Court of Appeal allow an appeal **6.27** against conviction they may remit the case to the Crown Court to consider whether to proceed under this section.' The section applies where the defendant successfully appeals against a conviction, any conviction, not just a conviction under the Protection from Harassment Act 1997. The Court of Appeal may remit the case to the Crown Court to consider whether it is 'necessary' to make a restraining order. The Court of Appeal may remit the case; they do not have a duty to do so. In exercising their discretion, it is suggested that the Court of Appeal should have in mind the relevant considerations discussed in paras 6.16 to 6.19 above. The Court of Appeal is unlikely to remit the case to the Crown Court unless they consider there is evidence that a restraining order is necessary, but their view does not bind the court to which the case is remitted.

The new s 5A(4) provides: **6.28**

Where—
(a) the Crown Court allows an appeal against conviction, or
(b) a case is remitted to the Crown Court under subsection (3),
the reference in subsection (1) to a court before which a person is acquitted of an offence is to be read as referring to that court.

A defendant who successfully appeals to the Crown Court against a conviction in the magistrates' court is considered to have been acquitted by the Crown Court. The Crown Court in which he is acquitted may still make a restraining order. The subsection also allows the Crown Court to make a restraining order when the Court of Appeal have remitted the case back to the Crown Court to consider whether a restraining order should be made.

H. DISCHARGE OF RESTRAINING ORDERS

6.29 Section 12(4) of the Act inserts a new s 5(7) into the Protection from Harassment Act 1997 which allows a court dealing with a person for an offence under that section, ie an alleged breach of the restraining order, to vary or discharge the restraining order by a further order. This provision applies whether the original order was made on conviction or acquittal. The court dealing with the offence does not have to be the same court as made the restraining order. This is in addition to the right which the prosecutor, the defendant, or the person mentioned in the order have to apply to the court that made the order for the order to be varied or discharged by a further order.

7

SURCHARGES

A. OVERVIEW

A surcharge is extra charge or payment. Surcharges have hitherto had limited **7.01** application in English law. They have most notably been imposed on local councillors or public officials who have acted improperly, or as a penalty for unpaid tax or VAT. The effect of these provisions is to change that radically. In effect, it will be a tax on criminal behaviour.

A surcharge under the Act is an amount of money the court will have a duty **7.02** to impose. The provisions for surcharges are divided into three categories. A surcharge is added to any conviction in the courts, to penalty notices for disorderly behaviour, and for repeated road traffic offences. The Government's intention is to make offenders pay a small sum of money to fund compensation for the victims of crime. The Act does not make provision for the establishment of a victims' fund into which surcharges will be paid. Instead, the proposal is 'that a certain portion of the consolidated fund will be ring fenced',[1] although it has been alleged that the amount of the fund available has been drastically reduced.[2] Given the difficulty currently being experienced by the courts in collecting fines,[3] it may be as well for the victims that they are not dependent on these surcharges being collected. To provide for surcharges, s 14 of the Act inserts new ss 161A and 161B into the Criminal Justice Act 2003.

---

[1] *Hansard*, HL col 206 (4 November 2004).
[2] ibid, col 276.
[3] Information on the DCA website estimates that £373 million was outstanding in June 2004.

B. SURCHARGE PAYABLE ON CONVICTION

7.03 The new s 161A(1) provides that 'a court when dealing with a person for one or more offences must also (subject to sections (2) and (3)) order him to pay a surcharge.' Whether the court is 'dealing with a person' is defined in s 161A(4). The court does not deal with a person if the court '(a) discharges him absolutely, or (b) makes an order under the Mental Health Act 1983 in respect of him.'

7.04 The new provision imposes a duty on the court to order a surcharge on a person convicted of an offence. It has no discretion not to do so, for example if to do so would impose financial hardship, or the surcharge may only be paid out of the proceeds of further crime. Unless s 161A(2) and (3) apply, all convictions will incur a surcharge no matter what the nature of the offence or what sentence is passed.

7.05 Section 161A(2) provides that 'subsection (1) does not apply in such cases as may be prescribed by an order made by the Secretary of State' and gives the Secretary of State the power to make an order setting out the circumstances when a surcharge should not be added by the court. The Government's intention was to introduce flexibility into the scheme once the surcharge had been operating. At the present time there is no order, and therefore no circumstances other than those prescribed by the Act when a surcharge will not be added by the court.

7.06 Section 161A(3) provides:

Where a court is dealing with an offender considers—
(a) that it would be appropriate to make a compensation order, but
(b) that he has insufficient means to pay both the surcharge and appropriate compensation,
the court must reduce the surcharge accordingly (if necessary to nil).

This section gives the court the discretion to reduce the surcharge if the offender does not have the financial resources to pay both a compensation order and a surcharge.

7.07 The Act does not specify what should happen where a person is convicted of more than one offence. Section 161A states that when dealing with a person for one or more offences the court must impose *a* surcharge. This question was raised in the House of Lords. The response was that for more than one offence the intention is for the surcharge to be levied on the punishment for the most serious of the offences.[4]

---

[4] *Hansard*, HL col 219 (4 November 2004).

C. THE AMOUNT

The new s 161B inserted by s 14 of the Act allows the Secretary of State to **7.08** specify the amount of surcharge by order. The Act does not specify the criteria the Secretary of State should apply when setting the amount or limit his power to increase the surcharge in the future. During the debates in the House of Lords the Government put forward the proposed figures.

For fixed penalty notices, including penalty notices for disorder, up to £80, the proposed surcharge level is between £5 and £10. For a fixed penalty notice, including penalty notices of disorder, which are imposed between £81 and £200, the proposed surcharge is £10. For a fine of up to £1,000, the proposed surcharge is £16. For all community penalties and fines of more than £1,000, the proposed surcharge is £16. For all community penalties and fines of more than £1,000, the proposed surcharge is £30. The surcharge is £30 for a custodial sentence that is suspended. It is also £30 for an immediate custodial sentence.[5]

The Secretary of State may also specify that the amount of the surcharge may **7.09** depend upon the offence or offences committed, how the offender is otherwise dealt with, or the age of the offender (s 161B(2)).

Section 164 of the Criminal Justice Act 2003 provides the criteria the court is **7.10** to apply when fixing a fine. Section 14 of the Act creates a new s 164(4A) so that the court when taking into account the financial circumstances of the offender must not reduce the fine on account of the surcharge unless the offender is unable to pay both. In reality if the offender does not have the means to pay both, the court will have to reduce the fine because they have no power to reduce the surcharge.

Section 161B(3) inserts a new para 13 in Pt 1 of Sch 9 to the Administration **7.11** of Justice Act 1970 to provide for the enforcement of a surcharge as if it were an order for costs or compensation.

Section 164B(4) amends Sch 5 to the Courts Act 2003 (collection of fines) to **7.12** allow the new provisions in the Courts Act 2003 which apply to the collection and enforcement of fines to apply to surcharges. The provisions in the Courts Act 2003 are currently being piloted. Accordingly, the new s 164(5) of the Criminal Justice Act 2003 gives the Secretary of State power to amend the provisions of Sch 5 as they apply to surcharges, in light of the pilot scheme. The order-making power in s 161B allows Sch 5 to the Courts Act 2003 provisions in their final form to apply or not apply to a surcharge as the Secretary of State decides.

---

[5] ibid, col 217.

D. INCREASE IN MAXIMUM ON-THE-SPOT PENALTY FOR DISORDERLY BEHAVIOUR

7.13 Section 3(2) of the Criminal Justice and Police Act 2001 (on-the-spot penalties for disorderly behaviour) provides that the Secretary of State may not specify an amount for the penalty which is more than a quarter of the amount of the maximum fine for which a person is liable on conviction of the offence. That section limits the maximum penalty that may be prescribed. For example, if the maximum fine a person would be liable to on conviction is £800, the maximum on-the-spot penalty would be £200.

7.14 Section 15(2) of the Act adds the words 'plus half the relevant surcharge' to s 3(2) so that a person who receives an on-the-spot penalty would have to pay a quarter of the maximum fine plus half of the relevant surcharge. 'Relevant surcharge' is defined in an new s 3(2A) inserted by s 15(3) of the Act as the surcharge payable 'by a person of that age who is fined the maximum amount for the offence'. If the relevant surcharge was £20, using the example above the person would have to pay £210.

E. HIGHER FIXED PENALTY FOR REPEATED ROAD TRAFFIC OFFENCES

7.15 Section 16(2) of the Act inserts a new s 53(3) into Road Traffic Offenders Act 1988 to allow a higher fixed penalty to be prescribed for repeat road traffic offenders, that is those who have committed an offence for which they were disqualified from driving or had penalty points endorsed on their licences within the previous three years. The period of three years was decided upon because that is the length of time an endorsement remains on a driving licence.

7.16 Section 16(3) of the Act inserts a new s 84(2) (regulations) into the Road Traffic Offenders Act 1988. This provides that in cases where a conditional offer has been made under s 75 of that Act which should have been a higher amount because it was a repeated road traffic offence under s 53 of that Act, then the fixed penalty clerk may issue a further 'surcharge notice' for the difference in the two amounts. Confusingly, this is not a surcharge of the kind imposed by s 161A of the Criminal Justice Act 2003, but in effect a higher fixed penalty, linked to the fact that it is a repeat offence. In effect the fixed penalty clerk is able to correct errors where the higher amount should have been charged but was not.

8

TRIAL BY JURY OF SAMPLE COUNTS ONLY

A. INTRODUCTION

The Act makes a radical change to the prosecution of sample counts, but the new provisions have no clear definitions to indicate when they should be applied. Therefore, in order to gain some understanding as to when and how the new sections will be utilized, it is helpful to look at the purpose behind the enactment. **8.01**

One of the stated aims of this Act was to punish offenders and 'to close loopholes where offenders were currently escaping justice'.[1] Sections 17 to 21 were introduced to close one of those loopholes, following recommendations from the Law Commission's consultation paper, *The Effective Prosecution of Multiple Offenders*.[2] **8.02**

Concerns had been identified in relation to the prosecution of multiple offences of fraud, although the new proposals are not limited to offences of fraud. The provisions will apply to any criminal trial where a defendant's offending is said to be too great to be accommodated in a single trial, although the Law Commission acknowledged that the problems identified would arise in only a limited number of offences other than fraud. Amongst that other limited number of offences would be internet pornography, innumerable similar thefts, and sex offences. **8.03**

---

[1] *Hansard*, HL col 949 (15 December 2003) *per* Baroness Scotland of Asthal.
[2] Law Com No 277.

8.04   Prior to the Court of Appeal decision in *R v Kidd*,[3] it was common practice in cases of multiple offending for the prosecution to frame an indictment containing a selected number of sample counts, which properly reflected the totality of other criminal offences of a similar nature committed by the defendant (D). This avoided the problem of an overloaded indictment and made the trial manageable. The sentencing tribunal would then proceed to sentence not just on the sample counts, but for the totality of the offending which the sample counts represented. This meant that D was being sentenced for offences of which he had never been convicted or which he had never admitted, whether by way of a guilty plea or by asking for other offences to be taken into consideration.

8.05   This was the exactly the point taken in *R v Kidd*. In that case D was a headmaster of a school and the allegations involved a series of indecent assaults. He was convicted of four counts on the indictment, which were presented as sample counts, and was sentenced not only for those four offences, but also for other offences of which the four were samples. On appeal, Lord Bingham CJ stated that:

> A defendant is not to be convicted of any offence with which he is charged unless and until his guilt is proved. Such guilt may be proved by his own admission or (on indictment) by the verdict of a jury. He may be sentenced only for an offence proved against him (by admission or verdict) or which he has admitted and asked the court to take into consideration when passing sentence.

Lord Bingham CJ went on to say that:

> Prosecuting authorities will wish, in the light of this decision . . . to include more counts in some indictments. We do not think this need be unduly burdensome or render the trial unmanageable.

8.06   The Law Commission did not challenge the validity of this decision but stated that it 'posed an intractable dilemma for prosecutors and the courts in cases of multiple theft and multiple fraud', leading to offenders escaping the appropriate sanctions. It recommended, therefore, that in such cases there should be a two-stage trial procedure.

8.07   The first stage takes place before a judge and jury with an indictment containing sample counts. Should a defendant be convicted by the jury of one or more counts on that indictment, then a second stage of the trial may follow, in which the defendant would be tried by a judge alone, in relation to scheduled offences linked to the specimen count of which the defendant had already been convicted. Not surprisingly these sections have been seen by many as an attack on trial by jury, with the Criminal Bar Association, amongst others, being firmly opposed to the provisions.

---

[3] [1998] 1 WLR 604.

B. APPLICATION BY PROSECUTION FOR CERTAIN COUNTS TO BE TRIED WITHOUT A JURY

Section 17 makes provision for the prosecution to apply to a judge for some **8.08** counts to be tried without a jury and sets out the conditions which must be met before such an order can be made. It also outlines matters to which the judge must pay regard in reaching a decision.

Section 17(1) provides that the prosecution may apply to a judge of the Crown **8.09** Court for a trial on indictment to take place on the basis that the trial of some, but not all, of the counts included in the indictment may be conducted without a jury. This application must be made at a preparatory hearing (s 18(1), see para 8.24 below). It is intended that applications under s 17(1) will only be made in cases of repeated similar offending, where previously sample counts would have been indicted.

C. THE THREE CONDITIONS

Section 17(2) provides that if an application is made under s 17(1) the judge **8.10** can only make an order for some, but not all, of the counts included in the indictment to be heard without a jury, if he is satisfied that three conditions are fulfilled. These three conditions are set out in s 17(3) to (5). They are that it is impracticable for the counts to be tried by a jury, that the counts can be regarded as sample counts, and that it is in the interests of justice for an order to be made.

1. That Trial by Jury is 'Impracticable'

The first condition in s 17(3) is that 'the number of counts included in the **8.11** indictment is likely to mean that a trial by jury involving all of those counts would be impracticable.' There is no definition of 'impracticable' in the Act, although there is clear guidance from the Court of Appeal that an indictment should not be overloaded.[4] The question of severance should be carefully considered at an early stage of any complex or lengthy trial in any event.

Bearing in mind the stated aim of these provisions, to ensure that a defendant **8.12** is to be sentenced for the totality of his proved offending, there is a balance to be struck between the making the trial manageable and the issues comprehensible to a jury, and the ability of a judge to sentence for the totality of a defendant's offending.

The first consideration, it is submitted, is that our system is based on the **8.13** assumption that even complex issues and evidence can be presented to a jury in a

---

[4] *R v Novac* (1977) 65 Cr App R 107 and *R v Kellard* [1995] 2 Cr App R 134.

way that they can understand. It is for the prosecution to show that jury trial, which should remain the norm, is likely to be impracticable. Section 17(6) provides that in reaching his decision the judge must have regard to any steps that might reasonably be taken to facilitate a trial by jury. The provision in s 17(2) should not become a means of remedying poor drafting of the indictment. If an indictment is properly and carefully drafted to reflect the full extent of a defendant's offending with relevant sample counts, it will only be in rare circumstances that an application under s 17 could be made. In the vast majority of criminal cases the proper use of sample counts on an indictment causes no problems to a sentencing judge.

8.14   Here are two typical situations.

Example 1
D is alleged to have indecently assaulted his stepdaughter almost daily over the course of two years. Obviously, it is as impracticable to indict him for a hundred individual assaults as it is to sentence him for those assaults. An indictment would be drafted containing sample counts, which reflected a number of offences over a period of time. There will normally be no problem in sentencing due to the serious nature of child abuse which will inevitably attract a substantial sentence even for the sample counts only.

Example 2
D dishonestly obtains welfare benefits over a period of four years amounting to £150,000. Again it would be impracticable to indict each offence separately, but in these circumstances, where the amount is a factor to be taken into account in sentencing,[5] a prosecutor might well apply to utilize the new provisions to ensure that D is sentenced for the totality of the offending.

8.15   The second condition in s 17(4) is that, if an order under s 17(2) were made, 'each count or group of counts which would accordingly be tried with a jury can be regarded as a sample of counts which could accordingly be tried without a jury'. Again there is no definition of a sample count but, as in any other case, r 9 of the Indictment Rules must be applied, that is, that the offences must be founded on the same facts or form part of a series of offences of the same or similar character, before counts can be linked.

8.16   In addition, it is submitted that the relationship between the sample counts and the linked offences should be such that the evidence on each sample count would be admissible on each of the offences in the schedule that are linked to that sample count, and vice versa. Questions of admissibility are to be determined by the laws of evidence, with the principles in the leading case of *DPP v P*[6] being applied.

---

[5] *R v Stewart* (1987) 9 Cr App R (S) 135.
[6] [1991] AC 421, HL.

Section 17(9) provides that for the purposes of this section and ss 18 to 20, a **8.17** count may not be regarded as a sample of other counts unless the defendant in respect of each count is the same person. It is difficult to see how the defendant could be anyone other than 'the same person' if the relevant criteria are to be satisfied before an order under s 17(2) can be made.

2. It is in the 'Interests of Justice'

The third condition in s 17(5) is that 'it is in the interests of justice for an order **8.18** under subsection (2) to be made.' This will be a balancing exercise between the rights of the defendant to a fair trial, as enshrined in Art 6 ECHR, and the ability of a sentencing judge to impose a fair sentence for the totality of offending. A likely problem is that the defendant may well perceive that a trial by a judge alone is inherently unfair and that the prosecution have 'cherry-picked' which counts should be heard by a jury and which by a judge.

The judge cannot make the order unless all three conditions are met. If they **8.19** are met, the judge has a discretion whether or not to make the order, since the Act only says that he 'may' do so. Once a judge has decided that a jury trial on all the counts is likely to be impracticable, however, it is not easy to see on what basis he could then decide not to make a section 17(2) order. Section 17(6) of the Act therefore provides that in deciding whether to make an order under s 17(2), the judge must have regard to any steps that might reasonably be taken to facilitate a trial by jury. This is closely linked to the condition that a jury trial is likely to be impracticable. If it can be facilitated by taking reasonable steps, it is not impracticable. This provision makes it clear that the judge must try to achieve a jury trial if he can.

The judge would have to consider whether a trial on sample counts would **8.20** adequately reflect the serious nature of the offending, such that a defendant could be properly sentenced for the totality of his offending or whether separate trials on groups of counts could take place. The cases where that would not be possible are likely to be rare.

Section 17(7) states that a step is not to be considered reasonable if it could **8.21** lead to the possibility of a defendant in the trial receiving a lesser sentence than would be the case if that step were not taken. This covers cases post *R v Kidd*,[7] where offenders could not be sentenced for the totality of their offending if they had not admitted guilt or been convicted of other similar offences. The judge will have to consider whether the sample counts in an indictment capable of being tried by a jury are sufficient to sentence a defendant adequately. In the vast majority of cases this should present no problem, if the indictment has been carefully considered and drawn up.

---

[7] [1998] 1 WLR 604.

3. Specifying the Counts

8.22 Section 17(8) provides that an order under s 17(2) must specify the counts that may be tried without a jury. It is intended that once the judge is satisfied that the conditions are met for an order to be made under s 17(2), the linked offences will be drawn up in a schedule to be attached to an indictment. These offences will be linked to a specified sample count on the indictment, to reflect the full extent of the alleged offending.

Example

8.23 D, the benefit fraudster above, is indicted on eight counts, each of which reflects a single offence in a six-month period covering the entire four years. If count 1, for instance, specified an offence on 1 January 2000, then the schedule linked to count 1 could include all the other offences committed between 2 January and 30 June 2000. Count 2 would indict an offence on 1 July 2000 and the schedule would include the remaining offences in the following six months and so on. Section 18 sets out the procedure that must be used in determining an application under s 17.

D. PROCEDURE FOR APPLICATIONS UNDER SECTION 17

1. Procedure for Determining the Application

8.24 Section 18(1) provides that the application *must* be determined at a preparatory hearing. It is not at the judge's discretion. Section 18(6) states that a preparatory hearing is to be given the same meaning as within the Criminal Justice Act 1987 and Pt 3 of the Criminal Procedure and Investigations Act 1996, which define a preparatory hearing by its purpose. At the hearing the judge will have to be satisfied that the application meets the three conditions set out in s 17 before he can make the order.

8.25 The purpose of such a preparatory hearing will be those purposes mentioned in s 7(1) of the Criminal Justice Act 1987 and in s 29(2) of the Criminal Procedure and Investigations Act 1996. Those stated purposes are to identify issues which are likely to be material to the verdict of the jury, assisting their comprehension of any such issues, expediting the proceedings before the jury, and assisting the judge's management of the trial. Section 18(2) of the Act extends them to include the purpose of determining the application under s 17. The hearing should be limited to these purposes and no other.[8]

8.26 Section 18(3) makes provision for s 29(1) of the Criminal Procedure and Investigations Act 1996 which gives a judge power to order that a preparatory hearing be held where the case appears complex or is likely to lead to a lengthy trial, to include a case where an application under s 17 of the Act has been made.

---

[8] *R v Gunarwardena* (1991) Cr App R 55.

In accordance with s 18(4) all parties to the preparatory hearing *must* be given **8.27** the opportunity to make representations with respect to the application. This will be the occasion when the defence must raise objections to the use of the procedure if they wish to challenge it.

2. Appeals

Under s 18(5), if either the prosecution or the defence do not accept the **8.28** judge's ruling that an order under s 17 should be made, there is a right of appeal to the Court of Appeal, but only with the leave of the judge or of the Court of Appeal. Section 9(11) of the Criminal Justice Act 1987 and s 35(1) of the Criminal Procedure and Investigations Act 1996, which govern interlocutory appeals against rulings made in the course of preparatory hearings under those Acts, are to have effect as if they also provided for an appeal from the determination by the judge under s 17.

3. Procedure following Conviction on the Sample Counts

In accordance with s 19(1), if an order is made under s 17(2) and a defendant is **8.29** found guilty by a jury on a count which can be regarded as a sample of other counts to be tried in those proceedings (contained in the schedules), those other counts may be tried without a jury. It is only where there has been a conviction by a jury of a sample count that a judge may proceed to the second stage of trial and consider offences linked in the schedules. If the jury acquit, then there is no procedure for the judge to hear the linked offences. It is not made clear what should happen to the linked offences, whether there should be a directed acquittal on them or whether they should lie on the file in the usual terms. The Law Commission was in favour of a presumption of a directed acquittal, unless exceptional circumstances dictated otherwise. It is submitted that there should be a directed acquittal rather than directing that they should lie on the file.

The Act is silent on what should happen if a defendant pleads guilty to the **8.30** sample counts on the indictment but not to the linked offences in the schedules. As there would be no conviction 'by a jury of a sample count' then the court could not go on to have a trial by a judge alone of the linked offences. Presumably if the Crown wished to proceed with those then there would have to be a jury trial in the usual way or other sample counts chosen with linked offences.

Section 19(2) gives the court conducting a trial without a jury, all the powers, **8.31** authorities, and jurisdiction which the court would have had if the trial had been conducted with a jury. Therefore, the court combines the roles of judge and jury and will determine both questions of fact and law. As this is a single trial with two stages, it is anticipated that the second stage will normally be heard by the same judge, with that judge being free to come to his or her own determination as to guilt on the linked offences. This poses the risk of inconsistent verdicts between the jury and a judge.

8.32   Except where the context otherwise requires, s 19(3) states that any reference in an enactment to a jury, the verdict of a jury, or the finding of a jury is to be read in relation to trials under s 17(2) as a reference to the court, the verdict of the court, or the findings of the court.

8.33   Under s 19(4)(a), if a defendant is convicted by a judge alone, following a hearing under s 17(2), the court *must* give a judgment which states the reasons for the conviction at, or as soon as reasonably practicable after, the time of the conviction. The Law Commission emphasized the importance of reasoned decisions, particularly where the judge was hearing a trial alone.[9] This was to ensure 'open justice and for the purposes of any appeal'.[10]

(a) *Appeals*

8.34   An appeal from a conviction by the court under s 17(2) is to be within twenty-eight days from the judgment mentioned in s 19(4)(a).

8.35   According to s 19(5), where there is a conviction by a jury of any count under the first stage of the trial, time does not begin to run under s 18(2) of the Criminal Appeal Act 1968 in relation to an appeal against that conviction until the date on which the proceedings end. As it has been emphasized that this is a single trial with two stages, this will be on the date that judgment is given in relation to any convictions at any trial without a jury.

8.36   Under s 19(6), in determining for the purposes of s 19(5) the date on which proceedings end, as for any other offence, the time period runs from the date of conviction and not sentence.

(b) *Issues of Insanity*

8.37   Section 19(7) states that nothing in ss 17 to 20 affects the requirement under s 4A of the Criminal Procedure (Insanity) Act 1964 that any question, finding, or verdict in that section be determined, made, or returned by a jury. The alterations made by the Act to the trial of an issue of unfitness to plead and insanity are dealt with in Chapter 9.

(c) *Rules of Court*

8.38   Section 20 provides that rules of court may make such provision as appear necessary or expedient in relation to ss 17 to 19. This includes the time limits for an application to be made under s 17, as the Act is silent as to this. At the time of writing, no rules are available. Given the wording of the Act, however, they are likely to be similar to the rules for preparatory hearings under the Criminal Justice Act 1987 (Preparatory Hearings) Rules 1997[11] and the

---

[9] *Murray v UK* [1995] 19 EHRR 193.
[10] Law Com No 277, para 7.41.
[11] SI 1997/1051

Criminal Procedure and Investigations Act 1996 (Preparatory Hearings) Rules 1997.[12]

8.39 Section 21 provides for the application of ss 17 to 20 to Northern Ireland which is outside the scope of this book.

---

[12] SI 1997/1052.

9

UNFITNESS TO PLEAD AND INSANITY

A. INTRODUCTION

The Act makes significant changes to the way in which the issue of fitness to **9.01** plead is to be tried, and the orders available to the court to deal with those who are found unfit to plead or not guilty by reason of insanity. In his report entitled 'Review of the Criminal Courts', published in October 2001, Lord Justice Auld recommended that the issue of fitness to plead be tried by a judge rather than a jury.[1] This recommendation was accepted by the Government. Clauses to effect these changes were inserted in the draft Mental Health Bill in June 2002. Controversy surrounding other aspects of the Mental Health Bill led to its being lost. The provisions have now been inserted into the Act in ss 22 to 26.

The new provisions apply only to those arraigned after the Act comes into **9.02** force.[2]

B. FITNESS TO PLEAD OR STAND TRIAL

The law and procedure for determining the issue of whether the defendant is **9.03** fit to plead or stand trial are set out in ss 4, 4A, and 5 of the Criminal Procedure (Insanity) Act 1964. Section 22(2) of the Act implements the recommendation of Lord Justice Auld that the issue of fitness to plead be tried by a judge and not

---

[1] Recommendation 51, paras 212–13.
[2] Schedule 12, para 8.

a jury. It does so by substituting for the words 'by a jury' in s 4(5) of the 1964 Act the words 'by the court without a jury'.

1. The Substantive Law

9.04   The Act does not change the substantive law on whether or not the defendant is fit to plead. The term 'fitness to plead' is, in practical terms, an incomplete, if not misleading description of the issue to be determined by a trial court. More commonly, the question is not whether an accused is physically or mentally competent to enter a plea, it is whether or not an accused is fit to stand trial. However, there may inevitably be an overlap between the two stages.

9.05   Section 4(1) of the Criminal Procedure (Insanity) Act 1964 applies where, on the trial of a person, the question arises whether the accused is under a disability such that, apart from this Act, it would constitute a bar to his being tried. The test remains as articulated 170 years ago in the case of *R v Pritchard*.[3] In that case the accused was a deaf mute. It was unclear whether he was a genuine mute or of sound or unsound mind. The jury empanelled to make the relevant findings were directed by Alderson B in the following terms:

> There are three points to be inquired into: First, whether the prisoner is mute of malice or not; secondly, whether he can plead to the indictment or not; thirdly, whether he is of sufficient intellect to comprehend the course of proceedings on the trial, so as to make a proper defence—to know that he might challenge [any jurors] to whom he may object— and to comprehend the details of the evidence . . . if you think that there is no certain mode of communicating the details of the trial to the prisoner, so that he can clearly understand them and be able properly to make his defence to the charge; you ought to find that he is not of sane mind. It is not enough, that he may have a general capacity of communicating on ordinary matters.[4]

9.06   The courts have, accordingly, sought to reconcile the statutory term 'disability' with the historical test set out in *R v Pritchard*. The court now considers whether an accused is capable of understanding the proceedings so as to:

- put forward his defence;
- challenge jurors;
- give proper instructions to his legal representatives; and
- follow the evidence.

9.07   Accordingly, an accused may be unfit to plead even if his condition falls outside of the definition of mental illness contained in the Mental Health Act 1983[5] or outside of the definition of insanity as set out in *R v M'Naughten*[6] (see

---

[3] *Pritchard* (1836) 7 C & P 303.
[4] ibid 304–6.
[5] Section 1.
[6] (1843) 8 ER 718.

R v Governor of Stafford Prison, ex p Emery).[7]

Conversely, an accused with a recognized mental illness and a high level of **9.08**
abnormality may nevertheless be fit to plead as long as he can satisfy the
requirements of the modern interpretation of the *Pritchard* test (see *R v Berry*).[8]
If the accused is unable to communicate with his legal advisers, he should be
found unfit (see *R v Sharp*).[9] Where an accused is fit to plead within the *Pritchard*
test, he is fit to plead even if his mental condition means that he may act against
his own best interests (see *R v Robertson*).[10]

By s 4(6) of the 1964 Act (as amended by s 22(3) of the Act), a court cannot **9.09**
make a determination of fitness to be tried, except on the written or oral evidence of two or more registered practitioners at least one of whom is duly
approved under the Mental Health Act 1983.

If the issue of fitness to plead is put forward by the defence, the onus of proof **9.10**
is upon the defence and is discharged if the court is satisfied on the balance of
probabilities that the accused is suffering from a disability (see *R v Robertson*). If
the Crown makes the allegation and the defence disputes the issue, the burden
rests upon the Crown (see *R v Podola*)[11] and the standard of proof is beyond
reasonable doubt.[12] There is no clear authority as to the standard or burden of
proof where the issue is raised, as it may be, by the court.

The question of fitness to stand trial is usually dealt with on arraignment. **9.11**
Under s 4(2) of the Criminal Procedure (Insanity) Act 1964, the court can
postpone consideration of the issue until later in the trial up to the opening
of the case for the defence. The question may not be determined after the
defendant has been acquitted on all counts (s 4(3)).

2. Determination of the Facts

Section 4A of the Criminal Procedure (Insanity) Act 1964 provides that once **9.12**
there has been a finding that the accused is under a disability, the trial shall not
continue. Instead, a jury decides whether the accused 'did the act or made the
omission charged against him as the offence', in a procedure referred to as the
'trial of the facts'.[13] That procedure remains in place. It ensures that a person
against whom there was not sufficient evidence to establish that he was the
person responsible for the acts or omissions, is acquitted. It also provides a
factual basis for the court and, where appropriate, the hospital authorities or
others to deal with the defendant.

---

[7] [1909] 2 KB 81.
[8] (1977) 66 Cr App R 156, CA.
[9] (1988) 41 Cr App R 197.
[10] [1968] 1 WLR 1767.
[11] [1960] 1 QB 325.
[12] *R v Robertson*, above.
[13] Section 48(6) of the Criminal Justice Act 2003 as amended by Sch 10, para 60 (which makes
provisions for trials without a jury) does not apply to this type of hearing.

9.13   Section 22(4) of the Act makes a consequential amendment to s 4A(1) so that the determination whether the accused is under a disability is made by the court and not the jury. If that determination is made on arraignment, a jury will be sworn in to decide whether he did the act or omission. If the determination takes place later in the trial, the jury that was trying him will make that determination (s 22(5)). The Act does not give the court a discretion to have the issue tried by another jury once the defendant is in charge of a jury. The Act does not appear to contemplate that circumstances may arise in which it is not appropriate for the original jury to continue to hear the case. Whether and to what extent the normal powers which the judge has to discharge a jury may be exercised in these circumstances are unclear.

9.14   By s 4A(2) of the 1964 Act, the determination of the facts takes place on the evidence (if any) already given in the trial and on such evidence as may be adduced or further adduced by the prosecution or adduced by the person appointed by the court under this section to put the case for the defence.

9.15   The jury has to be satisfied that the accused did the act or made the omission charged against him before it can make a finding. The standard of proof is the criminal standard of beyond reasonable doubt. The notion of 'act' or 'omission' is independent of any requisite mental element of a given charge, and consequently defences relating to state of mind (for example, provocation or diminished responsibility) are not open to the defence (see *R v Grant*[14] and *Antoine*[15]). If the jury are not so satisfied, then, by virtue of s 4A(4) of the 1964 Act, they shall acquit him as if the trial had proceeded to a conclusion.

9.16   The procedure relating to the 'trial of the facts' has been held to be consistent with the provisions of Art 6 ECHR. The Court of Appeal held that such a trial related to the determination of facts on behalf of a disabled person as opposed to a criminal trial (see *R v M*[16]).

9.17   Section 23 of the Act makes comparable changes to the determination of an issue of fitness to plead in Northern Ireland and falls outside the ambit of this book.

C. POWERS OF THE COURT TO DEAL WITH THOSE FOUND UNFIT TO PLEAD OR NOT GUILTY BY REASON OF INSANITY

9.18   Upon a special verdict that an accused was not guilty by reason of insanity or a finding that he 'did the act or made the omission charged against him', s 5 of the Criminal Procedure (Insanity) Act 1964 allowed a court disposing of a person under a disability, to make one of four orders, namely:

---

[14] [2002] QB 1030.
[15] [2001] 1 AC 340.
[16] [2002] 1 WLR 824.

- an order that the accused be admitted to hospital;[17]

or, unless the sentence for the offence to which the special verdict or findings relate is fixed by law:

- a guardianship order;[18]
- a supervision and treatment order;[19]
- an order for his absolute discharge.

An order for an accused to be admitted to hospital pursuant to s 5(1)(a) was **9.19** not a hospital order under s 37 of the Mental Health Act 1983. The powers under that section only arise when the accused was convicted, and so did not allow the court to impose a hospital order either with or without restriction under s 41 of that Act (see *Fairley*[20]).

Section 24(1) of the Act provides for the complete substitution of the existing **9.20** s 5 and creates a new s 5A. The new powers of disposal continue to apply where there is either a special verdict that an accused was not guilty by reason of insanity or a finding that he did the act or made the omission charged against him (s 5(1)).

The new s 5(2) provides: **9.21**

The court shall make in respect of the accused—
(a) a hospital order[21] (with or without a restriction order[22]);
(b) a supervision order; or
(c) an order for his absolute discharge.

A supervision order is a supervision order under the new Sch 1A to the 1964 Act which is inserted by the new s 5A(5) and Sch 2 to the Act.

The requirements of a supervision order under Sch 2 are broadly similar to **9.22** those of any other supervision order. The court may not make an order unless it is satisfied that the making of the order is the most suitable means of dealing with the accused. The supervision may be either by social services or by a probation officer, who must have indicated their willingness to undertake the supervision. The order may include a requirement for medical treatment on the evidence of at least two registered medical practitioners, one of whom is a registered mental health practitioner, that the defendant requires and may be susceptible to treatment, but does not need to be detained in hospital for it. Before making the order the court must be satisfied that arrangements have been

---

[17] Schedule 1 to the Criminal Procedure (Insanity and Unfitness to Plead) Act 1991.
[18] Within the meaning of the Mental Health Act 1983.
[19] Schedule 2 to the Criminal Procedure (Insanity and Unfitness to Plead) Act 1991
[20] [2003] EWCA Crim 1625.
[21] Under s 37 of the Mental Health Act 1983. There are consequential amendments to the Mental Health Act 1983, following the repeal of the power to make a hospital order under Sch 1 to the Criminal Procedure (Insanity and Unfitness to Plead) Act 1991.
[22] Under s 41 of the Mental Health Act 1983.

made for such treatment. The order lasts for up to two years, but may be revoked or amended within that time. The whole of Sch 2 can be found in Appendix A.

9.23 Where a person is admitted to hospital pursuant to a hospital order under s 37 of the Mental Health Act 1983, the individual is in a similar position to anyone admitted under the civil provisions of s 3 of the 1983 Act. The order for detention is valid for six months, but may be renewed thereafter if the medical grounds for continued detention are satisfied. A hospital order may be with or without restriction pursuant to s 41 of the Mental Health Act.

9.24 The power to make a restriction order exists where it appears to the court that, having regard to the nature of the offence, the antecedents of the offender and the risk of his committing further offences if set at large, it is necessary for the protection of the public from serious harm to place restrictions on his future release. Section 41 of the Mental Health Act allows the sentencing or disposing court to ensure that an individual remains detained even where the civil detention requirements have ceased to exist.

9.25 Unlike a hospital order made pursuant to s 37 of the Mental Health Act, a restriction order is not renewable and remains in force during the stated term of its currency, which may be without limit of time in certain cases. Release is then regulated by passage of time in the case of a specified restricted period, although the defendant may still be detained if the medical conditions justifying detention are satisfied. In the case of an restriction order without limit of time, the defendant may only be released on the order of the Secretary of State or by a Mental Health Review Tribunal. The effect of restriction is that a patient detained following an unfitness to plead disposal may be detained even if the condition from which he was suffering at the time of disposal no longer persists.

9.26 Where the sentence for the offence to which the special verdict or findings relate is fixed by law, and the court have power to make a hospital order, the new s 5(3) requires the court to make a hospital order with a restriction order.

9.27 The new ss 5A(1) to (3) make consequential amendments to the sections of the Mental Health Act 1983 that deal with the powers to make hospital and restriction orders, including the power to remand to hospital for reports and to make interim hospital orders, so that they now apply to orders made under this section and do not arise only when the defendant is convicted.

9.28 Where the court makes a hospital order under s 5(1) and the court also makes a restriction order which has not ceased to have effect, the Secretary of State, if satisfied after consultation with the responsible medical officer that the person can properly be tried, may remit the person for trial, either to the court of trial or to a prison (s 5(4)). On the person's arrival at the court or prison, the hospital and restriction orders cease to have effect. The Act is silent about the legal basis upon which the person is then detained. There is no provision about how the trial process is to be reactivated, nor about bringing him before a court if he is remitted to prison. There is nothing about him having access to legal advice. The Act is similarly silent about the basis upon which he is then to be tried. Do the findings of fact made by a previous jury bind the court at trial? What about those counts upon which he was 'acquitted' in a determination of the facts? Since the statute law has always made it clear that this procedure is not a trial, can the defendant plead *autrefois acquit*? Whilst the provision is only rarely likely to be used, it is likely to provide fertile ground for challenge and argument.

D. APPEALS

Section 16 of the Criminal Appeal Act 1968, as amended, gives the defendant   **9.29** a right to appeal against a finding that he is under a disability. The Court of Appeal may allow the appeal if they think the finding is unsafe, in which case the defendant may be tried for the offences with which he is charged. He may also appeal against any findings that he did the act or omission charged against him. If it allows the appeal, the Court of Appeal shall direct his acquittal. These powers are not affected by the Act.

Section 24 of the Act gives the Court of Appeal similar powers in relation to   **9.30** disposal of persons to whom the new ss 5 and 5A apply as the trial court. It does this by modifying ss 6 (substitution of finding of insanity or findings of unfitness to plead) and 14 (substitution of findings of unfitness to plead, etc) of the Criminal Appeals Act 1968.

Section 25 inserts new ss 16A and 16B to the Criminal Appeal Act 1968. The   **9.31** new s 16A provides a right of appeal (subject to leave or a trial judge certification) in relation to the imposition of a hospital order or interim hospital order by the Crown Court pursuant to that court's section 5 or 5A powers. The new s 16B gives the Court of Appeal the power, if it thinks the appellant should be dealt with differently, to dispose of any appeal by quashing, substituting, or varying the original order, so as to make the order they think is appropriate.

Section 26 gives effect to Sch 3 to the new Act (unfitness to stand trial and   **9.32** insanity: courts-martial, etc), as it relates to courts-martial.

E. THE ROLE OF THE LEGAL REPRESENTATIVE

It is apparent from the foregoing that the issue of fitness to plead is a mental   **9.33** health issue. As such, and as set out in para 213 of the Auld report, the matter is often the subject of agreement between the defence and prosecution. Mental health issues are not ordinarily adversarial, as it is the case that all interested parties have the best interests of the patient or potential patient in mind when conducting proceedings.

Criminal proceedings are by their nature adversarial. The best interests of a   **9.34** defendant qua defendant may not correspond with the best interests of a defendant qua patient or potential patient. The provisions of the old law and the Act may therefore place advocates in a criminal trial, both prosecution and defence, and particularly the defence, in a position where a conflict of interest between those two roles arises or may arise. This may be particularly acute if the judge raises the issue of fitness to plead during the course of a trial in which the defendant does not wish the issue to be raised, for example because he has a good defence on the merits. The new Act does nothing to address the duality of the roles of the trial advocate.

10

MISCELLANEOUS

A. POWERS OF AUTHORIZED OFFICERS EXECUTING WARRANTS

Under the Magistrates' Courts Act 1980, as amended, there are now persons **10.01** authorized under s 125A or s 125B for the purpose of executing warrants for the enforcement of fines and other orders. Those persons authorized by those two sections are civilian enforcement officers[1] and approved enforcement agencies.[2]

Section 27 gives further powers to authorized officers executing warrants of **10.02** arrest, commitment, detention, or distress, by inserting a new Sch 4A into the Magistrates' Courts Act 1980. Section 27(1) inserts s 125BA into the 1980 Act to give effect to the new Sch 4A in which the new powers are contained. Just to confuse things, the new Sch 4A is found in Sch 4 of the Act. Section 27(2) of the Act inserts Sch 4A after Sch 4 to the Magistrates' Courts Act 1980. Amazing!

Paragraph 1 of Sch 4A defines 'authorized officer' to mean a person entitled **10.03** to execute the warrant by virtue of s 125A (civilian enforcement officers) and s 125B of the Magistrates' Courts Act 1980 (approved enforcement agencies). It also defines premises to include any place and, in particular, include any vehicle,

---

[1] Section 125A(2)(a) defines civilian enforcement officers and includes employees of local authorities, police authorities, and magistrates' courts committees.

[2] Section 125B(2) defines 'approved enforcement agencies'. They are agencies approved under s 31A of the Justices of the Peace Act 1997, applying the criteria in the Approved Enforcement Agencies Regulations 2000.

vessel, aircraft, or hovercraft; any offshore installation within the meaning of the Mineral Workings (Offshore Installations) Act 1971; and any tent or moveable structure.

1. Entry to Execute Warrant of Arrest, etc

10.04 Paragraph 2 gives the power to an authorized officer to enter and search any premises for the purpose of executing a warrant of arrest, commitment, or detention issued in proceedings for or in connection with any criminal offence. This power may only be used to the extent that it is reasonably required for that purpose and only if the officer has reasonable grounds for believing that the person he is seeking is on the premises.[3] If the premises consists of two or more separate dwellings the power is limited to the common parts of the premises used by the occupiers of the separate dwellings and any such dwelling in which the officer has reasonable grounds for believing that the person whom he is seeking may be.[4]

2. Entry to Levy Distress

10.05 Distress is an ancient remedy which allows the debtor's money and goods to the value of the debt to be seized. Because it involves acts which would otherwise be tortious, authority to levy distress is granted by the issue of a distress warrant. A magistrates' court has power[5] to issue a distress warrant where a sum adjudged to be paid by a conviction or order of the magistrates' court is unpaid. An authorized officer may enter and search any premises in order to execute a distress warrant issued under s 76 of the Magistrates' Courts Act 1980. The power may be exercised only to the extent that it is reasonably required for that purpose.[6]

3. Searching Arrested Persons

10.06 Paragraph 4 of Sch 4A makes provision for an authorized officer to search a person arrested under a warrant of arrest, commitment, or detention issued in proceedings for or in connection with any criminal offence. There is no power to search a person arrested or committed for a purely civil matter, such as non-payment of maintenance. It would allow the search of a witness who had failed to answer a witness summons in a criminal case, and a warrant for their arrest had been issued, since that would have been issued in proceedings for a criminal offence. It is unclear whether a warrant of arrest for non-payment of a fine is

---

[3] Paragraph 2(2).
[4] Paragraph 2(3).
[5] Under Magistrates' Courts Act 1980, s 76.
[6] Paragraph 3.

issued 'in connection with a criminal offence'. Arguably, the offence is done and proved. The warrant is issued in connection with the non-payment of a financial penalty imposed, not the offence itself.

Paragraph 4(5) limits these powers of search. They are not to be read as authorizing the officer to require a person to remove any of his clothing in public other than an outer coat, a jacket, or gloves. However, officers are specifically authorized to search a person's mouth. **10.07**

Provided that the general condition in para 4(1) is satisfied, an authorized officer may search the arrested person if he has reasonable grounds for believing that the arrested person may present a danger to himself or others (para 4(2)). Obviously, the power is intended to allow the arresting officer to search for possible weapons, but it is not limited to that. Paragraph 4(6) authorizes an officer searching a person under this section to seize and retain any item he finds if he has reasonable grounds for believing that a person searched might use it to cause injury to himself or another. He may not seize and retain anything else, unless, presumably, the authorized officer finds something the possession of which is itself unlawful, such as illegal drugs or stolen property, when he may be able to do so under other powers. **10.08**

An authorized officer may also search an arrested person for anything which he might use to assist him to escape from lawful custody,[7] but only if the officer has reasonable grounds for believing that the arrested person may have concealed any such item on him[8] and only to the extent that it is reasonably required.[9] He may seize and retain anything he finds if he has reasonable grounds for believing that the person might use it to assist him to escape from lawful custody (para 4(7)). **10.09**

4. Use of Force

Paragraph 5 of Sch 4A provides that an authorized officer may use reasonable force, if necessary, in the exercise of a power conferred on him by this Schedule. What is reasonable force will depend on all the circumstances. The use of excessive force will render the search of the premises or persons, or the arrest unlawful. **10.10**

B. DISCLOSURE ORDERS FOR THE PURPOSE OF EXECUTING WARRANTS

Section 125C of the Magistrates' Courts Act 1980 already provides for basic personal information held by a relevant public authority to be supplied to a **10.11**

---

[7] Paragraph 4(3).
[8] Paragraph 4(4)(a).
[9] Paragraph 4(4)(b).

magistrates' court to facilitate the enforcement of a warrant. Section 28 inserts s 125CA into the Magistrates' Courts Act 1980, which sets out the power to make a disclosure order. Under s 125CA(1), a magistrates' court may make a disclosure order if it is satisfied that it is necessary to do so for the purpose of executing a warrant to which this section applies. Section 125CA(2) defines these as warrants of arrest, detention, commitment, and distress, issued by a justice of the peace in connection with the enforcement of a fine or other order imposed or made on conviction. Under s 125CA(4) such an order may only be made on the application of a person entitled to execute the warrant.

10.12   The order requires the person to whom it is directed to supply to the designated officer for the court the name, date of birth, national insurance number, and his address or any of his addresses of the person to whom the warrant relates. The section applies to the Crown as it applies to other persons.[10] The main recipients are obviously likely to be the Inland Revenue, the Department of Work and Pensions, and local authorities. These are organizations to which the public are required to give information, sometimes with an expectation that it will be kept confidential, which is then used for a quite different purpose. It is hard to envisage circumstances in which a court would issue a warrant against someone whose name it does not know. It is therefore unlikely to be necessary for that information to be required for the purposes of execution. The disclosure of an address is already permitted under other legislation.[11] Disclosure of a national insurance number gives access to other information about the individual concerned.

1. Use of Information Supplied under Disclosure Order

10.13   Section 28 of this Act also inserts s 125CB into the Magistrates' Courts Act 1980, which details what use may be made of any information supplied under a disclosure order. It also creates an either way offence if a person intentionally or recklessly discloses information supplied under a disclosure order otherwise than as permitted, or uses the information otherwise than for the purpose of facilitating the execution of a warrant.

10.14   Section 125CB(1) provides that the information supplied to a person under the order may be supplied by him to:

(a) the applicant for the order or any other person entitled to execute the warrant concerned;

(b) any employee of a body or person who, for the purposes of section 125B above, is an approved enforcement agency in relation to the warrant;

(c) any justices' clerk or other person appointed under section 2(1) of the Courts Act 2003.

---

[10] Section 125CA(5).
[11] For example, where a child has gone missing or to make orders for maintenance.

The offence for improper disclosure is created by s 125CB(2). If a person **10.15** intentionally or recklessly discloses information otherwise than as permitted under s 125CB(1) above or uses it otherwise than for the purpose of facilitating the execution of the warrant concerned, then he commits an offence.

Under s 125CB(3), it is not an offence to disclose any information in accord- **10.16** ance with any enactment or order of a court or for the purpose of any proceedings before a court or to disclose information which has previously been lawfully disclosed to the public. Section 125CB(4) sets out the penalties on conviction, which on summary conviction is a fine not exceeding the statutory maximum, and on indictment is a fine.

C. PROCEDURE ON BREACH OF COMMUNITY PENALTY, ETC

Section 29 of the new Act brings into effect Sch 5 to the Act, and concerns the **10.17** procedure to be followed by magistrates' courts in the event of breaches of the following orders:

(a) supervision requirements of detention and training orders (para 2);

(b) suspended sentence supervision orders (para 3);

(c) community orders under the Powers of Criminal Courts (Sentencing) Act 2000 (para 4);

(d) curfew orders and exclusion orders (para 5);

(e) attendance centre orders (para 6);

(f) community orders under the Criminal Justice Act 2003 (para 7);

(g) suspended sentence orders under the Criminal Justice Act 2003 (para 8).

The effect of paras 2 to 8 of Sch 5 to the Act is to remove the geographical **10.18** jurisdictional constraints implicit in the existing statutory regime. The Schedule is couched in similar terms in respect of breaches of any of the orders cited above. Instead of having to be brought back before the court that made the order, the offender will usually be brought before the court in the area in which he resides. Whilst this may be more convenient for the offender, it may mean that the supervisor has to travel to a different part of the country in order to give evidence. It also means that the court dealing with the breach may not have all the information that was available to the court that made the original order. The Schedule also allows the court dealing with an offender to amend the orders where there has been a change of residence.

D. PROSECUTION APPEALS

Section 30 of the Act amends s 58 of the Criminal Justice Act 2003. Part 9 of **10.19** that Act introduced new rights for the prosecution to appeal against rulings made by a Crown Court judge during the trial, including a ruling that there was no case to answer. Section 58(13) provided that the applicable time for the prosecution to apply to appeal was 'any time (whether before or after the commencement of the trial) before the *start of the judge's* summing-up to a jury'. Section 30(1) replaces the words in italics with 'time when the judge starts his'. The new wording makes no substantive change, but fits more happily with the change made by s 30(2) to deal with trials by a judge without a jury.

10.20 Section 30(2) of the Act is partly to correct an omission by oversight in the Criminal Justice Act 2003, under Pt 7 of which judges may try cases of fraud or alleged jury tampering without a jury. The previous wording which set out time limits by reference to the summing-up to a jury did not fit for non-jury trials. Section 30(2) therefore introduces a new s 58(14) into that Act. It provides that the reference to the time when the judge starts his summing-up to the jury includes the time when the judge would start his summing-up to the jury, but for the making of an order under Pt 7. The interpretation section of the Criminal Justice Act 2003 (s 74) is amended by Sch 10, para 60 to the Act to bring the trial of offences linked to sample counts by a judge alone within Pt 7, with such modifications as the Secretary of State may by order specify.

E. INTERMITTENT CUSTODY

10.21 Section 31 of the Act brings into effect Sch 6 to the Act. The main provision is in para 7. This inserts a new s 264A into the Criminal Justice Act 2003. The remainder of the Schedule makes consequential amendments to other sections of the 2003 Act. Section 264 of that Act deals with consecutive terms of imprisonment, but omitted to deal with intermittent custody orders.[12] The new section deals with the calculation of the periods to be served where the offender is sentenced to two or more terms of imprisonment to be served consecutively, each of which is a term to which an intermittent custody order relates.

10.22 Under an intermittent custody order, the prisoner will serve custodial periods in short blocks of a few days at a time, with the licence period running between these blocks. The effect of the amendment is that the offender is not to be treated as having served all the required custodial days until he has served the aggregate of the custodial days in relation to each term. Once the custodial days have been served, the offender remains on licence until the expiry of the relevant time which is the aggregate of all the custodial days and the longest of the total licence periods in relation to those terms.

---

[12] Criminal Justice Act 2003, s 183.

F. CONCLUSION

The amendments made under ss 30 and 31, whilst being minor and technical, **10.23** required yet another amendment to the long title of the Act. The continually changing nature of the bill drew attention in Parliament to the observation by outside concerned organizations that: 'This appears now to be less of a domestic violence Bill than a general crime Bill.'[13]

It was anticipated that inconvenience will be caused to practitioners when **10.24** such far-ranging general criminal and procedural provisions are included in legislation which will be referred to in short as the 'Domestic Violence Act'. This remains to be seen, and it may be that criminal practitioners have developed an immunity to the occupational hazard of misleadingly named and ever-changing criminal legislation.

---

[13] HL Vol 658, col 1423 (11 March 2004).

11

VICTIMS, ETC

A. SUMMARY

The provisions in Pt 3 of the Act set out the rights that some victims have to support, advice, and information. Prior to this Act support for victims, who may be witnesses, was provided by voluntary organizations and within various codes of practice, for example the Director of Public Prosecutions is responsible for issuing a Code for Crown Prosecutors under s 10 of the Prosecution of Offences Act 1986. **11.01**

Chapter 1 of Pt III of the Act provides for a statutory code of practice for victims. The procedure for issuing the code is prescribed by s 33 and the effect of non-compliance with the code is provided for by s 34. **11.02**

Chapter 2 of Pt III of the Act provides victims of a sexual or violent offence with the right to make representations or receive information concerning licence conditions or supervision requirements where the offender has been sentenced to imprisonment or detention. Corresponding provisions in relation to offenders subject to hospital orders, hospital directions, and transfer directions are contained in ss 36 to 44. The interpretation of ss 35 to 44 is contained in s 46. **11.03**

Chapter 3 of Pt III of the Act allows for investigations by the Parliamentary Commissioner in respect of complaints arising from the duties imposed by the code of practice and the duties of the local probation boards under ss 35 to 44 of the Act. A Commissioner for Victims and Witnesses is provided for by s 48. The functions duties and authorities within his remit are specified in ss 49 to 53 of the Act. Section 54 of the Act provides for disclosure of information in relation to compliance with the code, the duties of the local probation boards, **11.04** and the carrying out of the functions of the Commissioner. Section 55 places a duty on the Secretary of State to appoint a Victims' Advisory Panel. Section 56 gives the Secretary of State the power to pay grants to assist victims, witnesses, and other persons affected by offences. Section 57 provides for the recovery of criminal injuries compensation from offenders.

B. CHAPTER 1: THE VICTIMS' CODE

11.05 Section 32 of the Act requires the Home Secretary to publish a statutory code of practice for victims.[1] The code represents a minimum level of service in England and Wales. It supersedes the Victims' Charter. The Victims' Charter was published in 1990; it explained what happens after an offence has been reported to the police and the standards of service which a victim should expect. It was revised in 1996 and again in 2001 when the Home Office received responses to 'A Review of the Victims' Charter'. The Government expect the new code to be published for consultation in January or February 2006. Following the publication there will be a consultation period with the proposed code being laid before Parliament in the summer of 2006. The code should be implemented by December 2006.

11.06 Section 32(2) allows the code to restrict the application of the provisions to specified classes of victims. The proposals for those entitled to receive services under the draft code are set out in s 4 of the draft. It is divided into two sections, 'Which crimes?' and 'Which people?'. The crimes covered by the draft code are damage and deprivation of property, injury, and sexual offences. Those provided for are the victims, parents or guardians and, where a person has died, the victim's family spokesperson. Only individuals or businesses with fewer than nine employees are entitled to receive services.

11.07 Section 32(3) permits the code to include provision requiring or permitting services which are to be provided to a victim to be provided to others. For example, the draft code allows a parent or guardian to receive services where the person entitled is under 17. If the parent or guardian, however, is under investigation or has been charged in respect of the criminal conduct of which the young person is a victim then they are not entitled to receive services.

11.08 Section 32(4) provides for the code to make different provision for different purposes. Each organization required to provide services will necessarily provide different services. For example, the obligations of the Crown Prosecution Service are different from the obligations of the Criminal Injuries Compensation Authority, because their roles within the Criminal Justice System are different.

---

[1] A draft version of the code is available at http://www.cjsonline.gov.uk/citizen/victims/domviolence.html.

The most important limitation is in s 32(5) of the Act, which provides: **11.09**

The code may not require anything to be done by—
(a) a person acting in a judicial capacity;
(b) a person acting in the discharge of a function of a member of the Crown Prosecution Service which involves the exercise of discretion.

The provision limits the code so that judges and magistrates will not be subject to obligations under the code. The Crown Prosecution Service does have obligations according to the draft code, but the code cannot affect their decisions whether or not to prosecute. The provision allows judicial decisions to remain independent from the code.

Section 32(6) provides for victims to receive services regardless of whether **11.10** there has been a charge or conviction. An example of such service is at para 9.4 of the draft code where 'Victim Support must provide the Victim Support line, a national telephone service that offers advice to victims and others affected by crime'. Victim Support, an independent charity set up in the 1950s, has now contracted with the Home Office to provide certain services to victims.

Section 33(1) to (7) set out the procedure for bringing the code into effect. **11.11** The Home Secretary is required to consult with the Lord Chancellor and the Attorney-General when drafting the code. An agreed final version of the code will be laid before Parliament before it is brought into operation. The code may be revised under s 33(8); however, s 33(9) limits the revision so that future amendments to the code cannot reduce the rights of victims.

Section 34 provides for the effect of non-compliance: **11.12**

(1) If a person fails to perform a duty imposed on him by a code issued under section 32, the failure does not of itself make him liable to criminal or civil proceedings.
(2) But the code is admissible in evidence in criminal or civil proceedings and a court may take into account a failure to comply with the code in determining a question in the proceedings.

The code is a statutory code, breach of which cannot give rise to an action in itself. In a claim for negligence, however, the code would be admissible in evidence.

C. CHAPTER 2: REPRESENTATION AND INFORMATION

Sections 35 to 44 provide for victims to receive information and make repre- **11.13** sentations in respect of licence conditions or supervision requirements in the event of the offender's release. This Act repeals s 69 of the Criminal Justice and Court Services Act 2000.[2] Sections 36 to 44 of this Act put in place provisions where the offender is subject to orders under the Mental Health Act 1983.

---

[2] Section 69 of the Criminal Justice and Court Services Act sets out the duties of the local probation boards in connection with victims of sexual or violent crimes.

11.14 Section 35 provides for victims to receive information and make representations. 'The offender' must have been convicted of a sexual or violent offence and received a sentence of:

- imprisonment for a term of 12 months or more;
- detention during Her Majesty's pleasure;
- detention for a period of twelve months or more under s 91 of the Powers of Criminal Courts (Sentencing) Act 2000 (offenders under 18 convicted of certain serious offences);
- detention and training order of twelve months or more.

11.15 The local probation board have a duty to take reasonable steps to find out whether the person who appears to be the victim, or to act for the victim, wishes to make representations or receive information in respect of licence conditions or supervision requirements, in the event of the offender's release. Any representations made must be passed on to those deciding licence conditions or supervision requirements.

11.16 Sections 36, 37, and 38 place the same duty on local probation boards in respect of victims of those who are mentally ill who wish to make representations or receive information. The duty under these sections is in relation to an offender who is convicted, or who is found not guilty by reason of insanity, or in respect of whom findings are made following a determination that he is unfit to take part in the trial, and who is made the subject of a hospital order and restriction order.

11.17 The court may make a hospital order under s 37 of the Mental Health Act 1983. At the same time the court can make a restriction order under s 41 of that Act. To make a restriction order the court must be satisfied that the order is necessary to protect the public from serious harm. The restrictions under s 41 are that there is no periodic review as provided for by s 20 of the Mental Health Act 1983. Discharge, transfer, and leave of absence are restricted unless consent is given by the Home Secretary. A restriction order may or may not specify a time limit. As the patient 'offender' is subject to a hospital order, the representations and information will relate to discharge and conditions of discharge.

11.18 Sections 39, 40, and 41 place the same duties on local probation boards; however, the 'offender' is subject to a hospital direction and a limitation direction. Hospital and limitation directions are made under ss 45A and 45B of the Mental Health Act 1983. The court may make a 'hospital direction' which is a direction that the offender be detained in a specified hospital. A 'limitation direction' is that the offender is subject to the restrictions in s 41 of the Mental Health Act 1983. The option applies where the court has heard evidence that the offender is suffering from a psychopathic disorder and the making of a hospital order is appropriate. The responsible medical officers will have the option of seeking the patient's transfer to prison at any time before his release date if no further treatment is necessary or likely to be beneficial. The representations and information made by or given to the victim will depend on whether the offender is being discharged from hospital in which case they would relate to the conditions on discharge. In the case of release from prison it would be about conditions or supervision requirements.

Section 42, 43, and 44 place the same duties on the local probation boards   11.19
where the offender, whilst serving his sentence, is subject to a transfer direction and a restriction direction made by the Secretary of State. A transfer direction is made under s 47 of the Mental Health Act 1983. The direction allows the prisoner, who is serving a sentence, to be removed and detained in a hospital. The restriction direction is that the offender is subject to the restrictions under s 41 of the Mental Health Act 1983. The victim may wish to make representations and receive information in respect of conditions upon discharge.

D. CHAPTER 3: OTHER MATTERS RELATING TO VICTIMS ETC

Section 47 of the Act puts into effect Sch 7 to the Act. The Act extends the   11.20
Parliamentary Ombudsman's jurisdiction to allow him to investigate breaches under the Victims' Code and also complaints in respect of the duties imposed on the local probation boards under ss 35 to 44. The Commissioner must send a report of the results of the investigation, to the person to whom the complaint relates. Following the investigation, if a person has failed to perform a relevant duty and the failure has not or will not be remedied, the Commissioner can lay before each House of Parliament a special report on the case.

The provision for the appointment of a Commissioner for Victims and   11.21
Witnesses is provided for in ss 48 to 53 of the Act. The Commissioner's functions include promoting the interests of victims and witnesses, reviewing the Victims' Code, reporting to the Secretary of State, and advising Ministers on issues relating to victims and witnesses. The authorities within the Commissioner's remit are specified in Sch 9 to this Act. They are government departments and agencies involved in one way or another with the criminal process. Section 53 provides for the Commissioner to add, omit, or change the description of the authority.

Section 54 provides that a person may disclose information to those bound by   11.22
the Victims' Code, local probation boards, and the Commissioner and author-ities within his remit. Disclosure must be connected to compliance with the Victims' Code, ss 35 to 44, or the carrying out of the duties of the Commissioner.

Section 55 converts the Victims' Advisory Panel into a statutory body. A   11.23
Victims' Advisory Panel consisting of ten victims and chaired by Lord Falconer was set up in February 2003. The panel may provide reports if consulted by the Secretary of State on matters relating to victims or witnesses. If they do so, the Secretary of State must arrange for publication of the report and for it to be laid before Parliament.

11.24   Section 56 provides for the Secretary of State to pay grants to persons or organizations which help victims and witnesses.

11.25   Section 57 inserts four new provisions into the Criminal Compensation Act 1995 to provide for the recovery of compensation from offenders. The offender must have been convicted of an offence in respect of the criminal injury. The offender must be given a recovery notice and the basis on which he may be entitled to a review is set out in the new s 7C.

E. CONCLUSION

11.26   The provisions in Pt III of the Act go further than any other legislative measures, but the provisions do not extend to all victims and more could have been put in place for victims of domestic violence. The draft code does not explicitly require specialist services for adult and child victims of domestic violence. The witness service is only available in the criminal courts. Every day victims of domestic violence have to face their abusers in the civil courts; whether it be whilst they are obtaining an injunction or during Children Act 1989 proceedings. The majority of civil courts have a shortage of waiting rooms leaving many victims sitting in the same waiting area as their abuser. Respondents in Family Law Act 1996 proceedings may not be entitled to public funding, resulting in victims being cross-examined by their abuser.

11.27   The police have an obligation under the draft code to notify a vulnerable victim no later than one working day after the day of the event if they do not charge the suspect. A victim may be subject to further abuse on the suspect's immediate release.

11.28   The Act does not consider the issue of public funding for legal representation. Not all victims are eligible for public funding to obtain an injunction. Victims in receipt of disability living allowance have been refused public funding because their income is above the threshold.

11.29   Another example of difficulties victims may face is in respect of the immigration rules. A spouse or a partner has to complete a two-year probationary period before they are allowed to have recourse to public funds. In 1999, the Government introduced a concession for those who could prove that the relationship ended because of domestic violence. The private nature of domestic violence means it is difficult for victims to obtain proof.

11.30   Sections 35 to 44 of the Act provide for victims to receive information and make representations. Domestic violence is characterized by its repetitive nature; however, many of the assaults will not result in custodial sentences of twelve months or more. Once services have been established one hopes they will be continually improved and extended.

Domestic Violence, Crime and Victims Act 2004

CONTENTS

PART 1
DOMESTIC VIOLENCE ETC

PART 2
CRIMINAL JUSTICE

PART 3
VICTIMS ETC

CHAPTER 1
THE VICTIMS' CODE

CHAPTER 2
REPRESENTATIONS AND INFORMATION

CHAPTER 3
OTHER MATTERS RELATING TO VICTIMS ETC

PART 4

SUPPLEMENTARY

DOMESTIC VIOLENCE, CRIME AND VICTIMS ACT 2004

PART 1
DOMESTIC VIOLENCE ETC

Amendments to Part 4 of the Family Law Act 1996

1. Breach of non-molestation order to be a criminal offence

In Part 4 of the Family Law Act 1996 (c. 27) (family homes and domestic violence), after section 42 insert—

'42A. Offence of breaching non-molestation order

(1) A person who without reasonable excuse does anything that he is prohibited from doing by a non-molestation order is guilty of an offence.

(2) In the case of a non-molestation order made by virtue of section 45(1), a person can be guilty of an offence under this section only in respect of conduct engaged in at a time when he was aware of the existence of the order.

(3) Where a person is convicted of an offence under this section in respect of any conduct, that conduct is not punishable as a contempt of court.

(4) A person cannot be convicted of an offence under this section in respect of any conduct which has been punished as a contempt of court.

(5) A person guilty of an offence under this section is liable—

    (a) on conviction on indictment, to imprisonment for a term not exceeding five years, or a fine, or both;

    (b) on summary conviction, to imprisonment for a term not exceeding 12 months, or a fine not exceeding the statutory maximum, or both.

(6) A reference in any enactment to proceedings under this Part, or to an order under this Part, does not include a reference to proceedings for an offence under this section or to an order made in such proceedings.

    "Enactment" includes an enactment contained in subordinate legislation within the meaning of the Interpretation Act 1978 (c. 30).'

2. Additional considerations if parties are cohabitants or former cohabitants

(1) Section 41 of the Family Law Act 1996 (c. 27) (which requires a court, when considering the nature of the relationship of cohabitants or former cohabitants, to have regard to their non-married status) is repealed.

(2) In section 36(6)(e) of that Act (court to have regard to nature of parties' relationship when considering whether to give right to occupy to cohabitant or former cohabitant with no existing right), after 'relationship' insert 'and in particular the level of commitment involved in it'.

3. 'Cohabitants' in Part 4 of 1996 Act to include same-sex couples

In section 62(1)(a) of the Family Law Act 1996 (definition of 'cohabitant' for the purposes of Part 4 of that Act), for the words after ' "cohabitants" are' substitute 'two persons who, although not married to each other, are living together as husband and wife or (if of the same sex) in an equivalent relationship; and'.

103

4. Extension of Part 4 of 1996 Act to non-cohabiting couples

In section 62(3) of the Family Law Act 1996 (definition of 'associated' persons for the purposes of Part 4 of that Act), after paragraph (e) insert—

'(ea) they have or have had an intimate personal relationship with each other which is or was of significant duration;'.

Causing or allowing the death of a child or vulnerable adult

5. The offence

(1) A person ('D') is guilty of an offence if—
  (a) a child or vulnerable adult ('V') dies as a result of the unlawful act of a person who—
    (i) was a member of the same household as V, and
    (ii) had frequent contact with him,
  (b) D was such a person at the time of that act,
  (c) at that time there was a significant risk of serious physical harm being caused to V by the unlawful act of such a person, and
  (d) either D was the person whose act caused V's death or—
    (i) D was, or ought to have been, aware of the risk mentioned in paragraph (c),
    (ii) D failed to take such steps as he could reasonably have been expected to take to protect V from the risk, and
    (iii) the act occurred in circumstances of the kind that D foresaw or ought to have foreseen.

(2) The prosecution does not have to prove whether it is the first alternative in subsection (1)(d) or the second (sub-paragraphs (i) to (iii)) that applies.

(3) If D was not the mother or father of V—
  (a) D may not be charged with an offence under this section if he was under the age of 16 at the time of the act that caused V's death;
  (b) for the purposes of subsection (1)(d)(ii) D could not have been expected to take any such step as is referred to there before attaining that age.

(4) For the purposes of this section—
  (a) a person is to be regarded as a 'member' of a particular household, even if he does not live in that household, if he visits it so often and for such periods of time that it is reasonable to regard him as a member of it;
  (b) where V lived in different households at different times, 'the same household as V' refers to the household in which V was living at the time of the act that caused V's death.

(5) For the purposes of this section an 'unlawful' act is one that—
  (a) constitutes an offence, or
  (b) would constitute an offence but for being the act of—
    (i) a person under the age of ten, or
    (ii) a person entitled to rely on a defence of insanity.
  Paragraph (b) does not apply to an act of D.

(6) In this section—
  'act' includes a course of conduct and also includes omission;
  'child' means a person under the age of 16;
  'serious' harm means harm that amounts to grievous bodily harm for the purposes of the Offences against the Person Act 1861 (c. 100);

'vulnerable adult' means a person aged 16 or over whose ability to protect himself from violence, abuse or neglect is significantly impaired through physical or mental disability or illness, through old age or otherwise.

(7) A person guilty of an offence under this section is liable on conviction on indictment to imprisonment for a term not exceeding 14 years or to a fine, or to both.

6. Evidence and procedure: England and Wales

(1) Subsections (2) to (4) apply where a person ('the defendant') is charged in the same proceedings with an offence of murder or manslaughter and with an offence under section 5 in respect of the same death ('the section 5 offence').

(2) Where by virtue of section 35(3) of the Criminal Justice and Public Order Act 1994 (c. 33) a court or jury is permitted, in relation to the section 5 offence, to draw such inferences as appear proper from the defendant's failure to give evidence or refusal to answer a question, the court or jury may also draw such inferences in determining whether he is guilty—

(a) of murder or manslaughter, or

(b) of any other offence of which he could lawfully be convicted on the charge of murder or manslaughter,

even if there would otherwise be no case for him to answer in relation to that offence.

(3) The charge of murder or manslaughter is not to be dismissed under paragraph 2 of Schedule 3 to the Crime and Disorder Act 1998 (c. 37) (unless the section 5 offence is dismissed).

(4) At the defendant's trial the question whether there is a case for the defendant to answer on the charge of murder or manslaughter is not to be considered before the close of all the evidence (or, if at some earlier time he ceases to be charged with the section 5 offence, before that earlier time).

(5) An offence under section 5 is an offence of homicide for the purposes of the following enactments—

sections 24 and 25 of the Magistrates' Courts Act 1980 (c. 43) (mode of trial of child or young person for indictable offence);

section 51A of the Crime and Disorder Act 1998 (sending cases to the Crown Court: children and young persons);

section 8 of the Powers of Criminal Courts (Sentencing) Act 2000 (c. 6) (power and duty to remit young offenders to youth courts for sentence).

7. Evidence and procedure: Northern Ireland

(1) Subsections (2) to (4) apply where a person ('the defendant') is charged in the same proceedings with an offence of murder or manslaughter and with an offence under section 5 in respect of the same death ('the section 5 offence').

(2) Where by virtue of Article 4(4) of the Criminal Evidence (Northern Ireland) Order 1988 (S.I. 1988/1987 (N.I. 20)) a court or jury is permitted, in relation to the section 5 offence, to draw such inferences as appear proper from the defendant's failure to give evidence or refusal to answer a question, the court or jury may also draw such inferences in determining whether he is guilty—

(a) of murder or manslaughter, or

(b) of any other offence of which he could lawfully be convicted on the charge of murder or manslaughter, even if there would otherwise be no case for him to answer in relation to that offence.

(3) Where a magistrates' court is considering under Article 37 of the Magistrates' Courts (Northern Ireland) Order 1981 (S.I. 1981/1675 (N.I. 26)) whether to commit the defendant for trial for the offence of murder or manslaughter, if there is sufficient evidence to put him upon trial for the section 5 offence there is deemed to be sufficient evidence to put him upon trial for the offence of murder or manslaughter.

(4) At the defendant's trial the question whether there is a case to answer on the charge of murder or manslaughter is not to be considered before the close of all the evidence (or, if at some earlier time he ceases to be charged with the section 5 offence, before that earlier time).

(5) An offence under section 5 is an offence of homicide for the purposes of the following provisions—
Article 17 of the Criminal Justice (Children) (Northern Ireland) Order 1998 (S.I. 1998/1504 (N.I. 9)) (mode of trial of child for indictable offence);
Article 32 of that Order (power and duty to remit children to youth courts for sentence).

8. Evidence and procedure: courts-martial

(1) Section 6(1), (2) and (4) has effect in relation to proceedings before courts-martial with the following adaptations.

(2) A reference to an offence of murder or manslaughter or an offence under section 5 is to be read as a reference to an offence under—
   (a) section 70 of the Army Act 1955 (3 & 4 Eliz. 2 c. 18),
   (b) section 70 of the Air Force Act 1955 (3 & 4 Eliz. 2 c. 19), or
   (c) section 42 of the Naval Discipline Act 1957 (c. 53),
for which the offence referred to in section 6 is the corresponding civil offence (within the meaning of that Act).

(3) A reference to the court or jury is to be read as a reference to the court.

Domestic homicide reviews

9. Establishment and conduct of reviews

(1) In this section 'domestic homicide review' means a review of the circumstances in which the death of a person aged 16 or over has, or appears to have, resulted from violence, abuse or neglect by—
   (a) a person to whom he was related or with whom he was or had been in an intimate personal relationship, or
   (b) a member of the same household as himself,
held with a view to identifying the lessons to be learnt from the death.

(2) The Secretary of State may in a particular case direct a specified person or body within subsection (4) to establish, or to participate in, a domestic homicide review.

(3) It is the duty of any person or body within subsection (4) establishing or participating in a domestic homicide review (whether or not held pursuant to a direction under subsection (2)) to have regard to any guidance issued by the Secretary of State as to the establishment and conduct of such reviews.

(4) The persons and bodies within this subsection are—
   (a) in relation to England and Wales—
   chief officers of police for police areas in England and Wales;
   local authorities;
   local probation boards established under section 4 of the Criminal Justice and Court Services Act 2000 (c. 43);
   Strategic Health Authorities established under section 8 of the National Health Service Act 1977 (c. 49);
   Primary Care Trusts established under Section 16A of that Act.
   Local Health Boards established under section 16BA of that Act;
   NHS trusts established under section 5 of the National Health Service and Community Care Act 1990 (c. 19);
   (b) in relation to Northern Ireland—
   the Chief Constable of the Police Service of Northern Ireland; the Probation Board for Northern Ireland;
   Health and Social Services Boards established under Article 16 of the Health and Personal Social Services (Northern Ireland) Order 1972 (S.I. 1972/1265 (N.I. 14));
   Health and Social Services trusts established under Article 10 of the Health and Personal Social Services (Northern Ireland) Order 1991 (S.I. 1991/194 (N.I. 1)).
(5) In subsection (4)(a) 'local authority' means—
   (a) in relation to England, the council of a district, county or London borough, the Common Council of the City of London and the Council of the Isles of Scilly;
   (b) in relation to Wales, the council of a county or county borough.
(6) The Secretary of State may by order amend subsection (4) or (5).

PART 2
CRIMINAL JUSTICE

Assault, harassment etc

10. Common assault to be an arrestable offence

(1) In Schedule 1A to the Police and Criminal Evidence Act 1984 (c. 60) (specific offences which are arrestable offences), before paragraph 15 (but after the heading '*Criminal Justice Act 1988*') insert—
   '**14A. Common assault'**
(2) In Article 26(2) of the Police and Criminal Evidence (Northern Ireland) Order 1989 (S.I. 1989/1341 (N.I. 12)) (specific offences which are arrestable offences), after paragraph (m) insert—
   '(n) an offence under section 42 of the Offences against the Person Act 1861 (c. 100) (common assault etc).'

11. Common assault etc as alternative verdict

In section 6 of the Criminal Law Act 1967 (c. 58) (trial of offences), after subsection (3) (alternative verdicts on trial on indictment) insert—

'(3A) For the purposes of subsection (3) above an offence falls within the jurisdiction of the court of trial if it is an offence to which section 40 of the Criminal Justice Act 1988 applies (power to join in indictment count for common assault etc.), even if a count charging the offence is not included in the indictment.

(3B) A person convicted of an offence by virtue of subsection (3A) may only be dealt with for it in a manner in which a magistrates' court could have dealt with him.'

12. Restraining orders: England and Wales

(1) In section 5 of the Protection from Harassment Act 1997 (c. 40) (power to make restraining order where defendant convicted of offence under section 2 or 4 of that Act), in subsection (1) omit 'under section 2 or 4'.

(2) After subsection (3) of that section insert—

'(3A) In proceedings under this section both the prosecution and the defence may lead, as further evidence, any evidence that would be admissible in proceedings for an injunction under section 3.'

(3) After subsection (4) of that section insert—

'(4A) Any person mentioned in the order is entitled to be heard on the hearing of an application under subsection (4).'

(4) After subsection (6) of that section insert—

'(7) A court dealing with a person for an offence under this section may vary or discharge the order in question by a further order.'

(5) After that section insert—

'5A. Restraining orders on acquittal

(1) A court before which a person ("the defendant") is acquitted of an offence may, if it considers it necessary to do so to protect a person from harassment by the defendant, make an order prohibiting the defendant from doing anything described in the order.

(2) Subsections (3) to (7) of section 5 apply to an order under this section as they apply to an order under that one.

(3) Where the Court of Appeal allow an appeal against conviction they may remit the case to the Crown Court to consider whether to proceed under this section.

(4) Where—

(a) the Crown Court allows an appeal against conviction, or

(b) a case is remitted to the Crown Court under subsection (3),

the reference in subsection (1) to a court before which a person is acquitted of an offence is to be read as referring to that court.

(5) A person made subject to an order under this section has the same right of appeal against the order as if—

(a) he had been convicted of the offence in question before the court which made the order, and

(b) the order had been made under section 5.'

13. Restraining orders: Northern Ireland

(1) In Article 7 of the Protection from Harassment (Northern Ireland) Order 1997 (S.I. 1997/1180 (N.I. 9)) (power to make restraining order where defendant convicted of offence under Article 4 or 6 of that Order), in paragraph (1) omit 'under Article 4 or 6'.

(2) After paragraph (3) of that Article insert—

'(3A) In proceedings under this Article both the prosecution and the defence may lead, as further evidence, any evidence that would be admissible in proceedings for an injunction under Article 5.'

(3) After paragraph (4) of that Article insert—

'(4A) Any person mentioned in the order is entitled to be heard on the hearing of an application under paragraph (4).'

(4) After paragraph (6) of that Article insert—

'(7) A court dealing with a person for an offence under this Article may vary or discharge the order in question by a further order.'

(5) After that Article insert—

'7A. Restraining orders on acquittal

(1) A court before which a person ("the defendant") is acquitted of an offence may, if it considers it necessary to do so to protect a person from harassment by the defendant, make an order prohibiting the defendant from doing anything described in the order.

(2) Paragraphs (3) to (7) of Article 7 apply to an order under this Article as they apply to an order under that one.

(3) Where the Court of Appeal allow an appeal against conviction they may remit the case to the Crown Court to consider whether to proceed under this Article.

(4) Where—

(a) a county court allows an appeal against conviction, or

(b) a case is remitted to the Crown Court under paragraph (3),

the reference in paragraph (1) to a court before which a person is acquitted of an offence is to be read as referring to that court.

(5) A person made subject to an order under this Article has the same right of appeal against the order as if—

(a) he had been convicted of the offence in question before the court which made the order, and

(b) the order had been made under Article 7.'

Surcharges

14. Surcharge payable on conviction

(1) In Chapter 1 of Part 12 of the Criminal Justice Act 2003 (c. 44) (general provisions about sentencing), after section 161 insert—

'Surcharges

161A. Court's duty to order payment of surcharge

(1) A court when dealing with a person for one or more offences must also (subject to subsections (2) and (3)) order him to pay a surcharge.

(2) Subsection (1) does not apply in such cases as may be prescribed by an order made by the Secretary of State.

(3) Where a court dealing with an offender considers—

(a) that it would be appropriate to make a compensation order, but

(b) that he has insufficient means to pay both the surcharge and appropriate compensation,

the court must reduce the surcharge accordingly (if necessary to nil).

(4) For the purposes of this section a court does not "deal with" a person if it—

(a) discharges him absolutely, or

(b) makes an order under the Mental Health Act 1983 in respect of him.

161B. Amount of surcharge

(1) The surcharge payable under section 161A is such amount as the Secretary of State may specify by order.

(2) An order under this section may provide for the amount to depend on—

(a) the offence or offences committed,

(b) how the offender is otherwise dealt with (including, where the offender is fined, the amount of the fine),

(c) the age of the offender.

This is not to be read as limiting section 330(3) (power to make different provision for different purposes etc).'

(2) In section 164 of that Act (fixing of fines), after subsection (4) insert—

'(4A) In applying subsection (3), a court must not reduce the amount of a fine on account of any surcharge it orders the offender to pay under section 161A, except to the extent that he has insufficient means to pay both.'

(3) In Part 1 of Schedule 9 to the Administration of Justice Act 1970 (c. 31) (cases where payment enforceable as on summary conviction), after paragraph 12 insert—

'13 Where under section 161A of the Criminal Justice Act 2003 a court orders the payment of a surcharge.'

(4) In Schedule 5 to the Courts Act 2003 (c. 39) (collection of fines), in paragraph 1(1) (application of Schedule), after 'a fine' insert 'or a surcharge imposed under section 161A of the Criminal Justice Act 2003'.

(5) The Secretary of State may by order—

(a) make provision amending Schedule 5 (collection of fines) or Schedule 6 (discharge of fines by unpaid work) to the Courts Act 2003 in its application by virtue of subsection (3) or (4) to surcharges;

(b) make provision for any part of Schedule 5, or the whole or any part of Schedule 6, not to apply to surcharges;

(c) make amendments to any enactment that are consequential on provision made under paragraph (a) or (b).

15. Increase in maximum on-the-spot penalty for disorderly behaviour

(1) In Chapter 1 of Part 1 of the Criminal Justice and Police Act 2001 (c. 16) (on-the-spot penalties for disorderly behaviour), section 3 is amended as follows.

(2) In subsection (2) (maximum penalty that may be prescribed), at the end insert 'plus a half of the relevant surcharge'.

(3) After that subsection insert—

'(2A) The "relevant surcharge", in relation to a person of a given age, is the amount payable by way of surcharge under section 161A of the Criminal Justice Act 2003 by a person of that age who is fined the maximum amount for the offence.'

16. Higher fixed penalty for repeated road traffic offences

(1) The Road Traffic Offenders Act 1988 (c. 53) is amended as follows.

(2) In section 53 (amount of fixed penalty), after subsection (2) insert—

'(3) In particular, in relation to England and Wales an order made under subsection (1)(a) may prescribe a higher fixed penalty in a case where, in the period of three years ending with the date of the offence in question, the offender committed an offence for which—

(a) he was disqualified from driving, or

(b) penalty points were endorsed on the counterpart of any licence held by him.'

(3) At the end of section 84 (regulations) (which becomes subsection (1)) insert—

'(2) The Secretary of State may by regulations provide that where—

(a) a conditional offer has been issued under section 75 of this Act,

(b) the amount of the penalty stated in the offer is not the higher amount applicable by virtue of section 53(3) of this Act, and

(c) it subsequently appears that that higher amount is in fact applicable,

the fixed penalty clerk may issue a further notice (a "surcharge notice") requiring payment of the difference between the two amounts.

(3) Regulations under subsection (2) above may—

(a) provide for this Part of this Act to have effect, in cases to which the regulations apply, with such modifications as may be specified;

(b) make provision for the collection and enforcement of amounts due under surcharge notices.'

Trial by jury of sample counts only

17. Application by prosecution for certain counts to be tried without a jury

(1) The prosecution may apply to a judge of the Crown Court for a trial on indictment to take place on the basis that the trial of some, but not all, of the counts included in the indictment may be conducted without a jury.

(2) If such an application is made and the judge is satisfied that the following three conditions are fulfilled, he may make an order for the trial to take place on the basis that the trial of some, but not all, of the counts included in the indictment may be conducted without a jury.

(3) The first condition is that the number of counts included in the indictment is likely to mean that a trial by jury involving all of those counts would be impracticable.

(4) The second condition is that, if an order under subsection (2) were made, each count or group of counts which would accordingly be tried with a jury can be regarded as a sample of counts which could accordingly be tried without a jury.

(5) The third condition is that it is in the interests of justice for an order under subsection (2) to be made.

(6) In deciding whether or not to make an order under subsection (2), the judge must have regard to any steps which might reasonably be taken to facilitate a trial by jury.

(7) But a step is not to be regarded as reasonable if it could lead to the possibility of a defendant in the trial receiving a lesser sentence than would be the case if that step were not taken.

(8) An order under subsection (2) must specify the counts which may be tried without a jury.

(9) For the purposes of this section and sections 18 to 20, a count may not be regarded as a sample of other counts unless the defendant in respect of each count is the same person.

18. Procedure for applications under section 17

(1) An application under section 17 must be determined at a preparatory hearing.

(2) Section 7(1) of the 1987 Act and section 29(2) of the 1996 Act are to have effect as if the purposes there mentioned included the purpose of determining an application under section 17.

(3) Section 29(1) of the 1996 Act is to have effect as if the grounds on which a judge of the Crown Court may make an order under that provision included the ground that an application under section 17 has been made.

(4) The parties to a preparatory hearing at which an application under section 17 is to be determined must be given an opportunity to make representations with respect to the application.

(5) Section 9(11) of the 1987 Act and section 35(1) of the 1996 Act are to have effect as if they also provided for an appeal to the Court of Appeal to lie from the determination by a judge of an application under section 17.

(6) In this section—

'preparatory hearing' means a preparatory hearing within the meaning of the 1987 Act or Part 3 of the 1996 Act;

'the 1987 Act' means the Criminal Justice Act 1987 (c. 38);

'the 1996 Act' means the Criminal Procedure and Investigations Act 1996 (c. 25).

19. Effect of order under section 17(2)

(1) The effect of an order under section 17(2) is that where, in the course of the proceedings to which the order relates, a defendant is found guilty by a jury on a count which can be regarded as a sample of other counts to be tried in those proceedings, those other counts may be tried without a jury in those proceedings.

(2) Where the trial of a count is conducted without a jury because of an order under section 17(2), the court is to have all the powers, authorities and jurisdiction which the court would have had if the trial of that count had been conducted with a jury (including power to determine any question and to make any finding which would be required to be determined or made by a jury).

(3) Except where the context otherwise requires, any reference in an enactment to a jury, the verdict of a jury or the finding of a jury is to be read, in relation to the trial of a count conducted without a jury because of an order under section 17(2), as a reference to the court, the verdict of the court or the finding of the court.

(4) Where the trial of a count is conducted without a jury because of an order under section 17(2) and the court convicts the defendant of that count—

(a) the court must give a judgment which states the reasons for the conviction at, or as soon as reasonably practicable after, the time of the conviction, and

(b) the reference in section 18(2) of the Criminal Appeal Act 1968 (c. 19) (notice of appeal or of application for leave to appeal to be given within 28 days from date of conviction etc) to the date of the conviction is to be read as a reference to the date of the judgment mentioned in paragraph (a).

(5) Where, in the case of proceedings in respect of which an order under section 17(2) has been made, a jury convicts a defendant of a count, time does not begin to run under section 18(2) of the Criminal Appeal Act 1968 in relation to an appeal against that conviction until the date on which the proceedings end.

(6) In determining for the purposes of subsection (5) the date on which proceedings end, any part of those proceedings which takes place after the time when matters relating to sentencing begin to be dealt with is to be disregarded.

(7) Nothing in this section or section 17, 18 or 20 affects the requirement under section 4A of the Criminal Procedure (Insanity) Act 1964 (c. 84) that any question, finding or verdict mentioned in that section be determined, made or returned by a jury.

20. Rules of court

(1) Rules of court may make such provision as appears to the authority making them to be necessary or expedient for the purposes of sections 17 to 19.

(2) Without limiting subsection (1), rules of court may in particular make provision for time limits within which applications under section 17 must be made or within which other things in connection with that section or section 18 or 19 must be done.

(3) Nothing in this section is to be taken as affecting the generality of any enactment conferring powers to make rules of court.

21. Application of sections 17 to 20 to Northern Ireland

(1) In their application to Northern Ireland, sections 17 to 20 have effect subject to the modifications in Schedule 1.

(2) Sections 17 to 20 do not apply in relation to a trial to which section 75 of the Terrorism Act 2000 (c. 11) (trial without jury for certain offences) applies.

Unfitness to plead and insanity

22. Procedure for determining fitness to plead: England and Wales

(1) The Criminal Procedure (Insanity) Act 1964 is amended as follows.

(2) In section 4 (finding of unfitness to plead), in subsection (5) (question of fitness to be determined by a jury), for the words from 'by a jury' to the end substitute 'by the court without a jury'.

(3) In subsection (6) of that section, for 'A jury' substitute 'The court'.

(4) In subsection (1) of section 4A (finding that the accused did the act or omission charged against him), for 'jury' substitute 'court'.

(5) For subsection (5) of that section substitute—

'(5) Where the question of disability was determined after arraignment of the accused, the determination under subsection (2) is to be made by the jury by whom he was being tried.'

23. Procedure for determining fitness to be tried: Northern Ireland

(1) The Mental Health (Northern Ireland) Order 1986 (S.I. 1986/595 (N.I. 4)) is amended as follows.

(2) In Article 49 (finding of unfitness to be tried), in paragraph (4) (question of fitness to be determined by a jury), for the words from 'by a jury' to the end substitute 'by the court without a jury'.

(3) In paragraph (4A) of that Article, for 'A jury' substitute 'The court'.

(4) In paragraph (1) of Article 49A (finding that the accused did the act or omission charged against him), for 'jury' substitute 'court'.

(5) For paragraph (5) of that Article substitute—

'(5) Where the question of fitness to be tried was determined after arraignment of the accused, the determination under paragraph (2) is to be made by the jury by whom he was being tried.'

24. Powers of court on finding of insanity or unfitness to plead etc

(1) For section 5 of the Criminal Procedure (Insanity) Act 1964 (c. 84) substitute—

'5. Powers to deal with persons not guilty by reason of insanity or unfit to plead etc.

(1) This section applies where—

(a) a special verdict is returned that the accused is not guilty by reason of insanity; or

(b) findings have been made that the accused is under a disability and that he did the act or made the omission charged against him.

(2) The court shall make in respect of the accused—

(a) a hospital order (with or without a restriction order);

(b) a supervision order; or

(c) an order for his absolute discharge.

(3) Where—

(a) the offence to which the special verdict or the findings relate is an offence the sentence for which is fixed by law, and

(b) the court have power to make a hospital order,

the court shall make a hospital order with a restriction order (whether or not they would have power to make a restriction order apart from this subsection).

(4) In this section—

"hospital order" has the meaning given in section 37 of the Mental Health Act 1983;

"restriction order" has the meaning given to it by section 41 of that Act;

"supervision order" has the meaning given in Part 1 of Schedule 1A to this Act.

5A. Orders made under or by virtue of section 5

(1) In relation to the making of an order by virtue of subsection (2)(a) of section 5 above, section 37 (hospital orders etc) of the Mental Health Act 1983 ("the 1983 Act") shall have effect as if—

(a) the reference in subsection (1) to a person being convicted before the Crown Court included a reference to the case where section 5 above applies;

(b) the words after "punishable with imprisonment" and before "or is convicted" were omitted; and

   (c) for subsections (4) and (5) there were substituted—

     "(4) Where an order is made under this section requiring a person to be admitted to a hospital ('a hospital order'), it shall be the duty of the managers of the hospital specified in the order to admit him in accordance with it."

(2) In relation to a case where section 5 above applies but the court have not yet made one of the disposals mentioned in subsection (2) of that section—

   (a) section 35 of the 1983 Act (remand to hospital for report on accused's mental condition) shall have effect with the omission of the words after paragraph (b) in subsection (3);

   (b) section 36 of that Act (remand of accused person to hospital for treatment) shall have effect with the omission of the words "(other than an offence the sentence for which is fixed by law)" in subsection (2);

   (c) references in sections 35 and 36 of that Act to an accused person shall be construed as including a person in whose case this subsection applies; and

   (d) section 38 of that Act (interim hospital orders) shall have effect as if—

     (i) the reference in subsection (1) to a person being convicted before the Crown Court included a reference to the case where section 5 above applies; and

     (ii) the words "(other than an offence the sentence for which is fixed by law)" in that subsection were omitted.

(3) In relation to the making of any order under the 1983 Act by virtue of this Act, references in the 1983 Act to an offender shall be construed as including references to a person in whose case section 5 above applies, and references to an offence shall be construed accordingly.

(4) Where—

   (a) a person is detained in pursuance of a hospital order which the court had power to make by virtue of section 5(1)(b) above, and

   (b) the court also made a restriction order, and that order has not ceased to have effect,

the Secretary of State, if satisfied after consultation with the responsible medical officer that the person can properly be tried, may remit the person for trial, either to the court of trial or to a prison.

    On the person's arrival at the court or prison, the hospital order and the restriction order shall cease to have effect.

(5) Schedule 1A to this Act (supervision orders) has effect with respect to the making of supervision orders under subsection (2)(b) of section 5 above, and with respect to the revocation and amendment of such orders.

(6) In relation to the making of an order under subsection (2)(c) of section 5 above, section 12(1) of the Powers of Criminal Courts (Sentencing) Act 2000 (absolute and conditional discharge) shall have effect as if—

   (a) the reference to a person being convicted by or before a court of such an offence as is there mentioned included a reference to the case where section 5 above applies; and

   (b) the reference to the court being of opinion that it is inexpedient to inflict punishment included a reference to it thinking that an order for absolute discharge would be most suitable in all the circumstances of the case.'

(2) Before Schedule 2 to the Criminal Procedure (Insanity) Act 1964 (c. 84) insert the Schedule set out in Schedule 2 to this Act.

(3) In section 6 of the Criminal Appeal Act 1968 (c. 19) (substitution of finding of insanity or findings of unfitness to plead etc) and in section 14 of that Act (substitution of findings of unfitness to plead etc), for subsections (2) and (3) substitute—

'(2) The Court of Appeal shall make in respect of the accused—

    (a) a hospital order (with or without a restriction order);

    (b) a supervision order; or

    (c) an order for his absolute discharge.

(3) Where—

    (a) the offence to which the appeal relates is an offence the sentence for which is fixed by law, and

    (b) the court have power to make a hospital order,

the court shall make a hospital order with a restriction order (whether or not they would have power to make a restriction order apart from this subsection).

(4) Section 5A of the Criminal Procedure (Insanity) Act 1964 ('the 1964 Act') applies in relation to this section as it applies in relation to section 5 of that Act.

(5) Where the Court of Appeal make an interim hospital order by virtue of this section—

    (a) the power of renewing or terminating it and of dealing with the appellant on its termination shall be exercisable by the court below and not by the Court of Appeal; and

    (b) the court below shall be treated for the purposes of section 38(7) of the Mental Health Act 1983 (absconding offenders) as the court that made the order.

(6) Where the Court of Appeal make a supervision order by virtue of this section, any power of revoking or amending it shall be exercisable as if the order had been made by the court below.

(7) In this section—

"hospital order" has the meaning given in section 37 of the Mental Health Act 1983;

"interim hospital order" has the meaning given in section 38 of that Act;

"restriction order" has the meaning given to it by section 41 of that Act;

"supervision order" has the meaning given in Part 1 of Schedule 1A to the 1964 Act.'

(4) Section 14A of the Criminal Appeal Act 1968 (c. 19) (power to order admission to hospital where, on appeal against verdict of not guilty by reason of insanity, Court of Appeal substitutes verdict of acquittal) is repealed.

(5) Section 5 of the Criminal Procedure (Insanity and Unfitness to Plead) Act 1991 (c. 25) and Schedules 1 and 2 to that Act are repealed.

25. Appeal against order made on finding of insanity or unfitness to plead etc

After section 16 of the Criminal Appeal Act 1968 insert—

'Appeal against order made in cases of insanity or unfitness to plead

16A. Right of appeal against hospital order etc.

(1) A person in whose case the Crown Court—

    (a) makes a hospital order or interim hospital order by virtue of section 5 or 5A of the Criminal Procedure (Insanity) Act 1964, or

(b) makes a supervision order under section 5 of that Act,

may appeal to the Court of Appeal against the order.

(2) An appeal under this section lies only—

(a) with the leave of the Court of Appeal; or

(b) if the judge of the court of trial grants a certificate that the case is fit for appeal.

16B. Disposal of appeal under s. 16A

(1) If on an appeal under section 16A of this Act the Court of Appeal consider that the appellant should be dealt with differently from the way in which the court below dealt with him—

(a) they may quash any order which is the subject of the appeal; and

(b) they may make such order, whether by substitution for the original order or by variation of or addition to it, as they think appropriate for the case and as the court below had power to make.

(2) The fact that an appeal is pending against an interim hospital order under the Mental Health Act 1983 shall not affect the power of the court below to renew or terminate the order or deal with the appellant on its termination.

(3) Where the Court of Appeal make an interim hospital order by virtue of this section—

(a) the power of renewing or terminating it and of dealing with the appellant on its termination shall be exercisable by the court below and not by the Court of Appeal; and

(b) the court below shall be treated for the purposes of section 38(7) of the said Act of 1983 (absconding offenders) as the court that made the order.

(4) The fact that an appeal is pending against a supervision order under section 5 of the Criminal Procedure (Insanity) Act 1964 shall not affect the power of the court below to revoke the order, or of a magistrates' court to revoke or amend it.

(5) Where the Court of Appeal make a supervision order by virtue of this section, the power of revoking or amending it shall be exercisable as if the order had been made by the court below.'

26. Courts-martial etc

Schedule 3 (unfitness to stand trial and insanity: courts-martial etc) has effect.

Miscellaneous

27. Powers of authorized officers executing warrants

(1) After section 125B of the Magistrates' Courts Act 1980 (c. 43) insert—

'125BA. Powers of persons authorized under section 125A or 125B

Schedule 4A to this Act, which confers powers on persons authorized under section 125A or 125B for the purpose of executing warrants for the enforcement of fines and other orders, shall have effect.'

(2) After Schedule 4 to that Act insert the Schedule set out in Schedule 4 to this Act.

28. Disclosure orders for purpose of executing warrants

After section 125C of the Magistrates' Courts Act 1980 insert—

'125CA. Power to make disclosure order

(1) A magistrates' court may make a disclosure order if satisfied that it is necessary to do so for the purpose of executing a warrant to which this section applies.

(2) This section applies to a warrant of arrest, commitment, detention or distress issued by a justice of the peace in connection with the enforcement of a fine or other order imposed or made on conviction.

(3) A disclosure order is an order requiring the person to whom it is directed to supply the designated officer for the court with any of the following information about the person to whom the warrant relates—
   (a) his name, date of birth or national insurance number;
   (b) his address (or any of his addresses).

(4) A disclosure order may be made only on the application of a person entitled to execute the warrant.

(5) This section applies to the Crown as it applies to other persons.

125CB. Use of information supplied under disclosure order

(1) Information supplied to a person under a disclosure order, or under this subsection, may be supplied by him to—
   (a) the applicant for the order or any other person entitled to execute the warrant concerned;
   (b) any employee of a body or person who, for the purposes of section 125B above, is an approved enforcement agency in relation to the warrant;
   (c) any justices' clerk or other person appointed under section 2(1) of the Courts Act 2003.

(2) A person who intentionally or recklessly—
   (a) discloses information supplied under a disclosure order otherwise than as permitted by subsection (1) above, or
   (b) uses information so supplied otherwise than for the purpose of facilitating the execution of the warrant concerned,
   commits an offence.

(3) But it is not an offence under subsection (2) above—
   (a) to disclose any information in accordance with any enactment or order of a court or for the purposes of any proceedings before a court; or
   (b) to disclose any information which has previously been lawfully disclosed to the public.

(4) A person guilty of an offence under subsection (2) above is liable—
   (a) on summary conviction, to a fine not exceeding the statutory maximum;
   (b) on conviction on indictment, to a fine.

(5) In this section "disclosure order" has the meaning given by section 125CA(3) above.'

29. Procedure on breach of community penalty etc

Schedule 5 (procedure on breach of community penalty etc) has effect.

30. Prosecution appeals

(1) In section 58(13) of the Criminal Justice Act 2003 (c. 44) (which defines 'applicable time'), for 'start of the judge's' substitute 'time when the judge starts his'.

(2) After section 58(13) of that Act insert—

   '(14) The reference in subsection (13) to the time when the judge starts his summing-up to the jury includes the time when the judge would start his summing-up to the jury but for the making of an order under Part 7.'

31. Intermittent custody

Schedule 6 (intermittent custody) has effect.

PART 3
VICTIMS ETC

CHAPTER 1
THE VICTIMS' CODE

32. Code of practice for victims

(1) The Secretary of State must issue a code of practice as to the services to be provided to a victim of criminal conduct by persons appearing to him to have functions relating to—

   (a) victims of criminal conduct, or

   (b) any aspect of the criminal justice system.

(2) The code may restrict the application of its provisions to—

   (a) specified descriptions of victims;

   (b) victims of specified offences or descriptions of conduct;

   (c) specified persons or descriptions of persons appearing to the Secretary of State to have functions of the kind mentioned in subsection (1).

(3) The code may include provision requiring or permitting the services which are to be provided to a victim to be provided to one or more others—

   (a) instead of the victim (for example where the victim has died);

   (b) as well as the victim.

(4) The code may make different provision for different purposes, including different provision for—

   (a) different descriptions of victims;

   (b) persons who have different functions or descriptions of functions;

   (c) different areas.

(5) The code may not require anything to be done by—

   (a) a person acting in a judicial capacity;

   (b) a person acting in the discharge of a function of a member of the Crown Prosecution Service which involves the exercise of a discretion.

(6) In determining whether a person is a victim of criminal conduct for the purposes of this section, it is immaterial that no person has been charged with or convicted of an offence in respect of the conduct.

(7) In this section—

   'criminal conduct' means conduct constituting an offence;

   'specified' means specified in the code.

33. Procedure

(1) Subsections (2) to (7) apply in relation to a code of practice required to be issued under section 32.

(2) The Secretary of State must prepare a draft of the code.

(3) In preparing the draft the Secretary of State must consult the Attorney-General and the Lord Chancellor.

(4) After preparing the draft the Secretary of State must—

    (a) publish the draft;

    (b) specify a period during which representations about the draft may be made to him.

(5) The Secretary of State must—

    (a) consider in consultation with the Attorney-General and the Lord Chancellor any representations made to him before the end of the specified period about the draft;

    (b) if he thinks it appropriate, modify the draft in the light of any such representations.

(6) After the Secretary of State has proceeded under subsection (5) he must lay the code before Parliament.

(7) When he has laid the code before Parliament the Secretary of State must bring it into operation on such day as he appoints by order.

(8) The Secretary of State may from time to time revise a code previously brought into operation under this section; and subsections (2) to (7) apply to a revised code as they apply to the code as first prepared.

(9) But the Secretary of State may revise a code under subsection (8) only if it appears to him that the proposed revisions would not result in—

    (a) a significant reduction in the quality or extent of the services to be provided under the code, or

    (b) a significant restriction in the description of persons to whom services are to be provided under the code.

34. Effect of non-compliance

(1) If a person fails to perform a duty imposed on him by a code issued under section 32, the failure does not of itself make him liable to criminal or civil proceedings.

(2) But the code is admissible in evidence in criminal or civil proceedings and a court may take into account a failure to comply with the code in determining a question in the proceedings.

CHAPTER 2

REPRESENTATIONS AND INFORMATION

Imprisonment or detention

35. Victims' rights to make representations and receive information

(1) This section applies if—

    (a) a court convicts a person ('the offender') of a sexual or violent offence, and

    (b) a relevant sentence is imposed on him in respect of the offence.

(2) But section 39 applies (instead of this section) if a hospital direction and a limitation direction are given in relation to the offender.

(3) The local probation board for the area in which the sentence is imposed must take all reasonable steps to ascertain whether a person who appears to the board to be the victim of the offence or to act for the victim of the offence wishes—

(a) to make representations about the matters specified in subsection (4);

(b) to receive the information specified in subsection (5).

(4) The matters are—

(a) whether the offender should be subject to any licence conditions or supervision requirements in the event of his release;

(b) if so, what licence conditions or supervision requirements.

(5) The information is information about any licence conditions or supervision requirements to which the offender is to be subject in the event of his release.

(6) If a person whose wishes have been ascertained under subsection (3) makes representations to the local probation board mentioned in that subsection or the relevant local probation board about a matter specified in subsection (4), the relevant local probation board must forward those representations to the persons responsible for determining the matter.

(7) If a local probation board has ascertained under subsection (3) that a person wishes to receive the information specified in subsection (5), the relevant local probation board must take all reasonable steps—

(a) to inform the person whether or not the offender is to be subject to any licence conditions or supervision requirements in the event of his release,

(b) if he is, to provide the person with details of any licence conditions or supervision requirements which relate to contact with the victim or his family, and

(c) to provide the person with such other information as the relevant local probation board considers appropriate in all the circumstances of the case.

(8) The relevant local probation board is—

(a) in a case where the offender is to be supervised on release by an officer of a local probation board, that local probation board;

(b) in any other case, the local probation board for the area in which the prison or other place in which the offender is detained is situated.

Hospital orders

36. Victims' rights: preliminary

(1) This section applies if the conditions in subsections (2) and (3) are met.

(2) The first condition is that one of these applies in respect of a person ('the patient') charged with a sexual or violent offence—

(a) the patient is convicted of the offence;

(b) a verdict is returned that the patient is not guilty of the offence by reason of insanity;

(c) a finding is made—

(i) under section 4 of the Criminal Procedure (Insanity) Act 1964 (c. 84) that the patient is under a disability, and

(ii) under section 4A of that Act that he did the act or made the omission charged against him as the offence.

(3) The second condition is that a hospital order with a restriction order is made in respect of the patient by a court dealing with him for the offence.

(4) The local probation board for the area in which the determination mentioned in subsection (2)(a), (b) or (c) is made must take all reasonable steps to ascertain whether a person who appears to the board to be the victim of the offence or to act for the victim of the offence wishes—

    (a) to make representations about the matters specified in subsection (5);

    (b) to receive the information specified in subsection (6).

(5) The matters are—

    (a) whether the patient should be subject to any conditions in the event of his discharge from hospital;

    (b) if so, what conditions.

(6) The information is information about any conditions to which the patient is to be subject in the event of his discharge from hospital.

37. Representations

(1) This section applies if section 36 applies.

(2) If—

    (a) a person makes representations about a matter specified in section 36(5) to the local probation board mentioned in section 36(4) or the relevant local probation board, and

    (b) it appears to the relevant local probation board that the person is the victim of the offence or acts for the victim of the offence,

the relevant local probation board must forward the representations to the persons responsible for determining the matter.

(3) The duty in subsection (2) applies only while the restriction order made in respect of the patient is in force.

(4) The Secretary of State must inform the relevant local probation board if he is considering—

    (a) whether to give a direction in respect of the patient under section 42(1) of the Mental Health Act 1983 (c. 20) (directions lifting restrictions),

    (b) whether to discharge the patient under section 42(2) of that Act, either absolutely or subject to conditions, or

    (c) if the patient has been discharged subject to conditions, whether to vary the conditions.

(5) A Mental Health Review Tribunal must inform the relevant local probation board if—

    (a) an application is made to the tribunal by the patient under section 69, 70 or 75 of the Mental Health Act 1983 (applications concerning restricted patients), or

    (b) the Secretary of State refers the patient's case to the tribunal under section 71 of that Act (references concerning restricted patients).

(6) Subsection (7) applies if—

    (a) the relevant local probation board receives information under subsection (4) or (5), and

    (b) a person who appears to the relevant local probation board to be the victim of the offence or to act for the victim of the offence—

      (i) when his wishes were ascertained under section 36(4), expressed a wish to make representations about a matter specified in section 36(5), or

      (ii) has made representations about such a matter to the relevant local probation board or the local probation board mentioned in section 36(4).

(7) The relevant local probation board must provide the information to the person.

(8) The relevant local probation board is—

    (a) if the patient is to be discharged subject to a condition that he reside in a particular area, the local probation board for the area;

    (b) in any other case, the local probation board for the area in which the hospital in which the patient is detained is situated.

38. Information

(1) This section applies if section 36 applies.

(2) Subsection (3) applies if a person who appears to the relevant local probation board to be the victim of the offence or to act for the victim of the offence—

    (a) when his wishes were ascertained under section 36(4), expressed a wish to receive the information specified in section 36(6), or

    (b) has subsequently informed the relevant local probation board that he wishes to receive that information.

(3) The relevant local probation board must take all reasonable steps—

    (a) to inform that person whether or not the patient is to be subject to any conditions in the event of his discharge;

    (b) if he is, to provide that person with details of any conditions which relate to contact with the victim or his family;

    (c) if the restriction order in respect of the patient is to cease to have effect, to notify that person of the date on which it is to cease to have effect;

    (d) to provide that person with such other information as the board considers appropriate in all the circumstances of the case.

(4) The Secretary of State must inform the relevant local probation board—

    (a) whether the patient is to be discharged;

    (b) if he is, whether he is to be discharged absolutely or subject to conditions;

    (c) if he is to be discharged subject to conditions, what the conditions are to be;

    (d) if he has been discharged subject to conditions—

      (i) of any variation of the conditions by the Secretary of State;

      (ii) of any recall to hospital under section 42(3) of the Mental Health Act 1983 (c. 20);

    (e) if the restriction order is to cease to have effect by virtue of action to be taken by the Secretary of State, of the date on which the restriction order is to cease to have effect.

(5) Subsections (6) and (7) apply (instead of subsection (4)) if—

    (a) an application is made to a Mental Health Review Tribunal by the patient under section 69, 70 or 75 of the Mental Health Act 1983 (c. 20) (applications concerning restricted patients), or

    (b) the Secretary of State refers the patient's case to a Mental Health Review Tribunal under section 71 of that Act (references concerning restricted patients).

(6) The tribunal must inform the relevant local probation board—

    (a) of the matters specified in subsection (4)(a) to (c);

(b) if the patient has been discharged subject to conditions, of any variation of the conditions by the tribunal;

(c) if the restriction order is to cease to have effect by virtue of action to be taken by the tribunal, of the date on which the restriction order is to cease to have effect.

(7) The Secretary of State must inform the relevant local probation board of the matters specified in subsection (4)(d) and (e).

(8) The duties in subsections (3) to (7) apply only while the restriction order is in force.

(9) The relevant local probation board has the meaning given in section 37(8).

Hospital directions

39. Victims' rights: preliminary

(1) This section applies if—

(a) a person ('the offender') is convicted of a sexual or violent offence,

(b) a relevant sentence is imposed on him in respect of the offence, and

(c) a hospital direction and a limitation direction are given in relation to him by a court dealing with him for the offence.

(2) The local probation board for the area in which the hospital direction is given must take all reasonable steps to ascertain whether a person who appears to the board to be the victim of the offence or to act for the victim of the offence wishes—

(a) to make representations about the matters specified in subsection (3);

(b) to receive the information specified in subsection (4).

(3) The matters are—

(a) whether the offender should, in the event of his discharge from hospital, be subject to any conditions and, if so, what conditions;

(b) whether the offender should, in the event of his release from hospital, be subject to any licence conditions or supervision requirements and, if so, what licence conditions or supervision requirements;

(c) if the offender is transferred to a prison or other institution in which he might have been detained if he had not been removed to hospital, whether he should, in the event of his release from prison or another such institution, be subject to any licence conditions or supervision requirements and, if so, what licence conditions or supervision requirements.

(4) The information is—

(a) information about any conditions to which the offender is to be subject in the event of his discharge;

(b) information about any licence conditions or supervision requirements to which the offender is to be subject in the event of his release.

40. Representations

(1) This section applies if section 39 applies.

(2) If—

(a) a person makes representations about a matter specified in section 39(3) to the local probation board mentioned in section 39(2) or the relevant local probation board, and

(b) it appears to the relevant local probation board that the person is the victim of the offence or acts for the victim of the offence, the relevant local probation board must forward the representations to the persons responsible for determining the matter.

(3) If the representations are about a matter specified in section 39(3)(a), the duty in subsection (2) applies only while the limitation direction given in relation to the offender is in force.

(4) The Secretary of State must inform the relevant local probation board if he is considering—

    (a) whether to give a direction in respect of the offender under section 42(1) of the Mental Health Act 1983 (c. 20) (directions lifting restrictions),

    (b) whether to discharge the offender under section 42(2) of that Act, either absolutely or subject to conditions, or

    (c) if the offender has been discharged subject to conditions, whether to vary the conditions.

(5) A Mental Health Review Tribunal must inform the relevant local probation board if—

    (a) an application is made to the tribunal by the offender under section 69, 70 or 75 of the Mental Health Act 1983 (applications concerning restricted patients), or

    (b) the Secretary of State refers the offender's case to the tribunal under section 71 of that Act (references concerning restricted patients).

(6) Subsection (7) applies if—

    (a) the relevant local probation board receives information under subsection (4) or (5), and

    (b) a person who appears to the relevant local probation board to be the victim of the offence or to act for the victim of the offence—

        (i) when his wishes were ascertained under section 39(2), expressed a wish to make representations about a matter specified in section 39(3)(a), or

        (ii) has made representations about such a matter to the relevant local probation board or the local probation board mentioned in section 39(2).

(7) The relevant local probation board must provide the information to the person.

(8) The relevant local probation board is—

    (a) if the offender is to be discharged from hospital subject to a condition that he reside in a particular area, the local probation board for the area;

    (b) if the offender is to be supervised on release by an officer of a local probation board, that local probation board;

    (c) in any other case, the local probation board for the area in which the hospital, prison or other place in which the offender is detained is situated.

41. Information

(1) This section applies if section 39 applies.

(2) Subsection (3) applies if a person who appears to the relevant local probation board to be the victim of the offence or to act for the victim of the offence—

    (a) when his wishes were ascertained under section 39(2), expressed a wish to receive the information specified in section 39(4), or

    (b) has subsequently informed the relevant local probation board that he wishes to receive that information.

(3) The relevant local probation board must take all reasonable steps—

    (a) to inform that person whether or not the offender is to be subject to any conditions in the event of his discharge;

    (b) if he is, to provide that person with details of any conditions which relate to contact with the victim or his family;

    (c) if the limitation direction in respect of the offender is to cease to have effect, to notify that person of the date on which it is to cease to have effect;

    (d) to inform that person whether or not the offender is to be subject to any licence conditions or supervision requirements in the event of his release;

    (e) if he is, to provide that person with details of any licence conditions or supervision requirements which relate to contact with the victim or his family;

    (f) to provide that person with such other information as the board considers appropriate in all the circumstances of the case.

(4) The Secretary of State must inform the relevant local probation board—

    (a) whether the offender is to be discharged;

    (b) if he is, whether he is to be discharged absolutely or subject to conditions;

    (c) if he is to be discharged subject to conditions, what the conditions are to be;

    (d) if he has been discharged subject to conditions—

        (i) of any variation of the conditions by the Secretary of State;

        (ii) of any recall to hospital under section 42(3) of the Mental Health Act 1983 (c. 20);

    (e) if the limitation direction is to cease to have effect by virtue of action to be taken by the Secretary of State, of the date on which the limitation direction is to cease to have effect.

(5) Subsections (6) and (7) apply (instead of subsection (4)) if—

    (a) an application is made to a Mental Health Review Tribunal by the offender under section 69, 70 or 75 of the Mental Health Act 1983 (c. 20) (applications concerning restricted patients), or

    (b) the Secretary of State refers the offender's case to a Mental Health Review Tribunal under section 71 of that Act (references concerning restricted patients).

(6) The tribunal must inform the relevant local probation board—

    (a) of the matters specified in subsection (4)(a) to (c);

    (b) if the offender has been discharged subject to conditions, of any variation of the conditions by the tribunal;

    (c) if the limitation direction is to cease to have effect by virtue of action to be taken by the tribunal, of the date on which the limitation direction is to cease to have effect.

(7) The Secretary of State must inform the relevant local probation board of the matters specified in subsection (4)(d) and (e).

(8) The duties in subsections (3)(a) to (c) and (4) to (7) apply only while the limitation direction is in force.

(9) The relevant local probation board has the meaning given in section 40(8).

Transfer directions

42. Victims' rights: preliminary

(1) This section applies if—

    (a) a person ('the offender') is convicted of a sexual or violent offence,

    (b) a relevant sentence is imposed on him in respect of the offence, and

    (c) while the offender is serving the sentence, the Secretary of State gives a transfer direction and a restriction direction in respect of him.

(2) The local probation board for the area in which the hospital specified in the transfer direction is situated must take all reasonable steps to ascertain whether a person who appears to the board to be the victim of the offence or to act for the victim of the offence wishes—

    (a) to make representations about the matters specified in subsection (3);

    (b) to receive the information specified in subsection (4).

(3) The matters are—

    (a) whether the offender should be subject to any conditions in the event of his discharge from hospital;

    (b) if so, what conditions.

(4) The information is information about any conditions to which the offender is to be subject in the event of his discharge from hospital.

43. Representations

(1) This section applies if section 42 applies.

(2) If—

    (a) a person makes representations about a matter specified in section 42(3) to the local probation board mentioned in section 42(2) or the relevant local probation board, and

    (b) it appears to the relevant local probation board that the person is the victim of the offence or acts for the victim of the offence,

    the relevant local probation board must forward the representations to the persons responsible for determining the matter.

(3) The duty in subsection (2) applies only while the restriction direction given in respect of the offender is in force.

(4) The Secretary of State must inform the relevant local probation board if he is considering—

    (a) whether to give a direction in respect of the offender under section 42(1) of the Mental Health Act 1983 (c. 20) (directions lifting restrictions),

    (b) whether to discharge the offender under section 42(2) of that Act, either absolutely or subject to conditions, or

    (c) if the offender has been discharged subject to conditions, whether to vary the conditions.

(5) A Mental Health Review Tribunal must inform the relevant local probation board if—

    (a) an application is made to the tribunal by the offender under section 69, 70 or 75 of the Mental Health Act 1983 (applications concerning restricted patients), or

    (b) the Secretary of State refers the offender's case to the tribunal under section 71 of that Act (references concerning restricted patients).

(6) Subsection (7) applies if—

    (a) the relevant local probation board receives information under subsection (4) or (5), and

    (b) a person who appears to the relevant local probation board to be the victim of the offence or to act for the victim of the offence—

      (i) when his wishes were ascertained under section 42(2), expressed a wish to make representations about a matter specified in section 42(3), or

      (ii) has made representations about such a matter to the relevant local probation board or the local probation board mentioned in section 42(2).

(7) The relevant local probation board must provide the information to the person.

(8) The relevant local probation board is—

    (a) if the offender is to be discharged subject to a condition that he reside in a particular area, the local probation board for the area;

    (b) in any other case, the local probation board for the area in which the hospital in which the offender is detained is situated.

44. Information

(1) This section applies if section 42 applies.

(2) Subsection (3) applies if a person who appears to the relevant local probation board to be the victim of the offence or to act for the victim of the offence—

    (a) when his wishes were ascertained under section 42(2), expressed a wish to receive the information specified in section 42(4), or

    (b) has subsequently informed the relevant local probation board that he wishes to receive that information.

(3) The relevant local probation board must take all reasonable steps—

    (a) to inform that person whether or not the offender is to be subject to any conditions in the event of his discharge;

    (b) if he is, to provide that person with details of any conditions which relate to contact with the victim or his family;

    (c) if the restriction direction in respect of the offender is to cease to have effect, to notify that person of the date on which it is to cease to have effect;

    (d) to provide that person with such other information as the board considers appropriate in all the circumstances of the case.

(4) The Secretary of State must inform the relevant local probation board—

    (a) whether the offender is to be discharged;

    (b) if he is, whether he is to be discharged absolutely or subject to conditions;

    (c) if he is to be discharged subject to conditions, what the conditions are to be;

    (d) if he has been discharged subject to conditions—

      (i) of any variation of the conditions by the Secretary of State;

      (ii) of any recall to hospital under section 42(3) of the Mental Health Act 1983 (c. 20);

    (e) if the restriction direction is to cease to have effect by virtue of action to be taken by the Secretary of State, of the date on which the restriction direction is to cease to have effect.

(5) Subsections (6) and (7) apply (instead of subsection (4)) if—

    (a) an application is made to a Mental Health Review Tribunal by the offender under section 69, 70 or 75 of the Mental Health Act 1983 (applications concerning restricted patients), or

    (b) the Secretary of State refers the offender's case to a Mental Health Review Tribunal under section 71 of that Act (references concerning restricted patients).

(6) The tribunal must inform the relevant local probation board—

    (a) of the matters specified in subsection (4)(a) to (c);

(b) if the offender has been discharged subject to conditions, of any variation of the conditions by the tribunal;

(c) if the restriction direction is to cease to have effect by virtue of action to be taken by the tribunal, of the date on which the restriction direction is to cease to have effect.

(7) The Secretary of State must inform the relevant local probation board of the matters specified in subsection (4)(d) and (e).

(8) The duties in subsections (3) to (7) apply only while the restriction direction is in force.

(9) The relevant local probation board has the meaning given in section 43(8).

Interpretation

45. Interpretation: sections 35 to 44

(1) In sections 35 to 44—

'court' does not include a court-martial or the Courts-Martial Appeal Court;

'hospital direction' has the meaning given in section 45A(3)(a) of the Mental Health Act 1983 (c. 20);

'hospital order' has the meaning given in section 37(4) of that Act;

'licence condition' means a condition in a licence;

'limitation direction' has the meaning given in section 45A(3)(b) of the Mental Health Act 1983;

'local probation board' means a local probation board established under section 4 of the Criminal Justice and Court Services Act 2000 (c. 43);

'relevant sentence' means any of these—

(a) a sentence of imprisonment for a term of 12 months or more;

(b) a sentence of detention during Her Majesty's pleasure;

(c) a sentence of detention for a period of 12 months or more under section 91 of the Powers of Criminal Courts (Sentencing) Act 2000 (c. 6) (offenders under 18 convicted of certain serious offences);

(d) a detention and training order for a term of 12 months or more;

'restriction direction' has the meaning given in section 49(2) of the Mental Health Act 1983;

'restriction order' has the meaning given in section 41(1) of that Act;

'supervision requirements' means requirements specified in a notice under section 103(6) of the Powers of Criminal Courts (Sentencing) Act 2000;

'transfer direction' has the meaning given in section 47(1) of the Mental Health Act 1983.

(2) For the purposes of sections 35 to 44, an offence is a sexual or violent offence if it is any of these—

(a) murder or an offence specified in Schedule 15 to the Criminal Justice Act 2003 (c. 44);

(b) an offence in respect of which the patient or offender is subject to the notification requirements of Part 2 of the Sexual Offences Act 2003 (c. 42));

(c) an offence against a child within the meaning of Part 2 of the Criminal Justice and Court Services Act 2000.

Northern Ireland

46. Victims of mentally disordered persons

(1) The Justice (Northern Ireland) Act 2002 (c. 26) is amended as follows.

(2) After section 69 (views on temporary release) insert—

'69A. Information about discharge and leave of absence of mentally disordered persons

(1) The Secretary of State must make a scheme requiring the Secretary of State to make available to persons falling within subsection (2) information about—
  (a) the discharge from hospital of, or
  (b) the grant of leave of absence from hospital to,
persons in respect of whom relevant determinations have been made.

(2) The persons referred to in subsection (1) are victims of the offences in respect of which the determinations were made who wish to receive the information.

(3) A relevant determination is made in respect of a person if—
  (a) a hospital order with a restriction order is made in respect of him by a court dealing with him for an offence, or
  (b) a transfer direction and a restriction direction are given in respect of him while he is serving a sentence of imprisonment in respect of an offence.

(4) The Secretary of State may from time to time make a new scheme or alterations to a scheme.

(5) The information to be made available under a scheme must include information as to any relevant conditions to which a person in respect of whom a relevant determination has been made is to be subject in the event of—
  (a) his discharge from hospital, or
  (b) the grant of leave of absence from hospital to him.

(6) A condition is relevant for the purposes of subsection (5) if it appears to the Secretary of State that it might affect a victim of an offence in respect of which the determination was made.

(7) A scheme may require the Secretary of State to take all reasonable steps to ascertain whether a person who appears to him to be the victim of an offence in respect of which a relevant determination has been made wishes to make representations about the matters specified in subsection (8).

(8) The matters are—
  (a) whether the person in respect of whom the determination has been made should be subject to any conditions in the event of his discharge from hospital or the grant of leave of absence from hospital to him;
  (b) if so, what conditions.

(9) A scheme that includes provision such as is mentioned in subsection (7) must specify how the representations are to be made.

(10) A scheme may require other information in relation to the discharge of, or the grant of leave of absence to, persons in respect of whom relevant determinations are made to be made available under the scheme.

(11) The other information may include, in cases of a description specified by the scheme or in which the Secretary of State considers it appropriate, the date on which it is anticipated that a person in respect of whom a relevant determination has been made will be discharged or granted leave of absence from hospital.

(12) Subsections (5) to (8) of section 68 apply in relation to a scheme made under this section as they apply in relation to a scheme made under that section.

(13) A scheme may make different provision in relation to different descriptions of persons in respect of whom a relevant determination is made.

69B. Views on leave of absence

(1) If a person who is the victim of an offence in respect of which a relevant determination has been made makes to the Secretary of State representations falling within subsection (2) the Secretary of State has the obligations specified in subsection (3).

(2) Representations fall within this subsection if they are to the effect that the grant of leave of absence to the person in respect of whom the determination has been made would threaten the safety, or otherwise adversely affect the well-being, of—

(a) the actual victim of the offence in respect of which the determination was made, or

(b) a person who is regarded for the purposes of a scheme under section 69A as a victim of that offence by virtue of section 68(5) (as applied by section 69A(12)).

(3) The Secretary of State must—

(a) have regard to the representations in deciding whether he should give his consent to leave of absence being granted, and

(b) inform the victim of any such decision.

(4) Section 69A(3) (relevant determination) applies for the purposes of this section.'

(3) In section 70 (supplementary), after subsection (3) insert—

'(4) In sections 68 and 69 references to a person serving a sentence of imprisonment in Northern Ireland include a person detained in hospital pursuant to a transfer direction and a restriction direction.

(5) In subsection (4) and section 69A(3)—

"restriction direction" has the meaning given in Article 55(2) of the Mental Health (Northern Ireland) Order 1986;

"transfer direction" has the meaning given in Article 53(2) of that Order.

(6) In section 69A(3)—

"hospital order" has the meaning given in Article 44(1) of the Mental Health (Northern Ireland) Order 1986;

"restriction order" has the meaning given in Article 47(1) of that Order;

"sentence of imprisonment" has the meaning given in Article 53(5) of that Order.

(7) In sections 69A and 69B "leave of absence" means leave of absence under Article 15 of the Mental Health (Northern Ireland) Order 1986.'

(4) In section 90(5) (statutory rules), in paragraph (b) after "section 68" insert "or 69A".

CHAPTER 3
OTHER MATTERS RELATING TO VICTIMS ETC

Parliamentary Commissioner

47. Investigations by Parliamentary Commissioner

Schedule 7 (which amends the Parliamentary Commissioner Act 1967 (c. 13)) has effect.

Commissioner for Victims and Witnesses

48. Commissioner for Victims and Witnesses

(1) The Secretary of State must appoint a Commissioner for Victims and Witnesses (referred to in this Part as the Commissioner).

(2) Before appointing the Commissioner the Secretary of State must consult the Attorney-General and the Lord Chancellor as to the person to be appointed.

(3) The Commissioner is a corporation sole.

(4) The Commissioner is not to be regarded—
   (a) as the servant or agent of the Crown, or
   (b) as enjoying any status, immunity or privilege of the Crown.

(5) The Commissioner's property is not to be regarded as property of, or held on behalf of, the Crown.

(6) Schedule 8 (which make further provision in connection with the Commissioner) has effect.

49. General functions of Commissioner

(1) The Commissioner must—
   (a) promote the interests of victims and witnesses;
   (b) take such steps as he considers appropriate with a view to encouraging good practice in the treatment of victims and witnesses;
   (c) keep under review the operation of the code of practice issued under section 32.

(2) The Commissioner may, for any purpose connected with the performance of his duties under subsection (1)—
   (a) make proposals to the Secretary of State for amending the code (at the request of the Secretary of State or on his own initiative);
   (b) make a report to the Secretary of State;
   (c) make recommendations to an authority within his remit;
   (d) undertake or arrange for or support (financially or otherwise) the carrying out of research;
   (e) consult any person he thinks appropriate.

(3) If the Commissioner makes a report to the Secretary of State under subsection (2)(b)—
   (a) the Commissioner must send a copy of the report to the Attorney-General and the Lord Chancellor;
   (b) the Secretary of State must lay a copy of the report before Parliament and arrange for the report to be published.

50. Advice

(1) If he is required to do so by a Minister of the Crown, the Commissioner must give advice to the Minister of the Crown in connection with any matter which—
   (a) is specified by the Minister, and
   (b) relates to victims or witnesses.

(2) If he is required to do so by or on behalf of an authority within his remit, the Commissioner must give advice to the authority in connection with the information provided or to be provided by or on behalf of the authority to victims or witnesses.

(3) In this section 'Minister of the Crown' Includes the Treasury.

51. Restrictions on exercise of functions

The Commissioner must not exercise any of his functions in relation to—
(a) a particular victim or witness;
(b) the bringing or conduct of particular proceedings;
(c) anything done or omitted to be done by a person acting in a judicial capacity or on the instructions of or on behalf of such a person.

52. 'Victims' and 'witnesses'

(1) This section applies for the purposes of sections 48 to 51.
(2) 'Victim' means—
    (a) a victim of an offence, or
    (b) a victim of anti-social behaviour.
(3) It is immaterial for the purposes of subsection (2)(a) that—
    (a) no complaint has been made about the offence;
    (b) no person has been charged with or convicted of the offence.
(4) 'Witness' means a person (other than a defendant)—
    (a) who has witnessed conduct in relation to which he may be or has been called to give evidence in relevant proceedings;
    (b) who is able to provide or has provided anything which might be used or has been used as evidence in relevant proceedings; or
    (c) who is able to provide or has provided anything mentioned in subsection (5) (whether or not admissible in evidence in relevant proceedings).
(5) The things referred to in subsection (4)(c) are—
    (a) anything which might tend to confirm, has tended to confirm or might have tended to confirm evidence which may be, has been or could have been admitted in relevant proceedings;
    (b) anything which might be, has been or might have been referred to in evidence given in relevant proceedings by another person;
    (c) anything which might be, has been or might have been used as the basis for any cross-examination in the course of relevant proceedings.
(6) For the purposes of subsection (4)—
    (a) a person is a defendant in relation to any criminal proceedings if he might be, has been or might have been charged with or convicted of an offence in the proceedings;
    (b) a person is a defendant in relation to any other relevant proceedings if he might be, has been or might have been the subject of an order made in those proceedings.
(7) In subsections (4) to (6) 'relevant proceedings' means—
    (a) criminal proceedings;
    (b) proceedings of any other kind in respect of anti-social behaviour.
(8) For the purposes of this section—
    (a) 'anti-social behaviour' means behaviour by a person which causes or is likely to cause harassment, alarm or distress to one or more persons not of the same household as the person;
    (b) a person is a victim of anti-social behaviour if the behaviour has caused him harassment, alarm or distress and he is not of the same household as the person who engages in the behaviour.

53. Authorities within Commissioner's remit

(1) For the purposes of this Part the authorities within the Commissioner's remit are those specified in Schedule 9.

(2) An authority specified in Schedule 9 that has functions in relation to an area outside England and Wales is within the Commissioner's remit only to the extent that it discharges its functions in relation to England and Wales.

(3) Subsection (2) does not apply in relation to the Foreign and Commonwealth Office.

(4) The Secretary of State may by order amend Schedule 9 by—

    (a) adding an authority appearing to him to exercise functions of a public nature;

    (b) omitting an authority;

    (c) changing the description of an authority.

(5) In preparing a draft of an order under subsection (4) the Secretary of State must consult the Attorney-General and the Lord Chancellor.

Disclosure of information

54. Disclosure of information

(1) A person may disclose information to a relevant authority for a purpose specified in subsection (2).

(2) The purposes are purposes connected with any of these—

    (a) compliance with the code issued under section 32;

    (b) compliance with sections 35 to 44;

    (c) the carrying out of the functions of the Commissioner.

(3) These are relevant authorities—

    (a) a person required to do anything under the code issued under section 32;

    (b) a local probation board established under section 4 of the Criminal Justice and Court Services Act 2000 (c. 43);

    (c) the Commissioner;

    (d) an authority within the Commissioner's remit.

(4) The Secretary of State may by order—

    (a) amend subsection (2) by adding any purpose appearing to him to be connected with the assistance of victims of offences or anti-social behaviour, witnesses of offences or anti-social behaviour or other persons affected by offences or anti-social behaviour;

    (b) amend subsection (3) by adding any authority appearing to him to exercise functions of a public nature.

(5) The reference in subsection (4)(a) to persons affected by offences does not include persons accused or convicted of offences.

(6) The Secretary of State may exercise the power in subsection (4) only after consulting the Attorney-General and the Lord Chancellor.

(7) Nothing in this section authorizes the making of a disclosure which contravenes the Data Protection Act 1998 (c. 29).

(8) This section does not affect a power to disclose which exists apart from this section.

Victims' Advisory Panel

55. Victims' Advisory Panel

(1) The Secretary of State must appoint persons to form a panel, to be known as the Victims' Advisory Panel.

(2) The Secretary of State must consult the Attorney-General and the Lord Chancellor before—
  (a) appointing a person to the Panel, or
  (b) removing a person from the Panel.

(3) The Secretary of State must consult the Panel at such times and in such manner as he thinks appropriate on matters appearing to him to relate to victims of offences or anti-social behaviour or witnesses of offences or anti-social behaviour.

(4) The Secretary of State may reimburse the members of the Panel for such of their travelling and other expenses as he thinks appropriate.

(5) If the Secretary of State consults the Panel under subsection (3) in a particular year, he must arrange for the Panel to prepare a report for the year—
  (a) summarising what the Panel has done in response to the consultation, and
  (b) dealing with such other matters as the Panel consider appropriate.

(6) If a report is prepared under subsection (5), the Secretary of State must—
  (a) arrange for it to be published, and
  (b) lay it before Parliament.

(7) The non-statutory Victims' Advisory Panel is to be treated as having been established in accordance with this section.

(8) If the Secretary of State consults the non-statutory Victims' Advisory Panel on a matter mentioned in subsection (3) before the date on which this section comes into force, the consultation is to be treated as taking place under subsection (3).

(9) The non-statutory Victims' Advisory Panel is the unincorporated body of persons known as the Victims' Advisory Panel established by the Secretary of State before the date on which this section comes into force.

(10) In this section 'year' means a period of 12 months beginning on 1 April.

Grants

56. Grants for assisting victims, witnesses etc

(1) The Secretary of State may pay such grants to such persons as he considers appropriate in connection with measures which appear to him to be intended to assist victims, witnesses or other persons affected by offences.

(2) The Secretary of State may make a grant under this section subject to such conditions as he considers appropriate.

Criminal injuries compensation

57. Recovery of criminal injuries compensation from offenders

(1) The Criminal Injuries Compensation Act 1995 (c. 53) is amended as follows.

(2) After section 7 insert—

'7A. Recovery of compensation from offenders: general

(1) The Secretary of State may, by regulations made by statutory instrument, make provision for the recovery from an appropriate person of an amount equal to all or part of the compensation paid in respect of a criminal injury.

(2) An appropriate person is a person who has been convicted of an offence in respect of the criminal injury.

(3) The amount recoverable from a person under the regulations must be determined by reference only to the extent to which the criminal injury is directly attributable to an offence of which he has been convicted.

(4) The regulations may confer functions in respect of recovery on—
    (a) claims officers;
    (b) if a Scheme manager has been appointed, persons appointed by the Scheme manager under section 3(4)(a).

(5) The regulations may not authorize the recovery of an amount in respect of compensation from a person to the extent that the compensation has been repaid in accordance with the Scheme.

7B. Recovery notices

(1) If, under regulations made under section 7A(1), an amount has been determined as recoverable from a person, he must be given a notice (a 'recovery notice') in accordance with the regulations which—
    (a) requires him to pay that amount, and
    (b) contains the information mentioned in subsection (2).

(2) The information is—
    (a) the reasons for the determination that an amount is recoverable from the person;
    (b) the basis on which the amount has been determined;
    (c) the way in which and the date before which the amount is required to be paid;
    (d) the means by which the amount may be recovered if it is not paid in accordance with the notice;
    (e) the grounds on which and the procedure by means of which he may seek a review if he objects to—
        (i) the determination that an amount is recoverable from him;
        (ii) the amount determined as recoverable from him.

(3) The Secretary of State may by order made by statutory instrument amend subsection (2) by—
    (a) adding information;
    (b) omitting information;
    (c) changing the description of information.

7C. Review of recovery determinations

(1) Regulations under section 7A(1) shall include provision for the review, in such circumstances as may be prescribed by the regulations, of—
    (a) a determination that an amount is recoverable from a person;
    (b) the amount determined as recoverable from a person.

(2) A person from whom an amount has been determined as recoverable under the regulations may seek such a review only on the grounds—

 (a) that he has not been convicted of an offence to which the injury is directly attributable;

 (b) that the compensation paid was not determined in accordance with the Scheme;

 (c) that the amount determined as recoverable from him was not determined in accordance with the regulations.

(3) Any such review must be conducted by a person other than the person who made the determination under review.

(4) The person conducting any such review may—

 (a) set aside the determination that the amount is recoverable;

 (b) reduce the amount determined as recoverable;

 (c) increase the amount determined as recoverable;

 (d) determine to take no action under paragraphs (a) to (c).

(5) But the person conducting any such review may increase the amount determined as recoverable if (but only if) it appears to that person that the interests of justice require the amount to be increased.

7D. Recovery proceedings

(1) An amount determined as recoverable from a person under regulations under section 7A(1) is recoverable from him as a debt due to the Crown if (but only if)—

 (a) he has been given a recovery notice in accordance with the regulations which complies with the requirements of section 7B, and

 (b) he has failed to pay the amount in accordance with the notice.

(2) In any proceedings for the recovery of the amount from a person, it is a defence for the person to show—

 (a) that he has not been convicted of an offence to which the injury is directly attributable;

 (b) that the compensation paid was not determined in accordance with the Scheme; or

 (c) that the amount determined as recoverable from him was not determined in accordance with regulations under section 7A.

(3) In any such proceedings, except for the purposes of subsection (2)(b), no question may be raised or finding made as to the amount that was, or ought to have been, the subject of an award.

(4) For the purposes of section 9 of the Limitation Act 1980 (time limit for actions for sums recoverable by statute to run from date on which cause of action accrued) the cause of action to recover that amount shall be taken to have accrued—

 (a) on the date on which the compensation was paid; or

 (b) if later, on the date on which a person from whom an amount is sought to be recovered was convicted of an offence to which the injury is directly attributable.

(5) If that person is convicted of more than one such offence and the convictions are made on different dates, the reference in subsection (4)(b) to the date on which he was convicted of such an offence shall be taken to be a reference to the

earlier or earliest (as the case may be) of the dates on which he was convicted of such an offence.'

(3) In section 9(7) (financial provisions: sums payable into Consolidated Fund), after 'section 3(1)(c)' insert ', or by virtue of regulations made under section 7A(1),'.

(4) In section 11, after subsection (8) insert—

'(8A) No regulations under section 7A(1) or order under section 7B(3) shall be made unless a draft of the regulations or order has been laid before Parliament and approved by a resolution of each House.'

PART 4
SUPPLEMENTARY

58. Amendments and repeals

(1) Schedule 10 (minor and consequential amendments) has effect.

(2) The provisions mentioned in Schedule 11 are repealed or revoked to the extent specified.

59. Transitional and transitory provisions

Schedule 12 (transitional and transitory provisions) has effect.

60. Commencement

The preceding provisions of this Act come into force in accordance with provision made by the Secretary of State by order.

61. Orders

(1) An order under this Act—
  (a) may make different provision for different purposes;
  (b) may include supplementary, incidental, saving or transitional provisions.

(2) Any power to make an order under this Act is exercisable by statutory instrument.

(3) A statutory instrument containing an order under section 9(6) or 33(7) is subject to annulment in pursuance of a resolution of either House of Parliament.

(4) No order may be made under section 14(5), 53(4) or 54(4) unless a draft of the order has been laid before Parliament and approved by a resolution of each House.

62. Extent

(1) Subject to the following provisions of this section, Parts 1 to 3 extend to England and Wales only.

(2) The following provisions extend also to Northern Ireland—
  section 5;
  section 9;
  sections 17 to 21;
  Schedule 1;
  section 56;

(3) The following provisions extend to Northern Ireland only—
  section 7;

section 10(2);
section 13;
section 23;
section 46.

(4) Section 8, so far as relating to proceedings before courts-martial constituted under a particular Act mentioned in subsection (2) of that section, has the same extent as that Act.

(5) An amendment, repeal or revocation in Schedule 3, 7, 8, 10 or 11 has the same extent as the provision to which it relates.

63. Short title

This Act may be cited as the Domestic Violence, Crime and Victims Act 2004.

SCHEDULES

SCHEDULE 1

Section 21

MODIFICATION OF SECTIONS 17 TO 20 FOR NORTHERN IRELAND

1. For section 18 substitute—

'18. Procedure for applications under section 17

(1) An application under section 17 must be determined—
   (a) at a preparatory hearing (within the meaning of the 1988 Order), or
   (b) at a hearing specified in, or for which provision is made by, Crown Court rules.

(2) The parties to a hearing mentioned in subsection (1) at which an application under section 17 is to be determined must be given an opportunity to make representations with respect to the application.

(3) Article 6(1) of the 1988 Order (which sets out the purposes of preparatory hearings) is to have effect as if the purposes there mentioned included the purpose of determining an application under section 17.

(4) Article 8(11) of the 1988 Order (appeal to Court of Appeal) is to have effect as if it also provided for an appeal to the Court of Appeal to lie from the determination by a judge of an application under section 17.

(5) In this section "the 1988 Order" means the Criminal Justice (Serious Fraud) (Northern Ireland) Order 1988.

18A. Appeals in respect of hearings under section 18(1)(b)

(1) An appeal shall lie to the Court of Appeal from the refusal by a judge at a hearing mentioned in section 18(1)(b) of an application under section 17 or from an order of a judge at such a hearing under section 17(2) which is made on the determination of such an application.

(2) Such an appeal may be brought only with the leave of the judge or the Court of Appeal.

(3) An order or a refusal of an application from which an appeal under this section lies is not to take effect—
   (a) before the expiration of the period for bringing an appeal under this section, or
   (b) if such an appeal is brought, before the appeal is finally disposed of or abandoned.

(4) On the termination of the hearing of an appeal under this section, the Court of Appeal may—
   (a) where the appeal is from an order, confirm or revoke the order, or
   (b) where the appeal is from a refusal of an application, confirm the refusal or make the order which is the subject of the application.

(5) In section 31(1) of the Criminal Appeal (Northern Ireland) Act 1980 (right of appeal to House of Lords) for "Act or" substitute "Act, section 18A of the Domestic Violence, Crime and Victims Act 2004,".

(6) In section 35 of that Act (bail) after "appeal under" insert "section 18A of the Domestic Violence, Crime and Victims Act 2004,".

(7) The Secretary of State may make an order containing provision, in relation to proceedings before the Court of Appeal under this section, which corresponds to any provision, in relation to appeals or other proceedings before that court, which is contained in the Criminal Appeal (Northern Ireland) Act 1980 (subject to any specified modifications).

(8) A statutory instrument containing an order under subsection (7) is subject to annulment in pursuance of a resolution of either House of Parliament.

18B. Reporting restrictions

(1) Sections 41 and 42 of the Criminal Procedure and Investigations Act 1996 are to apply in relation to—
   (a) a hearing of the kind mentioned in section 18(1)(b), and
   (b) any appeal or application for leave to appeal relating to such a hearing,
   as they apply in relation to a ruling under section 40 of that Act, but subject to the following modifications.

(2) Section 41(2) of that Act is to have effect as if for paragraphs (a) to (d) there were substituted—
   "(a) a hearing of the kind mentioned in section 18(1)(b) of the Domestic Violence, Crime and Victims Act 2004;
   (b) any appeal or application for leave to appeal relating to such a hearing."

(3) Section 41(3) of that Act is to have effect as if—
   (a) for "(2)" there were substituted "(2)(a) or an application to that judge for leave to appeal to the Court of Appeal", and
   (b) after "matter", in the second place where it occurs, there were inserted "or application".

(4) Section 41 of that Act is to have effect as if after subsection (3) there were inserted—
   "(3A) The Court of Appeal may order that subsection (1) shall not apply, or shall not apply to a specified extent, to a report of—
      (a) an appeal to that Court, or
      (b) an application to that Court for leave to appeal.
   (3B) The House of Lords may order that subsection (1) shall not apply, or shall not apply to a specified extent, to a report of—
      (a) an appeal to that House, or
      (b) an application to that House for leave to appeal."

(5) Section 41(4) of that Act is to have effect as if for "(3) the judge" there were substituted "(3), (3A) or (3B), the judge, the Court of Appeal or the House of Lords".

(6) Section 41(5) of that Act is to have effect as if for '(3) the judge' there were substituted "(3), (3A) or (3B), the judge, the Court of Appeal or the House of Lords".'

2. In section 19(3) after 'enactment' insert '(including any provision of Northern Ireland legislation)'.

3. In section 19(4)(b) for the words from 'section' to 'etc)' substitute 'section 16(1) of the Criminal Appeal (Northern Ireland) Act 1980 (notice of appeal or application for leave)'.

4. In section 19(5) for 'section 18(2) of the Criminal Appeal Act 1968' substitute 'section 16(1) of the Criminal Appeal (Northern Ireland) Act 1980'.

5. For section 19(7) substitute—

'(7) Nothing in this section or section 17, 18, 18A, 18B or 20 affects the requirement under Article 49A of the Mental Health (Northern Ireland) Order 1986 that any question, finding or verdict mentioned in that Article be determined, made or returned by a jury.'

6. For section 20(2) substitute—

'(2) Without limiting subsection (1), rules of court may in particular make provision—

    (a) for time limits within which applications under section 17 must be made or within which other things in connection with that section or sections 18 to 19 must be done;

    (b) in relation to hearings of the kind mentioned in section 18(1)(b).'

7. In section 20(3)—

(a) after 'section' insert 'or section 18(1)(b)';

(b) after 'enactment' insert '(including any provision of Northern Ireland legislation)'.

SCHEDULE 2

Section 24

SUPERVISION ORDERS ON FINDING OF INSANITY OR UNFITNESS TO PLEAD ETC

The following is the Schedule inserted before Schedule 2 to the Criminal Procedure (Insanity) Act 1964 (c. 84)—

'SCHEDULE 1A

Section 5A

SUPERVISION ORDERS

PART 1
PRELIMINARY

1. (1) In this Schedule "supervision order" means an order which requires the person in respect of whom it is made ("the supervised person") to be under the supervision of a social worker or an officer of a local probation board ("the supervising officer") for a period specified in the order of not more than two years.

(2) A supervision order may, in accordance with paragraph 4 or 5 below, require the supervised person to submit, during the whole of that period or such part of it as may be specified in the order, to treatment by or under the direction of a registered medical practitioner.

(3) The Secretary of State may by order direct that sub-paragraph (1) above shall be amended by substituting, for the period for the time being specified there, such period as may be specified in the order.

(4) An order under sub-paragraph (3) above may make in paragraph 11(2) below any amendment which the Secretary of State thinks necessary in consequence of any substitution made by the order.

(5) The power of the Secretary of State to make orders under sub-paragraph (3) above shall be exercisable by statutory instrument which shall be subject to annulment in pursuance of a resolution of either House of Parliament.

PART 2
MAKING AND EFFECT OF ORDERS

Circumstances in which orders may be made

2. (1) The court shall not make a supervision order unless it is satisfied that, having regard to all the circumstances of the case, the making of such an order is the most suitable means of dealing with the accused or appellant.

(2) The court shall not make a supervision order unless it is also satisfied—

(a) that the supervising officer intended to be specified in the order is willing to undertake the supervision; and

(b) that arrangements have been made for the treatment intended to be specified in the order.

Making of orders and general requirements

3. (1) A supervision order shall either—

(a) specify the local social services authority area in which the supervised person resides or will reside, and require him to be under the supervision of a social worker of the local social services authority for that area; or

(b) specify the local justice area in which that person resides or will reside, and require him to be under the supervision of an officer of a local probation board appointed for or assigned to that area.

(2) Before making such an order, the court shall explain to the supervised person in ordinary language—

(a) the effect of the order (including any requirements proposed to be included in the order in accordance with paragraph 4, 5 or 8 below); and

(b) that a magistrates' court has power under paragraphs 9 to 11 below to review the order on the application either of the supervised person or of the supervising officer.

(3) After making such an order, the court shall forthwith give copies of the order to an officer of a local probation board assigned to the court, and he shall give a copy—

(a) to the supervised person; and

(b) to the supervising officer.

(4) After making such an order, the court shall also send to the designated officer for the local justice area in which the supervised person resides or will reside ("the local justice area concerned")—

(a) a copy of the order; and

(b) such documents and information relating to the case as it considers likely to be of assistance to a court acting for that area in the exercise of its functions in relation to the order.

(5) Where such an order is made, the supervised person shall keep in touch with the supervising officer in accordance with such instructions as he may from time to time be given by that officer and shall notify him of any change of address.

Requirements as to medical treatment

4. (1) A supervision order may, if the court is satisfied as mentioned in sub-paragraph (2) below, include a requirement that the supervised person shall submit, during the whole of the period specified in the order or during such part of that period as may be so specified, to treatment by or under the direction of a registered medical practitioner with a view to the improvement of his mental condition.

(2) The court may impose such a requirement only if satisfied on the written or oral evidence of two or more registered medical practitioners, at least one of whom is duly registered, that the mental condition of the supervised person—

(a) is such as requires and may be susceptible to treatment; but

(b) is not such as to warrant the making of a hospital order within the meaning of the Mental Health Act 1983.

(3) The treatment required under this paragraph by any such order shall be such one of the following kinds of treatment as may be specified in the order, that is to say—

(a) treatment as a non-resident patient at such institution or place as may be specified in the order; and

(b) treatment by or under the direction of such registered medical practitioner as may be so specified;

but the nature of the treatment shall not be specified in the order except as mentioned in paragraph (a) or (b) above.

5. (1) This paragraph applies where the court is satisfied on the written or oral evidence of two or more registered medical practitioners that—

(a) because of his medical condition, other than his mental condition, the supervised person is likely to pose a risk to himself or others; and

(b) the condition may be susceptible to treatment.

(2) The supervision order may (whether or not it includes a requirement under paragraph 4 above) include a requirement that the supervised person shall submit, during the whole of the period specified in the order or during such part of that period as may be so specified, to treatment by or under the direction of a registered medical practitioner with a view to the improvement of the condition.

(3) The treatment required under this paragraph by any such order shall be such one of the following kinds of treatment as may be specified in the order, that is to say—

(a) treatment as a non-resident patient at such institution or place as may be specified in the order; and

(b) treatment by or under the direction of such registered medical practitioner as may be so specified;

but the nature of the treatment shall not be specified in the order except as mentioned in paragraph (a) or (b) above.

6. (1) Where the medical practitioner by whom or under whose direction the supervised person is being treated in pursuance of a requirement under paragraph 4 or 5 above is of the opinion that part of the treatment can be better or more conveniently given in or at an institution or place which—

(a) is not specified in the order, and

(b) is one in or at which the treatment of the supervised person will be given by or under the direction of a registered medical practitioner,

he may, with the consent of the supervised person, make arrangements for him to be treated accordingly.

(2) Such arrangements may provide for the supervised person to receive part of his treatment as a resident patient in an institution or place of any description.

(3) Where any such arrangements are made for the treatment of a supervised person—

(a) the medical practitioner by whom the arrangements are made shall give notice in writing to the supervising officer, specifying the institution or place in or at which the treatment is to be carried out; and

(b) the treatment provided for by the arrangements shall be deemed to be treatment to which he is required to submit in pursuance of the supervision order.

7. While the supervised person is under treatment as a resident patient in pursuance of arrangements under paragraph 6 above, the supervising officer shall carry out the supervision to such extent only as may be necessary for the purpose of the revocation or amendment of the order.

Requirements as to residence

8. (1) Subject to sub-paragraph (2) below, a supervision order may include requirements as to the residence of the supervised person.

(2) Before making such an order containing any such requirement, the court shall consider the home surroundings of the supervised person.

PART 3
REVOCATION AND AMENDMENT OF ORDERS

Revocation of order

9. (1) Where a supervision order is in force in respect of any person and, on the application of the supervised person or the supervising officer, it appears to a magistrates' court acting for the local justice area concerned that, having regard to circumstances which have arisen since the order was made, it would be in the interests of the health or welfare of the supervised person that the order should be revoked, the court may revoke the order.

(2) The court by which a supervision order was made may of its own motion revoke the order if, having regard to circumstances which have arisen since the order was made, it considers that it would be inappropriate for the order to continue.

Amendment of order by reason of change of residence

10. (1) This paragraph applies where, at any time while a supervision order is in force in respect of any person, a magistrates' court acting for the local justice area concerned is satisfied that the supervised person proposes to change, or has changed, his

residence from the area specified in the order to another local social services authority area or local justice area.

(2) Subject to sub-paragraph (3) below, the court may, and on the application of the supervising officer shall, amend the supervision order by substituting the other area for the area specified in the order.

(3) The court shall not amend under this paragraph a supervision order which contains requirements which, in the opinion of the court, cannot be complied with unless the supervised person continues to reside in the area specified in the order unless, in accordance with paragraph 11 below, it either—

(a) cancels those requirements; or

(b) substitutes for those requirements other requirements which can be complied with if the supervised person ceases to reside in that area.

Amendment of requirements of order

11. (1) Without prejudice to the provisions of paragraph 10 above, but subject to sub-paragraph (2) below, a magistrates' court for the local justice area concerned may, on the application of the supervised person or the supervising officer, by order amend a supervision order—

(a) by cancelling any of the requirements of the order; or

(b) by inserting in the order (either in addition to or in substitution for any such requirement) any requirement which the court could include if it were the court by which the order was made and were then making it.

(2) The power of a magistrates' court under sub-paragraph (1) above shall not include power to amend an order by extending the period specified in it beyond the end of two years from the day of the original order.

Amendment of requirements in pursuance of medical report

12. (1) Where the medical practitioner by whom or under whose direction the supervised person is being treated for his mental condition in pursuance of any requirement of a supervision order—

(a) is of the opinion mentioned in sub-paragraph (2) below, or

(b) is for any reason unwilling to continue to treat or direct the treatment of the supervised person,

he shall make a report in writing to that effect to the supervising officer and that officer shall apply under paragraph 11 above to a magistrates' court for the local justice area concerned for the variation or cancellation of the requirement.

(2) The opinion referred to in sub-paragraph (1) above is—

(a) that the treatment of the supervised person should be continued beyond the period specified in the supervision order;

(b) that the supervised person needs different treatment, being treatment of a kind to which he could be required to submit in pursuance of such an order;

(c) that the supervised person is not susceptible to treatment; or

(d) that the supervised person does not require further treatment.

Supplemental

13. (1) On the making under paragraph 9 above of an order revoking a supervision order, the designated officer for the local justice area concerned, or (as the case may be) the Crown Court, shall forthwith give copies of the revoking order to the supervising officer.

(2) A supervising officer to whom in accordance with sub-paragraph (1) above copies of a revoking order are given shall give a copy to the supervised person and to the person in charge of any institution in which the supervised person is residing.

14. (1) On the making under paragraph 10 or 11 above of any order amending a supervision order, the designated officer for the local justice area concerned shall forthwith—

(a) if the order amends the supervision order otherwise than by substituting a new area or a new place for the one specified in the supervision order, give copies of the amending order to the supervising officer;

(b) if the order amends the supervision order in the manner excepted by paragraph (a) above, send to the designated officer for the new local justice area concerned—

(i) copies of the amending order; and

(ii) such documents and information relating to the case as he considers likely to be of assistance to a court acting for that area in exercising its functions in relation to the order;

and in a case falling within paragraph (b) above, the designated officer for that area shall give copies of the amending order to the supervising officer.

(2) Where the designated officer for the court making the order is also the designated officer for the new local justice area—

(a) sub-paragraph (1)(b) above does not apply; but

(b) the designated officers shall give copies of the amending order to the supervising officer.

(3) Where in accordance with sub-paragraph (1) or (2) above copies of an order are given to the supervising officer, he shall give a copy to the supervised person and to the person in charge of any institution in which the supervised person is or was residing.'

SCHEDULE 3

Section 26

UNFITNESS TO STAND TRIAL AND INSANITY: COURTS-MARTIAL ETC

Army Act 1953 (3 & 4 Eliz. 2 c. 18) and Air Force Act 1955 (3 & 4 Eliz. 2 c. 19)

1. For section 116 of the Army Act 1955 and of the Air Force Act 1955 (provisions where accused found insane) substitute—

'Findings of unfitness to stand trial and insanity

115A. Fitness to stand trial

(1) This section applies where on a trial by court-martial of a person the question arises (at the instance of the defence or otherwise) whether the accused is fit to stand trial.

(2) For the purposes of this Act a person is unfit to stand trial if he is under a disability such that apart from the Criminal Procedure (Insanity) Act 1964 it would constitute a bar to his being tried on indictment in England and Wales.

(3) If, having regard to the nature of the supposed disability, the judge advocate is of opinion that it is expedient to do so and in the interests of the accused, he may postpone consideration of the question of fitness to stand trial until any time up to the opening of the case for the defence.

(4) If, before the question of fitness to stand trial falls to be determined, the court finds the accused not guilty on the charge or each of the charges on which he is being tried, that question shall not be determined.

(5) Subject to subsections (3) and (4) above, the question of fitness to stand trial shall be determined as soon as it arises.

(6) The question of fitness to stand trial shall be determined by the judge advocate sitting alone.

(7) A judge advocate shall not make a determination under subsection (6) above except on the written or oral evidence of two or more registered medical practitioners at least one of whom is duly approved.

115B. Finding that the accused did the act or made the omission charged

(1) This section applies where in accordance with section 115A(6) above it is determined by a judge advocate that the accused is unfit to stand trial.

(2) The trial shall not proceed or further proceed but it shall be determined by the court—

(a) on the evidence (if any) already given in the trial, and

(b) on such evidence as may be adduced or further adduced by the prosecution, or adduced by a person appointed by the judge advocate under this section to put the case for the defence,

whether it is satisfied, as respects the charge or each of the charges on which the accused was to be or was being tried, that he did the act or made the omission charged against him as the offence.

(3) If as respects that charge or any of those charges the court is satisfied as mentioned in subsection (2) above, it shall make a finding that the accused did the act or made the omission charged against him.

(4) If as respects that charge or any of those charges the court is not so satisfied, the court shall find the accused not guilty as if on the charge in question the trial had proceeded to a conclusion.

(5) Where the question of fitness to stand trial was determined after arraignment of the accused, the determination under subsection (2) above shall be made by the court-martial by whom he was being tried.

116. Findings of insanity

(1) Where, on the trial of a person by court-martial, the court is satisfied, as respects the charge or any of the charges on which he is being tried, that the accused did the act or made the omission charged against him as the offence but that at the time of that act or omission he was insane, the court shall find that the accused was not guilty of that offence by reason of insanity.

(2) No finding under subsection (1) above shall be made except on the written or oral evidence of two or more registered medical practitioners at least one of whom is duly approved.

116A. Powers to deal with person unfit to stand trial or not guilty by reason of insanity

(1) This section applies where, on a trial of a person by a court-martial—
   (a) the accused is found to be unfit to stand trial and to have done the act or made the omission charged against him; or
   (b) the accused is found not guilty by reason of insanity.
(2) The court shall make in respect of the accused—
   (a) a hospital order (with or without a restriction order);
   (b) a supervision order; or
   (c) an order for his absolute discharge.
(3) Where—
   (a) the offence to which the findings relate is an offence the sentence for which is fixed by law, and
   (b) the court has power to make a hospital order,
   the court shall make a hospital order with a restriction order (whether or not it would have power to make a restriction order apart from this subsection).
(4) The functions of the court under this section shall be exercised by the judge advocate (or, where subsection (5) below applies, the judicial officer) sitting alone, and section 95(2) and (3) above shall not apply.
(5) Any function of the court under this section exercisable after an adjournment or an appeal shall be exercisable by a judicial officer if—
   (a) the court ordering the adjournment, or (as the case may be) the Courts-Martial Appeal Court, so orders; or
   (b) the Judge Advocate General so directs.
(6) In this Act—
   "hospital order" has the meaning given in section 37 of the Mental Health Act 1983;
   "restriction order" has the meaning given to it by section 41 of that Act;
   "supervision order" means an order which requires the person in respect of whom it is made ("the supervised person") to be under the supervision of a person ("the supervising officer") for a period specified in the order of not more than two years.

116B. Orders under the Mental Health Act

(1) In relation to the making of an order by virtue of subsection (2)(a) of section 116A above, section 37 (hospital orders etc) of the Mental Health Act 1983 ("the 1983 Act") shall have effect as if—
   (a) the reference in subsection (1) to a person being convicted before the Crown Court included a reference to the case where section 116A above applies;
   (b) the words after "punishable with imprisonment" and before "or is convicted" were omitted; and
   (c) for subsections (4) and (5) there were substituted—
      "(4) Where an order is made under this section requiring a person to be admitted to a hospital ('a hospital order'), it shall be the duty of the managers of the hospital specified in the order to admit him in accordance with it."
(2) In relation to a case where section 116A above applies but the court have not yet made one of the disposals mentioned in subsection (2) of that section—
   (a) section 35 of the 1983 Act (remand to hospital for report on accused's mental condition) shall have effect with the omission of the words after paragraph (b) in subsection (3);

(b) section 36 of that Act (remand of accused person to hospital for treatment) shall have effect with the omission of the words "(other than an offence the sentence for which is fixed by law)" in subsection (2);

(c) references in sections 35 and 36 of that Act to an accused person shall be construed as including a person in whose case this subsection applies; and

(d) section 38 of that Act (interim hospital orders) shall have effect as if—

    (i) the reference in subsection (1) to a person being convicted before the Crown Court included a reference to the case where section 116A above applies; and

    (ii) the words "(other than an offence the sentence for which is fixed by law)" in that subsection were omitted.

(3) In relation to the making of any order under the 1983 Act by virtue of this Act, that Act shall apply—

(a) as if references to the Crown Court were references to a court-martial;

(b) as if references to an offender were references to a person in whose case section 116A above applies (references to an offence being construed accordingly); and

(c) with such further modifications as may be prescribed.

(4) The Secretary of State may by regulations make provision with respect to the admission to, detention in, and release from, hospital of any person in respect of whom an order is made under the 1983 Act by virtue of this Act.

Regulations under this subsection may in particular make provision for a person in respect of whom such an order has been made to be conveyed to, and detained in, a place of safety pending his admission to hospital.

(5) Where—

(a) a person is detained in pursuance of a hospital order which the court had power to make by virtue of section 116A(1)(a) above, and

(b) the court also made a restriction order, and that order has not ceased to have effect,

the Secretary of State, if satisfied after consultation with the responsible medical officer that the person can properly be tried, may either remit the person for trial before a court-martial or direct that he be tried before a civil court.

In this subsection "responsible medical officer" means the registered medical practitioner in charge of the person's treatment.

(6) The Secretary of State may by regulations make provision supplementing subsection (5) above, including in particular—

(a) provision for a person in whose case that subsection applies to be conveyed to a court or place of detention and to be detained in such a place;

(b) provision for the hospital order and the restriction order to cease to have effect at such time as may be prescribed.

116C. Supervision orders

(1) The court shall not make an order under section 116A(2)(b) above unless it is satisfied—

(a) that, having regard to all the circumstances of the case, the making of a supervision order is the most suitable means of dealing with the accused;

(b) that the supervising officer intended to be specified in the order is willing to undertake the supervision; and

(c) that arrangements have been made for any treatment which (under subsection (2) below) is intended to be specified in the order.

(2) An order under section 116A(2)(b) above may, in accordance with regulations under subsection (3) below, require the supervised person to submit, during the whole of that period or such part of it as may be specified in the order, to treatment by or under the direction of a registered medical practitioner.

(3) The Secretary of State may—

(a) by order direct that the definition of "supervision order" in section 116A(6) above shall be amended by substituting, for the period for the time being specified there, such period as may be specified in the order under this subsection;

(b) by regulations make further provision in relation to supervision orders.

(4) Regulations under subsection (3) above may in particular make provision—

(a) as to the procedure to be followed by a court-martial making a supervision order;

(b) as the requirements which may be specified in such an order;

(c) as to the descriptions of supervising officer who may be so specified;

(d) for treatment to be provided at a place other than the place specified in the order in accordance with arrangements made by the medical practitioner by whom or under whose direction the supervised person is being treated;

(e) for the amendment and revocation of any supervision order.

116D. Provisions supplementary to sections 115A to 116C

(1) In this section and sections 115A to 116C above—

"duly approved" means approved for the purposes of section 12 of the Mental Health Act 1983 by the Secretary of State as having special experience in the diagnosis and treatment of mental disorder (within the meaning of that Act);

"prescribed" means prescribed by regulations made by the Secretary of State.

(2) For the purposes of the provisions of sections 115A and 116 of this Act which permit a court to act on the written evidence of a registered medical practitioner or a registered medical practitioner who is duly approved, a report in writing purporting to be signed by a registered medical practitioner or a registered medical practitioner who is duly approved may, subject to subsection (3) below, be received in evidence without proof of the signature of the practitioner and without proof that he has the requisite qualifications or is duly approved; but the court may require the signatory of any such report to be called to give oral evidence.

(3) Where, in pursuance of a direction of the court, any such report is tendered in evidence otherwise than by or on behalf of the accused, then—

(a) if the accused is represented by counsel or a solicitor, a copy of the report shall be given to his counsel or solicitor;

(b) if the accused is not so represented, the substance of the report shall be disclosed to him; and

(c) the accused may require the signatory of the report to be called to give oral evidence, and evidence to rebut the evidence contained in the report may be called by the accused or on his behalf.

(4) The power of the Secretary of State to make regulations under sections 116A to 116C above, and orders under section 116C(3) above, shall be exercisable by statutory instrument which shall be subject to annulment in pursuance of a resolution of either House of Parliament.'

2. In section 225(1) of the Army Act 1955 and in section 223(1) of the Air Force Act 1955 (general provisions as to interpretation) insert at the appropriate places—

' "hospital order" has the meaning assigned to it by section 116A(6) of this Act;';
' "restriction order" has the meaning assigned to it by section 116A(6) of this Act;';
' "supervision order" has the meaning assigned to it by section 116A(6) of this Act;'.

Naval Discipline Act 1957 (c. 53)

3. For section 63 of the Naval Discipline Act 1957 (provisions where accused found insane) substitute—

'Findings of unfitness to stand trial and insanity

62A. Fitness to stand trial

(1) This section applies where on a trial by court-martial of a person the question arises (at the instance of the defence or otherwise) whether the accused is fit to stand trial.

(2) For the purposes of this Act a person is unfit to stand trial if he is under a disability such that apart from the Criminal Procedure (Insanity) Act 1964 it would constitute a bar to his being tried on indictment in England and Wales.

(3) If, having regard to the nature of the supposed disability, the judge advocate is of opinion that it is expedient to do so and in the interests of the accused, he may postpone consideration of the question of fitness to stand trial until any time up to the opening of the case for the defence.

(4) If, before the question of fitness to stand trial falls to be determined, the court finds the accused not guilty on the charge or each of the charges on which he is being tried, that question shall not be determined.

(5) Subject to subsections (3) and (4) above, the question of fitness to stand trial shall be determined as soon as it arises.

(6) The question of fitness to stand trial shall be determined by the judge advocate sitting alone.

(7) A judge advocate shall not make a determination under subsection (6) above except on the written or oral evidence of two or more registered medical practitioners at least one of whom is duly approved.

62B. Finding that the accused did the act or made the omission charged

(1) This section applies where in accordance with section 62A(6) above it is determined by a judge advocate that the accused is unfit to stand trial.

(2) The trial shall not proceed or further proceed but it shall be determined by the court—

(a) on the evidence (if any) already given in the trial, and

(b) on such evidence as may be adduced or further adduced by the prosecution, or adduced by a person appointed by the judge advocate under this section to put the case for the defence,

whether it is satisfied, as respects the charge or each of the charges on which the accused was to be or was being tried, that he did the act or made the omission charged against him as the offence.

(3) If as respects that charge or any of those charges the court is satisfied as mentioned in subsection (2) above, it shall make a finding that the accused did the act or made the omission charged against him.

(4) If as respects that charge or any of those charges the court is not so satisfied, the court shall find the accused not guilty as if on the charge in question the trial had proceeded to a conclusion.

(5) Where the question of fitness to stand trial was determined after arraignment of the accused, the determination under subsection (2) above shall be made by the court-martial by whom he was being tried.

63. Findings of insanity

(1) Where, on the trial of a person by court-martial, the court is satisfied, as respects the charge or any of the charges on which he is being tried, that the accused did the act or made the omission charged against him as the offence but that at the time of that act or omission he was insane, the court shall find that the accused was not guilty of that offence by reason of insanity.

(2) No finding under subsection (1) above shall be made except on the written or oral evidence of two or more registered medical practitioners at least one of whom is duly approved.

63A. Powers to deal with person unfit to stand trial or not guilty by reason of insanity

(1) This section applies where, on a trial of a person by a court-martial—
    (a) the accused is found to be unfit to stand trial and to have done the act or made the omission charged against him; or
    (b) the accused is found not guilty by reason of insanity.

(2) The court shall make in respect of the accused—
    (a) a hospital order (with or without a restriction order);
    (b) a supervision order; or
    (c) an order for his absolute discharge.

(3) Where—
    (a) the offence to which the finding relates is an offence the sentence for which is fixed by law, and
    (b) the court has power to make a hospital order,
the court shall make a hospital order with a restriction order (whether or not it would have power to make a restriction order apart from this subsection).

(4) The functions of the court under this section shall be exercised by the judge advocate (or, where subsection (5) below applies, the judicial officer) sitting alone, and sections 56A(3) and 57 above shall not apply.

(5) Any function of the court under this section exercisable after an adjournment or an appeal shall be exercisable by a judicial officer if—
    (a) the court ordering the adjournment, or (as the case may be) the Court-Martial Appeal Court, so orders; or
    (b) the Judge Advocate of Her Majesty's Fleet so directs.

(6) In this Act—
    "hospital order" has the meaning given in section 37 of the Mental Health Act 1983;
    "restriction order" has the meaning given to it by section 41 of that Act;
    "supervision order" means an order which requires the person in respect of whom it is made ("the supervised person") to be under the supervision of a person ("the supervising officer") for a period specified in the order of not more than two years.

63B. Orders under the Mental Health Act

(1) In relation to the making of an order by virtue of subsection (2)(a) of section 63A above, section 37 (hospital orders etc) of the Mental Health Act 1983 ("the 1983 Act") shall have effect as if—

    (a) the reference in subsection (1) to a person being convicted before the Crown Court included a reference to the case where section 63A above applies;

    (b) the words after "punishable with imprisonment" and before "or is convicted" were omitted; and

    (c) for subsections (4) and (5) there were substituted—

        "(4) Where an order is made under this section requiring a person to be admitted to a hospital ('a hospital order'), it shall be the duty of the managers of the hospital specified in the order to admit him in accordance with it."

(2) In relation to a case where section 63A above applies but the court has not yet made one of the disposals mentioned in subsection (2) of that section—

    (a) section 35 of the 1983 Act (remand to hospital for report on accused's mental condition) shall have effect with the omission of the words after paragraph (b) in subsection (3);

    (b) section 36 of that Act (remand of accused person to hospital for treatment) shall have effect with the omission of the words "(other than an offence the sentence for which is fixed by law)" in subsection (2);

    (c) references in sections 35 and 36 of that Act to an accused person shall be construed as including a person in whose case this subsection applies; and

    (d) section 38 of that Act (interim hospital orders) shall have effect as if—

        (i) the reference in subsection (1) to a person being convicted before the Crown Court included a reference to the case where section 63A above applies; and

        (ii) the words "(other than an offence the sentence for which is fixed by law)" in that subsection were omitted.

(3) In relation to the making of any order under the 1983 Act by virtue of this Act, that Act shall apply—

    (a) as if references to the Crown Court were references to a court-martial;

    (b) as if references to an offender were references to a person in whose case section 63A above applies (references to an offence being construed accordingly); and

    (c) with such further modifications as may be prescribed.

(4) The Secretary of State may by regulations make provision with respect to the admission to, detention in, and release from, hospital of any person in respect of whom an order is made under the 1983 Act by virtue of this Act.

    Regulations under this subsection may in particular make provision for a person in respect of whom such an order has been made to be conveyed to, and detained in, a place of safety pending his admission to hospital.

(5) Where—

    (a) a person is detained in pursuance of a hospital order which the court had power to make by virtue of section 63A(1)(a) above, and

    (b) the court also made a restriction order, and that order has not ceased to have effect,

the Secretary of State, if satisfied after consultation with the responsible medical officer that the person can properly be tried, may either remit the person for trial before a court-martial or direct that he be tried before a civil court.

In this subsection "responsible medical officer" means the registered medical practitioner in charge of the person's treatment.

(6) The Secretary of State may by regulations make provision supplementing subsection (5) above, including in particular—

   (a) provision for a person in whose case that subsection applies to be conveyed to a court or place of detention and to be detained in such a place;

   (b) provision for the hospital order and the restriction order to cease to have effect at such time as may be prescribed.

63C. Supervision orders

(1) The court shall not make an order under section 63A(2)(b) above unless it is satisfied—

   (a) that, having regard to all the circumstances of the case, the making of a supervision order is the most suitable means of dealing with the accused;

   (b) that the supervising officer intended to be specified in the order is willing to undertake the supervision; and

   (c) that arrangements have been made for any treatment which (under subsection (2) below) is intended to be specified in the order.

(2) An order under section 63A(2)(b) above may, in accordance with regulations under subsection (3) below, require the supervised person to submit, during the whole of that period or such part of it as may be specified in the order, to treatment by or under the direction of a registered medical practitioner.

(3) The Secretary of State may—

   (a) by order direct that the definition of "supervision order" in section 63A(6) above shall be amended by substituting, for the period for the time being specified there, such period as may be specified in the order under this subsection;

   (b) by regulations make further provision in relation to supervision orders.

(4) Regulations under subsection (3) above may in particular make provision—

   (a) as to the procedure to be followed by a court-martial making a supervision order;

   (b) as the requirements which may be specified in such an order;

   (c) as to the descriptions of supervising officer who may be so specified;

   (d) for treatment to be provided at a place other than the place specified in the order in accordance with arrangements made by the medical practitioner by whom or under whose direction the supervised person is being treated;

   (e) for the amendment and revocation of any supervision order.

63D. Provisions supplementary to sections 62A to 63C

(1) In this section and sections 62A to 63C above—

   "duly approved" means approved for the purposes of section 12 of the Mental Health Act 1983 by the Secretary of State as having special experience in the diagnosis and treatment of mental disorder (within the meaning of that Act);

   "prescribed" means prescribed by regulations made by the Secretary of State.

(2) For the purposes of the provisions of sections 62A and 63 of this Act which permit a court to act on the written evidence of a registered medical practitioner or a registered medical practitioner who is duly approved, a report in writing purporting to be signed by a registered medical practitioner or a registered medical practitioner who is duly approved may, subject to subsection (3) below, be received in evidence without

proof of the signature of the practitioner and without proof that he has the requisite qualifications or is duly approved; but the court may require the signatory of any such report to be called to give oral evidence.

(3) Where, in pursuance of a direction of the court, any such report is tendered in evidence otherwise than by or on behalf of the accused, then—

   (a) if the accused is represented by counsel or a solicitor, a copy of the report shall be given to his counsel or solicitor;

   (b) if the accused is not so represented, the substance of the report shall be disclosed to him; and

   (c) the accused may require the signatory of the report to be called to give oral evidence, and evidence to rebut the evidence contained in the report may be called by the accused or on his behalf.

(4) The power of the Secretary of State to make regulations under sections 63A to 63C above, and orders under section 63C(3) above, shall be exercisable by statutory instrument which shall be subject to annulment in pursuance of a resolution of either House of Parliament.'

4. In the proviso to section 56(3) of that Act (court-martial not to be adjourned for more than six days), after 'except with the consent of the accused and the prosecuting authority' insert, 'or for the purpose of exercising powers under section 63A of this Act,'.

5. In section 135(1) of that Act (general provisions as to interpretation) insert at the appropriate places—

   ' "hospital order" has the meaning assigned to it by section 63A(6) of this Act;';

   ' "restriction order" has the meaning assigned to it by section 63A(6) of this Act;';

   ' "supervision order" has the meaning assigned to it by section 63A(6) of this Act;'.

Courts-Martial (Appeals) Act 1968 (c. 20)

6. The Courts-Martial (Appeals) Act 1968 is amended as follows.

7. For section 16 substitute—

'16. Substitution of finding of insanity or findings of unfitness to stand trial etc.

(1) This section applies where, on an appeal against conviction, the Appeal Court, on the written or oral evidence of two or more registered medical practitioners at least one of whom is duly approved, are of opinion—

   (a) that the proper finding would have been one of not guilty by reason of insanity; or

   (b) that the case is not one where there should have been a finding of not guilty, but that there should have been findings that the accused was unfit to stand trial and that he did the act or made the omission charged against him.

(2) The Appeal Court shall make in respect of the appellant—

   (a) a hospital order (with or without a restriction order);

   (b) a supervision order; or

   (c) an order for his absolute discharge.

(3) Where—

   (a) the offence to which the appeal relates is an offence the sentence for which is fixed by law, and

   (b) the Appeal Court have power to make a hospital order,

the Appeal Court shall make a hospital order with a restriction order (whether or not they would have power to make a restriction order apart from this subsection).

(4) The provisions of, or made under, the sections specified below shall apply (with any necessary modifications) in relation to the Appeal Court as they apply in relation to a court-martial. The sections are—

    (c) where the relevant Service Act is the Army Act, sections 116B to 116D of that Act;

    (d) where the relevant Service Act is the Air Force Act, sections 116B to 116D of that Act;

    (e) where the relevant Service Act is the Naval Discipline Act, sections 63B to 63D of that Act.

(5) Where the Appeal Court make an interim hospital order by virtue of this section—

    (a) the power of renewing or terminating it and of dealing with the appellant on its termination shall be exercisable by a judicial officer and not by the Appeal Court; and

    (b) section 38(7) of the Mental Health Act 1983 (absconding offenders) shall have effect as if the reference to the court that made the order were a reference to a judicial officer.

(6) Where the Appeal Court make a supervision order by virtue of this section, any power of revoking or amending it shall be exercisable by a judicial officer and not by the Appeal Court.'

8. In section 21 (appeal against finding of not guilty by reason of insanity), in subsection (1), after 'except' insert 'section 8(2) and'.

9. In section 22 (consequences where appeal under section 21 allowed), at the beginning of subsection (4) insert 'Subject to section 23 below,'.

10. For section 23 substitute—

'23. Substitution of findings of unfitness to stand trial etc.

(1) This section applies where, on an appeal under section 21 of this Act, the Appeal Court, on the written or oral evidence of two or more registered medical practitioners at least one of whom is duly approved, are of opinion that—

    (a) the case is not one where there should have been a finding of not guilty; but

    (b) there should have been findings that the accused was unfit to stand trial and that he did the act or made the omission charged against him.

(2) The Appeal Court shall make in respect of the appellant—

    (a) a hospital order (with or without a restriction order);

    (b) a supervision order; or

    (c) an order for his absolute discharge.

(3) Where—

    (a) the offence to which the appeal relates is an offence the sentence for which is fixed by law, and

    (b) the Appeal Court have power to make a hospital order,

the Appeal Court shall make a hospital order with a restriction order (whether or not they would have power to make a restriction order apart from this subsection).

(4) The provisions of, or made under, the sections specified below shall apply (with any

necessary modifications) in relation to the Appeal Court as they apply in relation to a court-martial. The sections are—

(c) where the relevant Service Act is the Army Act, sections 116B to 116D of that Act;

(d) where the relevant Service Act is the Air Force Act, sections 116B to 116D of that Act;

(e) where the relevant Service Act is the Naval Discipline Act, sections 63B to 63D of that Act.

(5) Where the Appeal Court make an interim hospital order by virtue of this section—

(a) the power of renewing or terminating it and of dealing with the appellant on its termination shall be exercisable by a judicial officer and not by the Appeal Court; and

(b) section 38(7) of the Mental Health Act 1983 (absconding offenders) shall have effect as if the reference to the court that made the order were a reference to a judicial officer.

(6) Where the Appeal Court make a supervision order by virtue of this section, any power of revoking or amending it shall be exercisable by a judicial officer and not by the Appeal Court.'

11. (1) Section 24 (appeal against finding of unfitness to stand trial) is amended as follows.

(2) In subsection (1)—

(a) for 'his trial' substitute 'trial and to have done the act or made the omission charged against him';

(b) for 'the finding' substitute 'either or both of those findings'.

(3) In subsection (2), after 'except' insert 'section 8(2) and'.

12. For section 25 substitute—

'25. Disposal of Appeal Under s. 24

(1) This section applies to appeals under section 24 of this Act.

(2) Where the Appeal Court allow an appeal against a finding that the appellant is unfit to stand trial—

(a) the appellant may be tried accordingly for the offence with which he was charged; and

(b) the Court may make such orders as appear to them necessary or expedient pending any such trial for the custody, release or continued detention of the appellant.

(3) Where, otherwise than in a case falling within subsection (2) above, the Appeal Court allow an appeal against a finding that the appellant did the act or made the omission charged against him, the Court shall, in addition to quashing the finding, direct a finding of not guilty to be recorded (but not a finding of not guilty by reason of insanity).'

13. After that section insert—

'Appeal against order made in cases of insanity or unfitness to stand trial

25A. Right of appeal against hospital order etc.

(1) A person in whose case a court-martial—

(a) makes a hospital order or interim hospital order by virtue of the relevant Service Act, or

(b) makes a supervision order under the relevant Service Act,

may appeal to the Appeal Court against the order.

(2) An appeal under this section lies only with the leave of the Appeal Court.

25B. Disposal of appeal under s. 25A

(1) If on an appeal under section 25A of this Act the Appeal Court consider that the appellant should be dealt with differently from the way in which the court below dealt with him—

(a) they may quash any order which is the subject of the appeal; and

(b) they may make such order, whether by substitution for the original order or by variation of or addition to it, as they think appropriate for the case and as the court below had power to make.

(2) The fact that an appeal is pending against an interim hospital order under the Mental Health Act 1983 shall not affect the power of the court below to renew or terminate the order or deal with the appellant on its termination.

(3) Where the Appeal Court make an interim hospital order by virtue of this section—

(a) the power of renewing or terminating it and of dealing with the appellant on its termination shall be exercisable by a judicial officer and not by the Appeal Court; and

(b) section 38(7) of the said Act of 1983 (absconding offenders) shall have effect as if the reference to the court that made the order were a reference to a judicial officer.

(4) The fact that an appeal is pending against a supervision order under the relevant Service Act shall not affect any power conferred on any other court to revoke or amend the order.

(5) Where the Appeal Court make a supervision order by virtue of this section, any power of revoking or amending it shall be exercisable by a judicial officer and not by the Appeal Court.'

14. (1) Section 57 (interpretation) is amended as follows.

(2) In subsection (1) insert at the relevant places—

' "duly approved" means approved for the purposes of section 12 of the Mental Health Act 1983 by the Secretary of State as having special experience in the diagnosis and treatment of mental disorder (within the meaning of that Act);';

' "hospital order" has the meaning given in section 37 of the Mental Health Act 1983;';

' "interim hospital order" has the meaning given in section 38 of that Act;';

' "judicial officer" has the same meaning as in the relevant Service Act;';

' "restriction order" has the meaning given to it by section 41 of the Mental Health Act 1983;';

' "supervision order" means an order which requires the person in respect of whom it is made to be under the supervision of another person for a period specified in the order of not more than two years.'

(3) After subsection (2) insert—

'(2A) For the purposes of the provisions of sections 16 and 23 of this Act which permit the Appeal Court to act on the written evidence of a registered medical practitioner or a registered medical practitioner who is duly approved, a report in writing purporting to be signed by a registered medical practitioner or a registered medical practitioner who is duly approved may, subject to subsection (2B) below, be received in evidence without proof of the signature of the practitioner and without proof that he has the requisite qualifications or is duly approved; but the Appeal Court may require the signatory of any such report to be called to give oral evidence.

(2B) Where, in pursuance of a direction of the Appeal Court, any such report is tendered in evidence otherwise than by or on behalf of the appellant, then—

(a) if the appellant is represented by counsel or a solicitor, a copy of the report shall be given to his counsel or solicitor;

(b) if the appellant is not so represented, the substance of the report shall be disclosed to him; and

(c) the appellant may require the signatory of the report to be called to give oral evidence, and evidence to rebut the evidence contained in the report may be called by the appellant or on his behalf.'

15. (1) Schedule 3 (modifications in relation to prisoners of war) is amended as follows.

(2) In paragraph 3—

(a) in paragraph (a), for 'or 15' substitute, '14A, 15 or 25A';

(b) omit paragraph (b).

(3) After paragraph 3 insert—

'3A In relation to a protected prisoner of war, sections 16 and 23 of this Act shall each have effect as if the following subsection were substituted for subsection (4)—

"(4) The provisions of a Royal Warrant shall apply (with any necessary modifications) in relation to the Appeal Court as they apply in relation to a court-martial." '

SCHEDULE 4

Section 27

POWERS OF AUTHORIZED OFFICERS EXECUTING WARRANTS

The following is the Schedule inserted after Schedule 4 to the Magistrates' Courts Act 1980 (c. 43)—

'SCHEDULE 4A

Section 125BA

POWERS OF AUTHORIZED OFFICERS EXECUTING WARRANTS

Meaning of "Authorized Officer" etc

1. In this Schedule—

"authorized officer", in relation to a warrant, means a person who is entitled to execute the warrant by virtue of—

(a) section 125A of this Act (civilian enforcement officers); or
(b) section 125B of this Act (approved enforcement agencies);
"premises" includes any place and, in particular, includes—
(a) any vehicle, vessel, aircraft or hovercraft;
(b) any offshore installation within the meaning of the Mineral Workings (Offshore Installations) Act 1971; and
(c) any tent or movable structure.

Entry to execute warrant of arrest etc

2. (1) An authorized officer may enter and search any premises for the purpose of executing a warrant of arrest, commitment or detention issued in proceedings for or in connection with any criminal offence.
(2) The power may be exercised—
(a) only to the extent that it is reasonably required for that purpose; and
(b) only if the officer has reasonable grounds for believing that the person whom he is seeking is on the premises.
(3) In relation to premises consisting of two or more separate dwellings, the power is limited to entering and searching—
(a) any parts of the premises which the occupiers of any dwelling comprised in the premises use in common with the occupiers of any other such dwelling; and
(b) any such dwelling in which the officer has reasonable grounds for believing that the person whom he is seeking may be.

Entry to levy distress

3. (1) An authorized officer may enter and search any premises for the purpose of executing a warrant of distress issued under section 76 of this Act for default in paying a sum adjudged to be paid by a conviction.
(2) The power may be exercised only to the extent that it is reasonably required for that purpose.

Searching arrested persons

4. (1) This paragraph applies where a person is arrested in pursuance of a warrant of arrest, commitment or detention issued in proceedings for or in connection with any criminal offence.
(2) An authorized officer may search the arrested person, if he has reasonable grounds for believing that the arrested person may present a danger to himself or others.
(3) An authorized officer may also search the arrested person for anything which he might use to assist him to escape from lawful custody.
(4) The power conferred by sub-paragraph (3) above may be exercised—
(a) only if the officer has reasonable grounds for believing that the arrested person may have concealed on him anything of a kind mentioned in that sub-paragraph; and
(b) only to the extent that it is reasonably required for the purpose of discovering any such thing.
(5) The powers conferred by this paragraph to search a person are not to be read as authorising the officer to require a person to remove any of his clothing in public other than an outer coat, a jacket or gloves; but they do authorize the search of a person's mouth.

(6) An officer searching a person under sub-paragraph (2) above may seize and retain anything he finds, if the officer has reasonable grounds for believing that the person searched might use it to cause physical injury to himself or to any other person.

(7) An officer searching a person under sub-paragraph (3) above may seize and retain anything he finds, if he has reasonable grounds for believing that the person might use it to assist him to escape from lawful custody.

Use of force

5. An authorized officer may use reasonable force, if necessary, in the exercise of a power conferred on him by this Schedule.'

SCHEDULE 5

Section 29

PROCEDURE ON BREACH OF COMMUNITY PENALTY ETC

Interpretation

1. In this Schedule—
  'the Sentencing Act' means the Powers of Criminal Courts (Sentencing) Act 2000 (c. 6);
  'the 2003 Act' means the Criminal Justice Act 2003 (c. 44).

Detention and training orders

2. (1) Section 104 of the Sentencing Act (breach of supervision requirements of detention and training order) is amended as follows.

(2) In subsection (1) (issue of summons or warrant by justice of the peace)—
  (a) omit the words 'acting for a relevant petty sessions area';
  (b) in paragraph (a), omit the words 'before a youth court acting for the area';
  (c) in paragraph (b), omit the words 'requiring him to be brought before such a court'.

(3) For subsection (2) substitute—
  '(2) Any summons or warrant issued under this section shall direct the offender to appear or be brought—
  (a) before a youth court acting for the petty sessions area in which the offender resides; or
  (b) if it is not known where the offender resides, before a youth court acting for same petty sessions area as the justice who issued the summons or warrant.'

Suspended sentence supervision orders

3. (1) Section 123 of the Sentencing Act (breach of requirement of suspended sentence supervision order) is amended as follows.

(2) In subsection (1) (issue of summons or warrant by justice of the peace) omit the words 'acting for the petty sessions area for the time being specified in the order'.

(3) For subsection (2) substitute—

'(2) Any summons or warrant issued under this section shall direct the offender to appear or be brought—

  (a) before a magistrates' court for the petty sessions area in which the offender resides; or

  (b) if it is not known where the offender resides, before a magistrates' court acting for the petty sessions area for the time being specified in the suspended sentence supervision order.'

(4) After subsection (4) insert—

'(5) Where a magistrates' court dealing with an offender under this section would not otherwise have the power to amend the suspended sentence supervision order under section 124(3) below (amendment by reason of change of residence), that provision has effect as if the reference to a magistrates' court acting for the petty sessions area for the time being specified in the suspended sentence supervision order were a reference to the court dealing with the offender.'

Community orders under the Sentencing Act

4. (1) Schedule 3 to the Sentencing Act (breach, revocation and amendment of certain community orders), as it has effect on the day on which this Act is passed, is amended as follows.

(2) In paragraph 3(1) (issue of summons or warrant by justice of the peace) omit the words 'acting for the petty sessions area concerned'.

(3) In paragraph 3(2) (court before which offender to appear or be brought), for paragraph (c) substitute—

'(c) in the case of a relevant order which is not an order to which paragraph (a) or (b) applies, before a magistrates' court acting for the petty sessions area in which the offender resides or, if it is not known where he resides, before a magistrates' court acting for the petty sessions area concerned.'

(4) In paragraph 4 (powers of magistrates' court to deal with breach), after sub-paragraph (3) insert—

'(3A) Where a magistrates' court dealing with an offender under sub-paragraph (1)(a), (b) or (c) above would not otherwise have the power to amend the relevant order under paragraph 18 below (amendment by reason of change of residence), that paragraph has effect as if the reference to a magistrates' court acting for the petty sessions area concerned were a reference to the court dealing with the offender.'

Curfew orders and exclusion orders

5. (1) Schedule 3 to the Sentencing Act (breach, revocation and amendment of curfew orders and exclusion orders), as substituted by paragraph 125 of Schedule 32 to the 2003 Act, is amended as follows.

(2) In paragraph 3(1) (issue of summons or warrant by justice of the peace) omit the words 'acting for the petty sessions area concerned'.

(3) In paragraph 3(2) (court before which offender to appear or be brought), for paragraph (b) substitute—

'(b) in the case of a relevant order which is not an order to which paragraph (a) above applies, before a magistrates' court acting for the petty sessions area in which the offender resides or, if it is not known where he resides, before a magistrates' court acting for the petty sessions area concerned.'

(4) In paragraph 4 (powers of magistrates' court to deal with breach), after sub-paragraph (4) insert—

'(4A) Where a magistrates' court dealing with an offender under sub-paragraph (2)(a) or (b) above would not otherwise have the power to amend the relevant order under paragraph 15 below (amendment by reason of change of residence), that paragraph has effect as if the reference to a magistrates' court acting for the petty sessions area concerned were a reference to the court dealing with the offender.'

Attendance centre orders

6. (1) Schedule 5 to the Sentencing Act (breach, revocation and amendment of attendance centre orders) is amended as follows.

(2) In paragraph 1(1) (issue of summons or warrant by justice of the peace), omit the words—

(a) 'acting for a relevant petty sessions area';

(b) 'before a magistrates' court acting for the area';

(c) 'requiring him to be brought before such a court'.

(3) For paragraph 1(2) substitute—

'(2) Any summons or warrant issued under this paragraph shall direct the offender to appear or be brought—

(a) before a magistrates' court acting for the petty sessions area in which the offender resides; or

(b) if it is not known where the offender resides, before a magistrates' court acting for the petty sessions area in which is situated the attendance centre which the offender is required to attend by the order or by virtue of an order under paragraph 5(1)(b) below.'

(4) In paragraph 2 (powers of magistrates' court to deal with breach), after sub-paragraph (5) insert—

'(5A) Where a magistrates' court dealing with an offender under sub-paragraph (1)(a) above would not otherwise have the power to amend the order under paragraph 5(1)(b) below (substitution of different attendance centre), that paragraph has effect as if references to an appropriate magistrates' court were references to the court dealing with the offender.'

Community orders under the 2003 Act

7. (1) Schedule 8 to the 2003 Act (breach, revocation or amendment of community order) is amended as follows.

(2) In paragraph 7(2) (issue of summons or warrant by justice of the peace) omit the words 'acting for the petty sessions area concerned'.

(3) In paragraph 7(3) (court before which offender to appear or be brought), for paragraph (b) substitute—

'(b) in any other case, before a magistrates' court acting for the petty sessions area in which the offender resides or, if it is not known where he resides, before a magistrates' court acting for the petty sessions area concerned.'

(4) In paragraph 9 (powers of magistrates' court to deal with breach), after sub-paragraph (5) insert—

'(5A)Where a magistrates' court dealing with an offender under sub-paragraph (1)(a) would not otherwise have the power to amend the community order under paragraph 16 (amendment by reason of change of residence), that paragraph has effect as if the references to the appropriate court were references to the court dealing with the offender.'

(5) In paragraph 27 (provision of copies of orders), at the end of sub-paragraph (1)(c) insert

', and

(d) where the court acts for a petty sessions area other than the one specified in the order prior to the revocation or amendment, provide a copy of the revoking or amending order to a magistrates' court acting for the area so specified.'

Suspended sentence orders under the 2003 Act

8. (1) Schedule 12 to the 2003 Act (breach or amendment of suspended sentence order, and effect of further conviction) is amended as follows.

(2) In paragraph 6(2) (issue of summons or warrant by justice of the peace) omit the words 'acting for the petty sessions area concerned'.

(3) In paragraph 6(3) (court before which offender to appear or be brought), for paragraph (b) substitute—

'(b) in any other case, before a magistrates' court acting for the petty sessions area in which the offender resides or, if it is not known where he resides, before a magistrates' court acting for the petty sessions area concerned.'

(4) In paragraph 8 (powers of magistrates' court to deal with breach), after sub-paragraph (4) insert—

'(4A) Where a magistrates' court dealing with an offender under sub-paragraph (2)(c) would not otherwise have the power to amend the suspended sentence order under paragraph 14 (amendment by reason of change of residence), that paragraph has effect as if the references to the appropriate court were references to the court dealing with the offender.'

(5) In paragraph 22 (provision of copies of orders), at the end of sub-paragraph (1)(c) insert

', and

(d) where the court acts for a petty sessions area other than the one specified in the order prior to the revocation or amendment, provide a copy of the revoking or amending order to a magistrates' court acting for the area so specified.'

9. In Schedule 13 to the 2003 Act (transfer of suspended sentence orders to Scotland or Northern Ireland), in paragraph 12 (modifications of Schedule 12), after sub-paragraph (5) insert—

'(5A) In paragraph 6(3)(b), the words "before a magistrates' court acting for the petty sessions area in which the offender resides or, if it is not known where he resides," are omitted.'

Local Justice Areas

10. The power conferred by section 109(5)(b) of the Courts Act 2003 (c. 39) to amend or repeal any enactment, other than one contained in an Act passed in a later session, includes power to amend any such enactment as amended by this Schedule, but only for the purpose of making consequential provision in connection with the establishment of local justice areas under section 8 of that Act.

SCHEDULE 6

Section 31

INTERMITTENT CUSTODY

1. The Criminal Justice Act 2003 (c. 44) is amended as follows.

2. In section 244 (duty to release prisoners), in subsection (3)—
(a) in paragraph (c), for the words from 'which is not' to 'section 183(3)' substitute 'which for the purposes of section 183 (as read with section 263(2) or 264A(2) in the case of concurrent or consecutive sentences) is not a licence period';
(b) in paragraph (d), after 'consecutive sentences' insert 'none of which falls within paragraph (c)'.

3. In section 246 (power to release prisoners on licence before required to do so), in the definition of 'the required custodial days' in subsection (6)—
(a) in paragraph (b), after 'custody' insert 'which are consecutive';
(b) at the end of that paragraph insert', or
(c) in the case of two or more sentences of intermittent custody which are wholly or partly concurrent, the aggregate of the numbers so specified less the number of days that are to be served concurrently;'.

4. In section 249 (duration of licence), at the end of subsection (3) insert 'and subsection (2) has effect subject to section 264A(3) (consecutive terms: intermittent custody)'.

5. In section 250 (licence conditions), in subsection (7), for 'and section 264(3) and (4) (consecutive terms)' substitute ',section 264(3) and (4) (consecutive terms) and section 264A(3) (consecutive terms: intermittent custody)'.

6. In section 264 (consecutive terms), in subsection (1), after paragraph (b) insert, 'and (c) none of those terms is a term to which an intermittent custody order relates.'

7. After that section insert—

'264A. Consecutive terms: intermittent custody

(1) This section applies where—
    (a) a person ("the offender") has been sentenced to two or more terms of imprisonment which are to be served consecutively on each other,
    (b) the sentences were passed on the same occasion or, where they were passed on different occasions, the person has not been released under this Chapter at any time during the period beginning with the first and ending with the last of those occasions, and
    (c) each of the terms is a term to which an intermittent custody order relates.

(2) The offender is not to be treated as having served all the required custodial days in relation to any of the terms of imprisonment until he has served the aggregate of all the required custodial days in relation to each of them.

(3) After the number of days served by the offender in prison is equal to the aggregate of the required custodial days in relation to each of the terms of imprisonment, the offender is to be on licence until the relevant time and subject to such conditions as are required by this Chapter in respect of any of the terms of imprisonment, and none of the terms is to be regarded for any purpose as continuing after the relevant time.

(4) In subsection (3) "the relevant time" means the time when the offender would, but for his release, have served a term equal in length to the aggregate of—

(a) all the required custodial days in relation to the terms of imprisonment, and

(b) the longest of the total licence periods in relation to those terms.

(5) In this section—

"total licence period", in relation to a term of imprisonment to which an intermittent custody order relates, means a period equal in length to the aggregate of all the licence periods as defined by section 183 in relation to that term;

"the required custodial days", in relation to such a term, means the number of days specified under that section.'

SCHEDULE 7

Section 47

INVESTIGATIONS BY PARLIAMENTARY COMMISSIONER

1. The Parliamentary Commissioner Act 1967 (c. 13) is amended as follows.

2. (1) Section 5 (matters subject to investigation) is amended as follows.

(2) After subsection (1) insert—

'(1A) Subsection (1C) of this section applies if—

(a) a written complaint is duly made to a member of the House of Commons by a member of the public who claims that a person has failed to perform a relevant duty owed by him to the member of the public, and

(b) the complaint is referred to the Commissioner, with the consent of the person who made it, by a member of the House of Commons with a request to conduct an investigation into it.

(1B) For the purposes of subsection (1A) of this section a relevant duty is a duty imposed by any of these—

(a) a code of practice issued under section 32 of the Domestic Violence, Crime and Victims Act 2004 (code of practice for victims), or

(b) sections 35 to 44 of that Act (duties of local probation boards in connection with victims of sexual or violent offences).

(1C) If this subsection applies, the Commissioner may investigate the complaint.'

(3) In subsection (3) for 'investigation under this Act' substitute 'investigation under subsection (1) of this section'.

(4) After subsection (4) insert—

'(4A) Without prejudice to subsection (2) of this section, the Commissioner shall not conduct an investigation pursuant to a complaint under subsection (1A) of this section in respect of—

(a) action taken by or with the authority of the Secretary of State for the purposes of protecting the security of the State, including action so taken with respect to passports, or

(b) any action or matter described in any of paragraphs 1 to 4 and 6A to 11 of Schedule 3 to this Act.

(4B) Her Majesty may by Order in Council amend subsection (4A) of this section so as to exclude from paragraph (a) or (b) of that subsection such actions or matters as may be described in the Order.

(4C) Any statutory instrument made by virtue of subsection (4B) of this section shall be subject to annulment in pursuance of a resolution of either House of Parliament.'

3. (1) Section 7 (procedure in respect of investigations) is amended as follows.

(2) In subsection (1) after 'complaint under' insert 'section 5(1) of'.

(3) After subsection (1) insert—

'(1A) Where the Commissioner proposes to conduct an investigation pursuant to a complaint under section 5(1A) of this Act, he shall give the person to whom the complaint relates an opportunity to comment on any allegations contained in the complaint.'

(4) In subsection (2) for 'such investigation' substitute 'investigation under this Act'.

(5) In subsection (4)—

(a) after 'authority concerned' insert 'or the person to whom the complaint relates';

(b) for 'that department or authority' substitute 'that department, authority or person'.

4. (1) Section 8 (evidence) is amended as follows.

(2) In subsection (1) after 'investigation under' insert 'section 5(1) of'.

(3) After subsection (1) insert—

'(1A) For the purposes of an investigation pursuant to a complaint under section 5(1A) of this Act the Commissioner may require any person who in his opinion is able to furnish information or produce documents relevant to the investigation to furnish any such information or produce any such document.'

(4) In subsection (2) for 'such investigation' substitute 'investigation under this Act'.

5. (1) Section 10 (reports by Commissioner) is amended as follows.

(2) In subsection (2), after 'investigation under' insert 'section 5(1) of'.

(3) After subsection (2) insert—

'(2A) In any case where the Commissioner conducts an investigation pursuant to a complaint under section 5(1A) of this Act, he shall also send a report of the results of the investigation to the person to whom the complaint relates.'

(4) In subsection (3) after 'investigation under' insert 'section 5(1) of'.

(5) After subsection (3) insert—

'(3A) If, after conducting an investigation pursuant to a complaint under section 5(1A) of this Act, it appears to the Commissioner that—

(a) the person to whom the complaint relates has failed to perform a relevant duty owed by him to the person aggrieved, and

(b) the failure has not been, or will not be, remedied,

the Commissioner may, if he thinks fit, lay before each House of Parliament a special report upon the case.

(3B) For the purposes of subsection (3A) of this section "relevant duty" has the meaning given by section 5(1B) of this Act.'

(6) In subsection (5)(d) after 'subsection (2)' insert 'or (2A)'.

6. In section 12(1) (interpretation) for the definition of 'person aggrieved' substitute—
' "person aggrieved"—

(a) in relation to a complaint under section 5(1) of this Act, means the person who claims or is alleged to have sustained such injustice as is mentioned in section 5(1)(a) of this Act;

(b) in relation to a complaint under section 5(1A) of this Act, means the person to whom the duty referred to in section 5(1A)(a) of this Act is or is alleged to be owed;'.

SCHEDULE 8

Section 48

COMMISSIONER FOR VICTIMS AND WITNESSES

Deputy Commissioner

1. (1) The Secretary of State must appoint a Deputy Commissioner for Victims and Witnesses (referred to in this Schedule as the Deputy Commissioner).

(2) Before appointing the Deputy Commissioner the Secretary of State must consult the Attorney-General and the Lord Chancellor as to the person to be appointed.

(3) The Deputy Commissioner must act as the Commissioner—

(a) during any period when the office of Commissioner is vacant;

(b) at any time when the Commissioner is absent or is unable to act.

(4) The Deputy Commissioner is not to be regarded—

(a) as the servant or agent of the Crown, or

(b) as enjoying any status, immunity or privilege of the Crown.

Terms of appointment

2. (1) This paragraph applies in relation to a person appointed as the Commissioner or the Deputy Commissioner.

(2) The period for which the person is appointed must not exceed 5 years.

(3) Subject to sub-paragraph (4), the person is eligible for re-appointment.

(4) The person must not hold office for more than 10 years in total.

(5) The person may at any time resign from office by giving notice in writing to the Secretary of State.

(6) The Secretary of State may at any time remove the person from office if he is satisfied that the person—

    (a) has become bankrupt, has had his estate sequestrated or has made a composition or arrangement with, or granted a trust deed for, his creditors, or

    (b) is otherwise unable or unfit to carry out his functions.

(7) The Secretary of State must consult the Attorney-General and the Lord Chancellor before removing the person from office.

(8) Subject to sub-paragraphs (2) to (7), the person holds office on the terms specified by the Secretary of State after consulting the Attorney-General and the Lord Chancellor.

Staff

3. (1) The Commissioner may appoint such persons as members of his staff as he thinks fit.

(2) The Commissioner must obtain the approval of the Secretary of State to—

    (a) the number of persons appointed as members of his staff, and

    (b) their terms and conditions of service.

(3) No member of the staff of the Commissioner is to be regarded—

    (a) as the servant or agent of the Crown, or

    (b) as enjoying any status, immunity or privilege of the Crown.

Delegation

4. The Commissioner may authorize any member of his staff or the Deputy Commissioner to carry out any of his functions.

Pensions

5. (1) Schedule 1 to the Superannuation Act 1972 (c. 11) (kinds of employment and offices to which a scheme under section 1 of that Act may apply) is amended as set out in sub-paragraphs (2) and (3).

(2) At the end of the list headed 'Other Bodies' insert—

'Employment as a member of the staff of the Commissioner for Victims and Witnesses.'

(3) In the list headed 'Offices', in the appropriate places, insert—

'Commissioner for Victims and Witnesses.'

'Deputy Commissioner for Victims and Witnesses.'

(4) The Secretary of State must pay to the Minister for the Civil Service, at such times as the Minister for the Civil Service may direct, such sums as the Minister for the Civil Service may determine in respect of the increase attributable to sub-paragraphs (1) to (3) in the sums payable out of money provided by Parliament under the Superannuation Act 1972.

Finance

6. The Secretary of State must pay—

    (a) the remuneration of the Commissioner and the Deputy Commissioner;

    (b) such sums as he thinks fit in respect of the expenses of the Commissioner and the Deputy Commissioner.

Accounts

7. (1) The Commissioner must—
   (a) keep proper accounts and proper records in relation to the accounts;
   (b) prepare a statement of accounts in respect of each financial year, in the form directed by the Secretary of State;
   (c) send copies of the statement to the Secretary of State and the Comptroller and Auditor General, not later than the 31 August following the end of the financial year to which it relates.
(2) The Comptroller and Auditor General must—
   (a) examine, certify and report on the statement of accounts;
   (b) lay copies of the statement and of his report before Parliament.

Annual plan

8. (1) The Commissioner must, before the beginning of each financial year apart from the first, prepare a plan setting out how he intends to exercise his functions during the financial year (an annual plan).
(2) In preparing the plan, the Commissioner must consider whether to deal in the plan with any issues specified by the Secretary of State.
(3) The Commissioner must send a copy of the plan to the Secretary of State for his approval.
(4) The Secretary of State must consult the Attorney-General and the Lord Chancellor in deciding whether to approve the plan.
(5) If the Secretary of State does not approve the plan—
   (a) he must give the Commissioner his reasons for not approving it, and
   (b) the Commissioner must revise the plan.
(6) Sub-paragraphs (2) to (5) apply to a revised plan as they apply to the plan as first prepared.

Annual report

9. (1) The Commissioner must, as soon as possible after the end of each financial year, prepare a report on how he has exercised his functions during the financial year.
(2) The report for any financial year apart from the first must include—
   (a) the Commissioner's annual plan for the financial year, and
   (b) an assessment of the extent to which the plan has been carried out.
(3) The Commissioner must send a copy of the report to—
   (a) the Secretary of State,
   (b) the Attorney-General, and
   (c) the Lord Chancellor.
(4) The Secretary of State must—
   (a) lay a copy of the report before Parliament;
   (b) arrange for the report to be published.

Disqualification acts

10. (1) In Part 3 of Schedule 1 to the House of Commons Disqualification Act 1975 (c. 24) (offices the holders of which are disqualified) at the appropriate places insert—
'Commissioner for Victims and Witnesses.'
'Deputy Commissioner for Victims and Witnesses.'

(2) In Part 3 of Schedule 1 to the Northern Ireland Assembly Disqualification Act 1975 (c. 25) (offices the holders of which are disqualified) at the appropriate places insert—
'Commissioner for Victims and Witnesses.'
'Deputy Commissioner for Victims and Witnesses.'

Meaning of 'financial year'

11. In this Schedule 'financial year' means—
(a) the period beginning on the day on which section 48 comes into force and ending on the next 31 March (which is the first financial year), and
(b) each subsequent period of 12 months beginning on 1 April.

SCHEDULE 9

Section 53

AUTHORITIES WITHIN COMMISSIONER'S REMIT

Government departments

1. The Department for Constitutional Affairs.
2. The Department for Education and Skills.
3. The Department of Health.
4. The Department of Trade and Industry.
5. The Department for Transport.
6. The Department for Work and Pensions.
7. The Foreign and Commonwealth Office.
8. The Home Office.
9. The Office of the Deputy Prime Minister.

Customs and Excise

10. The Commissioners of Customs and Excise.

Police forces etc

11. A police force for a police area in England or Wales.
12. The Serious Fraud Office.
13. The National Criminal Intelligence Service.

14. The National Crime Squad.
15. The force of constables appointed under section 53 of the British Transport Commission Act 1949 (c. xxix).
16. The Ministry of Defence Police.

Criminal injuries compensation

17. The Criminal Injuries Compensation Appeals Panel.
18. The Criminal Injuries Compensation Authority.

Health and safety

19. The Health and Safety Commission.
20. The Health and Safety Executive.

Legal services

21. The Legal Services Commission.

Court administration

22. Persons exercising functions relating to the carrying on of the business of a court.

Criminal justice system

23. The Criminal Cases Review Commission.
24. The Crown Prosecution Service.
25. A local probation board established under section 4 of the Criminal Justice and Court Services Act 2000 (c. 43).
26. The Parole Board.
27. The Prison Service.
28. The Youth Justice Board for England and Wales.
29. A youth offending team established under section 39 of the Crime and Disorder Act 1998 (c. 37).

Maritime and coastguards

30. The Maritime and Coastguard Agency.

SCHEDULE 10

Section 58(1)

MINOR AND CONSEQUENTIAL AMENDMENTS

Colonial Prisoners Removal Act 1884 (c. 31)

1. In section 10 of the Colonial Prisoners Removal Act 1884 (application of Act to removal of criminal lunatics), in subsection (3), in paragraph (a) for the words from 'give' to the end substitute 'by warrant direct that he is to be detained in such hospital, within the meaning given by section 145(1) of the Mental Health Act 1983, as may be specified in the direction; and any such direction shall have the same effect as a hospital order under section 37 of that Act together with a restriction order under section 41 of that Act, made without limitation of time;'.

Children and Young Persons Act 1933 (c. 12)

2. In Schedule 1 to the Children and Young Persons Act 1933 (offences against children and young persons with respect to which special provisions of the Act apply), after 'Infanticide' insert—
'An offence under section 5 of the Domestic Violence, Crime and Victims Act 2004, in respect of a child or young person.'

Criminal Procedure (Insanity) Act 1964 (c. 84)

3. In section 8(2) of the Criminal Procedure (Insanity) Act 1964 (interpretation), after the definition of 'duly approved' insert—
' "local probation board" means a local probation board established under section 4 of the Criminal Justice and Court Services Act 2000;'.

Criminal Appeal Act 1968 (c. 19)

4. In section 15 of the Criminal Appeal Act 1968 (right of appeal against finding of disability), in subsection (1), for the words 'the jury has returned' substitute 'there have been'.

5. In section 37 of that Act (detention of defendant on appeal by the Crown to House of Lords), in subsection (4), for paragraph (b) substitute—
'(b) a hospital order made by virtue of section 5(2)(a) of the Criminal Procedure (Insanity) Act 1964 (powers to deal with persons not guilty by reason of insanity or unfit to plead etc),'.

6. In section 51 of that Act (interpretation), in subsection (2A), for '6, 14 or 14A' substitute '6 or 14'.

7. In Schedule 1 to the Children and Young Persons Act (Northern Ireland) 1968 (offences against children and young persons with respect to which special provisions of the Act apply), after 'Infanticide' insert—

> 'An offence under section 5 of the Domestic Violence, Crime and Victims Act 2004, in respect of a child or young person.'

Juries Act 1974 (c. 23)

8. (1) Section 11 of the Juries Act 1974 (ballot and swearing of jurors) is amended as follows.

(2) In subsection (5) omit paragraph (b).

(3) In subsection (6) omit ', (b)'.

Rehabilitation of Offenders Act 1974 (c. 53)

9. In section 1(3) of the Rehabilitation of Offenders Act 1974 (meaning of 'sentence' for the purposes of that Act), after 'other than' insert—

'(za) a surcharge imposed under section 161A of the Criminal Justice Act 2003;'.

Magistrates' Courts Act 1980 (c. 43)

10. In section 108 of the Magistrates' Courts Act 1980 (right of appeal to Crown Court), after subsection (3) insert—

'(4) Subsection (3)(d) above does not prevent an appeal against a surcharge imposed under section 161A of the Criminal Justice Act 2003.'

11. In section 139 of that Act (disposal of sums adjudged to be paid by conviction)—

(a) after paragraph (a) insert—

> '(aa) in the second place in payment to the fund mentioned in paragraph (c) below of surcharges imposed under section 161A of the Criminal Justice Act 2003;';

(b) in paragraph (b), for 'second' substitute 'third'.

Criminal Appeal (Northern Ireland) Act 1980 (c. 47)

12. In section 13A of the Criminal Appeal (Northern Ireland) Act 1980 (appeal against finding of unfitness to be tried), in subsection (1), for 'the jury has returned' substitute 'there has been'.

13. In section 19(1A)(a) of that Act (legal aid), after 'appeal under' insert 'section 18A of the Domestic Violence, Crime and Victims Act 2004,'.

Supreme Court Act 1981 (c. 54)

14. In section 55 of the Supreme Court Act 1981 (constitution of criminal division of Court of Appeal), in subsection (4)(a)(iii) omit the words 'of a jury'.

15. In section 81 of that Act (power of Crown Court to grant bail), in subsection (1A), for 'or 15' substitute ', 15 or 16A'.

Criminal Justice Act 1982 (c. 48)

16. In Schedule 1 to the Criminal Justice Act 1982 (offences excluded from early release provisions), in Part 2, after the entry relating to the Sexual Offences Act 2003 (c. 42) insert—

'Domestic Violence, Crime and Victims Act 2004

Section 5 (causing or allowing the death of a child or vulnerable adult).'

Representation of the People Act 1983 (c. 2)

17. In section 3A of the Representation of the People Act 1983 (disenfranchisement of offenders detained in mental hospitals), for subsection (5) substitute—
'(5) As respects any part of the United Kingdom, this section applies to any person in respect of whom a hospital order has been made by virtue of—
    (a) section 116A of the Army Act 1955 or the Air Force Act 1955 or section 63A of the Naval Discipline Act 1957, or
    (b) section 16 or 23 of the Courts-Martial (Appeals) Act 1968.'

Mental Health Act 1983 (c. 20)

18. In section 47 of the Mental Health Act 1983 (removal to hospital of persons serving sentences of imprisonment, etc), in subsection (5)(a), for the words 'under any enactment to which section 46 applies' substitute 'made in consequence of a finding of insanity or unfitness to stand trial'.

19. In section 69 of that Act (application to tribunals concerning patients subject to hospital orders etc), in subsection (2)(a)—
    (a) for 'below,' substitute 'below or';
    (b) omit 'or section 5(1) of the Criminal Procedure (Insanity) Act 1964'.

20. In section 71 of that Act (references by Home Secretary concerning restricted patients) omit subsections (5) and (6).

21. In section 79 of that Act (interpretation of Part 5), in subsection (1)—
    (a) for paragraph (a) substitute—
'(a) is treated by virtue of any enactment as subject to a hospital order and a restriction order; or';
    (b) omit paragraph (b).

22. In section 84 of that Act (removal to England and Wales of offenders found insane in Channel Islands and Isle of Man), in subsection (2), for the words from 'had been' to the end substitute 'were subject to a hospital order together with a restriction order, made without limitation of time'.

23. (1) Schedule 5 to that Act (transitional and saving provisions) is amended as follows.

(2) For paragraph 21 substitute—

'21. Any direction to which section 71(4) of the Mental Health Act 1959 applied immediately before the commencement of this Act shall have the same effect as a hospital order together with a restriction order, made without limitation of time.'

(3) In paragraph 37(2), for 'direction under section 46 of this Act' substitute 'hospital order together with a restriction order, made without limitation of time'.

Police and Criminal Evidence Act 1984 (c. 60)

24. In Schedule 5 to the Police and Criminal Evidence Act 1984 (serious arrestable offences), in Part 2, after paragraph 23 insert—

'*Domestic Violence, Crime and Victims Act 2004*

24. Section 5 (causing or allowing the death of a child or vulnerable adult).'

Prosecution of Offences Act 1985 (c. 23)

25. In section 16 of the Prosecution of Offences Act 1985 (defence costs), in subsection (4) (power of Court of Appeal to make defendant's costs order), after paragraph (c) insert 'or

(d) allows, to any extent, an appeal under section 16A of that Act (appeal against order made in cases of insanity or unfitness to plead);'.

Coroners Act 1988 (c. 13)

26. In section 16 of the Coroners Act 1988 (adjournment of inquest in event of criminal proceedings), in subsection (1)(a), after sub-paragraph (iii) insert—

'(iv) an offence under section 5 of the Domestic Violence, Crime and Victims Act 2004 (causing or allowing the death of a child or vulnerable adult); or'.

27. In section 17 of that Act (coroner to be informed of result of criminal proceedings), in subsections (1) and (2), at the end of paragraph (c) insert '; or

(d) an offence under section 5 of the Domestic Violence, Crime and Victims Act 2004 (causing or allowing the death of a child or vulnerable adult),'.

Criminal Justice Act 1988 (c. 33)

28. In section 41 of the Criminal Justice Act 1988 (power of Crown Court to deal with summary offence where person committed for either way offence), after subsection (4) insert—

'(4A) The committal of a person under this section in respect of an offence to which section 40 above applies shall not prevent him being found guilty of that offence under section 6(3) of the Criminal Law Act 1967 (alternative verdicts on trial on indictment); but where he is convicted under that provision of such an offence, the functions of the Crown Court under this section in relation to the offence shall cease.'

29. In Schedule 5 to the Police and Criminal Evidence (Northern Ireland) Order 1989 (serious arrestable offences), in Part 2, after paragraph 14 insert—

'Domestic Violence, Crime and Victims Act 2004

Section 5 (causing or allowing the death of a child or vulnerable adult).'

Criminal Justice Act 1991 (c. 53)

30. In section 24 of the Criminal Justice Act 1991 (recovery of fines etc by deductions from income support), after subsection (3) insert—

'(3A) This section applies in relation to a surcharge imposed under section 161A of the Criminal Justice Act 2003 as if any reference in subsection (1) or (3) above to a fine included a reference to a surcharge.'

Criminal Appeal Act 1995 (c. 35)

31. In section 9 of the Criminal Appeal Act 1995 (references by Criminal Cases Review Commission to Court of Appeal), in subsection (6), for the words 'a jury in England and Wales has returned' substitute 'in England and Wales there have been'.

32. In section 10 of that Act (which makes equivalent provision for Northern Ireland), in subsection (7), for the words 'a jury in Northern Ireland has returned' substitute 'in Northern Ireland there has been'.

Law Reform (Year and a Day Rule) Act 1996 (c. 19)

33. In section 2 of the Law Reform (Year and a Day Rule) Act 1996 (restriction on institution of proceedings for fatal offence), in subsection (3), at the end of paragraph (b) insert

', or

(c) an offence under section 5 of the Domestic Violence, Crime and Victims Act 2004 (causing or allowing the death of a child or vulnerable adult).'

Family Law Act 1996 (c. 27)

34. (1) Section 36 of the Family Law Act 1996 (one cohabitant or former cohabitant with no existing right to occupy) is amended as follows.

(2) In subsection (1)(c), for the words from 'live together as' to the end substitute 'cohabit or a home in which they at any time cohabited or intended to cohabit'.

(3) In subsection (6)(f), for 'lived together as husband and wife' substitute 'cohabited'.

35. In section 38 of that Act (neither cohabitant or former cohabitant entitled to occupy), in subsection (1)(a), for 'live or lived together as husband and wife' substitute 'cohabit or cohabited'.

36. (1) Section 42 of that Act (non-molestation orders) is amended as follows.

(2) After subsection (4) insert—

'(4A) A court considering whether to make an occupation order shall also consider whether to exercise the power conferred by subsection (2)(b).

(4B) In this Part 'the applicant', in relation to a non-molestation order, includes (where the context permits) the person for whose benefit such an order would be or is made in exercise of the power conferred by subsection (2)(b).'

(3) In subsection (5)(a) omit the words from 'or' to 'made'.

37. (1) Section 46 of that Act (undertakings) is amended as follows.

(2) In subsection (3), after 'under subsection (1)' insert 'instead of making an occupation order'.

(3) After that subsection insert—

'(3A) The court shall not accept an undertaking under subsection (1) instead of making a non-molestation order in any case where it appears to the court that—

(a) the respondent has used or threatened violence against the applicant or a relevant child; and

(b) for the protection of the applicant or child it is necessary to make a non-molestation order so that any breach may be punishable under section 42A.'

(4) In subsection (4), for 'it were an order of the court' substitute 'the court had made an occupation order or a non-molestation order in terms corresponding to those of the undertaking'.

38. (1) Section 47 of that Act (arrest for breach of occupation order or non-molestation order) is amended as follows.

(2) Omit subsection (1).

(3) In subsections (2) and (4), for 'a relevant order' substitute 'an occupation order'.

(4) In subsections (3) and (5), for 'the relevant order' substitute 'the occupation order'.

(5) In subsection (8), for the words up to the end of paragraph (b) substitute—

'If the court—

(a) has made a non-molestation order, or

(b) has made an occupation order but has not attached a power of arrest under subsection (2) or (3) to any provision of the order, or has attached that power only to certain provisions of the order,'.

39. In section 49 of that Act (variation and discharge of orders), in subsection (4) omit 'or non-molestation order'.

40. In section 62 of that Act (definitions), in subsection (1)(b), for ' "former cohabitants" is to be read accordingly, but' substitute ' "cohabit" and "former cohabitants" are to be read accordingly, but the latter expression'.

41. (1) In section 63 of that Act (interpretation of Part 4), subsection (1) is amended as follows.

(2) At the beginning of the definition of 'cohabitant' and 'former cohabitant' insert ' "cohabit",'.

(3) In the definition of 'relative'—

    (a) for 'or nephew' in paragraph (b) substitute ', nephew or first cousin';

    (b) for 'is living or has lived with another person as husband and wife' substitute 'is cohabiting or has cohabited with another person'.

42. (1) Schedule 7 to that Act (transfer of certain tenancies on divorce etc or on separation of cohabitants) is amended as follows.

(2) In paragraph 3(2), for 'to live together as husband and wife' substitute 'to cohabit'.

(3) In paragraph 4(b), for 'lived together as husband and wife' substitute 'cohabited'.

Protection from Harassment Act 1997 (c. 40)

43. (1) Section 5 of the Protection from Harassment Act 1997 (power to make restraining order where defendant convicted of offence under section 2 or 4 of that Act) is amended as follows.

(2) In the heading, at the end insert '**on conviction**'.

(3) In subsection (2) omit 'further'.

44. In section 7 of that Act (interpretation), in subsection (1), for 'sections 1 to 5' substitute 'sections 1 to 5A'.

Crime (Sentences) Act 1997 (c. 43)

45. (1) Section 47 of the Crime (Sentences) Act 1997 (power to specify hospital units) is amended as follows.

(2) Omit subsections (1)(d) and (2)(c).

(3) For subsection (4) substitute—

    '(4) A reference in this section to section 37 or 41 of the 1983 Act includes a reference to that section as it applies by virtue of—

        (a) section 5 of the Criminal Procedure (Insanity) Act 1964,

        (b) section 6 or 14 of the Criminal Appeal Act 1968,

        (c) section 116A of the Army Act 1955 or the Air Force Act 1955 or section 63A of the Naval Discipline Act 1957, or

        (d) section 16 or 23 of the Courts-Martial (Appeals) Act 1968.'

46. (1) Schedule 1 to that Act (transfers of prisoners within the British Islands) (as amended by Schedule 32 to the Criminal Justice Act 2003) is amended as follows.

(2) In paragraph 8 (restricted transfers from England and Wales to Scotland), in sub-paragraphs (2)(a) and (4)(a), for '264' substitute '264A'.

(3) In paragraph 9 (restricted transfers from England and Wales to Northern Ireland), in sub-paragraphs (2)(a) and (4)(a), for '264' substitute '264A'.

Protection from Harassment (Northern Ireland) Order 1997 (S.I. 1997/1180 (N.I. 9))

47. (1) Article 7 of the Protection from Harassment (Northern Ireland) Order 1997 (power to make restraining order where defendant convicted of offence under Article 4 or 6 of that Act) is amended as follows.

(2) In the heading, at the end insert '**on conviction**'.

(3) In paragraph (2) omit 'further'.

Crime and Disorder Act 1998 (c. 37)

48. In section 32 of the Crime and Disorder Act 1998 (racially or religiously aggravated harassment etc) omit subsection (7) (which is superseded by provision made by section 12(1) above).

Powers of Criminal Courts (Sentencing) Act 2000 (c. 6)

49. In section 132 of the Powers of Criminal Courts (Sentencing) Act 2000 (compensation orders: appeals etc), after subsection (4) insert—

'(4A) Where an order is made in respect of a person under subsection (3) or (4) above, the Court of Appeal or House of Lords shall make such order for the payment of a surcharge under section 161A of the Criminal Justice Act 2003, or such variation of the order of the Crown Court under that section, as is necessary to secure that the person's liability under that section is the same as it would be if he were being dealt with by the Crown Court.'

50. In section 136 of that Act (power to order statement as to financial circumstances of parent or guardian), in subsection (1), for 'or compensation' substitute ', compensation or surcharge'.

51. (1) Section 137 of that Act (power to order parent or guardian to pay fine, costs or compensation) is amended as follows.

(2) In the heading, for '**or compensation**' substitute '**, compensation or surcharge**'.

(3) After subsection (1) insert—

'(1A) Where but for this subsection a court would order a child or young person to pay a surcharge under section 161A of the Criminal Justice Act 2003, the court shall order that the surcharge be paid by the parent or guardian of the child or young person instead of by the child or young person himself, unless the court is satisfied—

(a) that the parent or guardian cannot be found; or

(b) that it would be unreasonable to make an order for payment, having regard to the circumstances of the case.'

(4) In subsection (3), for 'subsections (1) and (2)' substitute 'subsections (1) to (2)'.

52. (1) Section 138 of that Act (fixing of fine or compensation to be paid by parent or guardian) is amended as follows.

(2) In the heading, for '**or compensation**' substitute '**, compensation or surcharge**'.

(3) Before paragraph (a) of subsection (1) insert—

'(za) subsection (3) of section 161A of the Criminal Justice Act 2003 (surcharges) and subsection (4A) of section 164 of that Act (fixing of fines) shall have effect as if any reference in those subsections to the offender's means were a reference to those of the parent or guardian;'.

53. In section 142(1) of that Act (power of Crown Court to order search of persons before it)—
(a) before paragraph (a) insert—
   '(za) the Crown Court orders a person to pay a surcharge under section 161A of the Criminal Justice Act 2003,';
(b) in paragraph (d), for 'or compensation' substitute ', compensation or surcharge'.

Criminal Justice and Court Services Act 2000 (c. 43)

54. The Criminal Justice and Court Services Act 2000 is amended as follows.

55. Section 69 (duties in connection with victims of certain offences) (which is superseded by section 35 of this Act) is repealed.

56. In Schedule 4 (offences against children for the purposes of disqualification orders), in paragraph 3, after paragraph (sa) insert—
'(sb) he commits an offence under section 5 of the Domestic Violence, Crime and Victims Act 2004 (causing or allowing the death of a child or vulnerable adult) in respect of a child.'

Sexual Offences Act 2003 (c. 42)

57. (1) Section 133 of the Sexual Offences Act 2003 (general interpretation of Part 2) is amended as follows.
(2) In subsection (1)—
   (a) in the definition of 'admitted to a hospital', for paragraph (c) substitute—
      '(c) section 46 of the Mental Health Act 1983, section 69 of the Mental Health (Scotland) Act 1984 or Article 52 of the Mental Health (Northern Ireland) Order 1986;';
   (b) in the definition of 'detained in a hospital', for paragraph (c) substitute—
      '"(c) section 46 of the Mental Health Act 1983, section 69 of the Mental Health (Scotland) Act 1984 or Article 52 of the Mental Health (Northern Ireland) Order 1986;';
   (c) in the definition of 'restriction order', for paragraph (c) substitute—
      '"(c) a direction under section 46 of the Mental Health Act 1983, section 69 of the Mental Health (Scotland) Act 1984 or Article 52 of the Mental Health (Northern Ireland) Order 1986;'.
(3) After that subsection insert—
   '(1A) A reference to a provision specified in paragraph (a) of the definition of "admitted to a hospital", "detained in a hospital" or "restriction order" includes a reference to the provision as it applies by virtue of—
      (a) section 5 of the Criminal Procedure (Insanity) Act 1964,
      (b) section 6 or 14 of the Criminal Appeal Act 1968,
      (c) section 116A of the Army Act 1955 or the Air Force Act 1955 or section 63A of the Naval Discipline Act 1957, or
      (d) section 16 or 23 of the Courts-Martial (Appeals) Act 1968.'

58. In section 135 of that Act (interpretation: mentally disordered offenders), omit subsection (4)(c).

182

59. (1) Schedule 5 to that Act (other offences for the purposes of sexual offences prevention orders) is amended as follows.

(2) After paragraph 63 insert—

'63A An offence under section 5 of the Domestic Violence, Crime and Victims Act 2004 (causing or allowing the death of a child or vulnerable adult).'

(3) After paragraph 171 insert—

'171A An offence under section 5 of the Domestic Violence, Crime and Victims Act 2004 (causing or allowing the death of a child or vulnerable adult).'

(4) In paragraph 172, for '63' substitute '63A'.

Criminal Justice Act 2003 (c. 44)

60. In section 48 of the Criminal Justice Act 2003 (c. 44) (further provisions about trial without a jury), in subsection (6), for paragraphs (a) and (b) substitute 'the requirement under section 4A of the Criminal Procedure (Insanity) Act 1964 that any question, finding or verdict mentioned in that section be determined, made or returned by a jury'.

61. In section 50 of that Act (application of Part 7 to Northern Ireland), in subsection (13), for paragraphs (a) to (c) substitute—

'(a) for "section 4A of the Criminal Procedure (Insanity) Act 1964" substitute "Article 49A of the Mental Health (Northern Ireland) Order 1986", and

(b) for "that section" substitute "that Article".'

62. In section 74 of that Act (interpretation of Part 9), after subsection (6) insert—

'(7) In its application to a trial on indictment in respect of which an order under section 17(2) of the Domestic Violence, Crime and Victims Act 2004 has been made, this Part is to have effect with such modifications as the Secretary of State may by order specify.'

63. In section 151 of that Act (community order for persistent offender previously fined), in subsection (5), after 'compensation order' insert 'or a surcharge under section 161A'.

64. In section 305 of that Act (interpretation of Part 12), in subsection (1), insert at the appropriate place—

' "compensation order" has the meaning given by section 130(1) of the Sentencing Act;'.

65. In Schedule 15 to that Act (specified offences for the purposes of Chapter 5 of Part 12 of that Act), in Part 1 (specified violent offences), after paragraph 63 insert—

'63A An offence under section 5 of the Domestic Violence, Crime and Victims Act 2004 (causing or allowing the death of a child or vulnerable adult).'

66. In Schedule 17 to that Act (Northern Ireland offences specified for the purposes of section 229(4)), in Part 1 (specified violent offences), after paragraph 60 insert—

'60A An offence under section 5 of the Domestic Violence, Crime and Victims Act 2004 (causing or allowing the death of a child or vulnerable adult).'

SCHEDULE 11

Section 58(2)

REPEALS

Short title and chapter	Extent of repeal
Criminal Procedure (Insanity) Act 1964 (c. 84)	Section 7. In section 8— (a) the proviso to subsection (3); (b) in subsection (4), the words from, 'except' to 'courts-martial,'. Schedule 2.
Criminal Appeal Act 1968 (c. 19)	Section 14A.
Courts-Martial (Appeals) Act 1968 (c. 20)	In Schedule 3, paragraph 3(b).
Juries Act 1974 (c. 23)	In section 11, paragraph (b) of subsection (5) and '(b)' in subsection (6). In Schedule 1, paragraph 4(2).
Supreme Court Act 1981 (c. 54)	In section 55(4)(a)(iii), the words 'of a jury'.
Mental Health Act 1983 (c. 20)	In section 69(2)(a), the words 'or section 5(1) of the Criminal Procedure (Insanity) Act 1964'. Section 71(5) and (6). Section 79(1)(b).
Prosecution of Offences Act 1985 (c. 23)	In section 16(4), the word 'or' preceding paragraph (c).
Coroners Act 1988 (c. 13)	In section 16(1)(a), the word 'or' preceding sub-paragraph (iii). In section 17, in subsections (1) and (2) the word 'or' preceding paragraph (c).
Criminal Procedure (Insanity and Unfitness to Plead) Act 1991 (c.25)	Sections 3 and 5. In section 6 (a) the definition of 'local probation board' in subsection (1); (b) subsection (2). Schedules 1 and 2.
Law Reform (Year and a Day Rule) Act 1996 (c.19)	In section 2(3), the word 'or' preceding paragraph (b).
Family Law Act 1996 (c. 27)	Section 41. In section 42(5)(a), the words from 'or' to 'made'. Section 47(1). In section 49(4), the words 'or non-molestation order'.
Armed Forces Act 1996 (c. 46)	Section 8. Schedule 2.
Protection from Harassment Act 1997 (c. 40)	In section 5, the words 'under section 2 or 4' in subsection (1) and the word 'further' in subsection (2).

Crime (Sentences) Act 1997 (c. 43)	In section 47 (a) in subsection (1), paragraph (d) and the word 'or' preceding it; (b) in subsection (2), paragraph (c) and the word 'and' preceding it.
Protection from Harassment (Northern Ireland) Order 1997 (S.I.1997/1180(N.I.9))	In Article 7, the words 'under Article 4 or 6' in paragraph (1) and the word 'further' in paragraph (2).
Crime and Disorder Act 1998 (c. 37)	Section 32(7).
Access to Justice Act 1999 (c. 22)	In Schedule 13, paragraph 163.
Powers of Criminal Courts (Sentencing) Act 2000 (c. 6)	In Schedule 9, paragraph 133.
Care Standards Act 2000 (c. 14)	In Schedule 4, paragraph 16.
Criminal Justice and Court Services Act 2000 (c. 43)	Section 69. In Schedule 7, paragraphs 99 to 102.
Sexual Offences Act 2003 (c. 42)	Section 135(4)(c).
Criminal Justice Act 2003 (c. 44)	In section 246(6), in the definition of 'the required custodial days', the word 'or' preceding paragraph (b). In section 264(1), the word 'and' preceding paragraph (b).

SCHEDULE 12

Section 59

TRANSITIONAL AND TRANSITORY PROVISIONS

1. (1) Section 1 and paragraphs 37 to 39 of Schedule 10 apply only in relation to conduct occurring on or after the commencement of that section.

(2) In relation to an offence committed before the commencement of section 154(1) of the Criminal Justice Act 2003 (c. 44), the reference to 12 months in subsection (5)(b) of section 42A of the Family Law Act 1996 (inserted by section 1 of this Act) is to be read as a reference to six months.

2. In section 5, the reference in subsection (1)(a) to an unlawful act does not include an act that (or so much of an act as) occurs before the commencement of that section.

3. (1) This paragraph has effect, in relation to any time before the commencement of the repeal (by paragraph 51 of Schedule 3 to the Criminal Justice Act 2003) of section 6 of the Magistrates' Courts Act 1980 (c. 43), where—

(a) a magistrates' court is considering under subsection (1) of that section whether to commit a person ('the accused') for trial for an offence of murder or man-slaughter, and

(b) the accused is charged in the same proceedings with an offence under section 5 above in respect of the same death.

(2) If there is sufficient evidence to put the accused on trial by jury for the offence under section 5, there is deemed to be sufficient evidence to put him on trial by jury for the offence of murder or manslaughter.

4. Section 10 applies only in relation to offences committed on or after the commencement of that section.

5. (1) Section 12(1) and paragraphs 43(3) and 48 of Schedule 10 do not apply where the conviction occurs before the commencement of those provisions.

(2) Section 12(2) applies only in relation to applications made on or after the commencement of that provision.

(3) Section 12(4) and paragraphs 43(2) and 44 of Schedule 10 do not apply where the acquittal (or, where subsection (5) of the inserted section 5A applies, the allowing of the appeal) occurs before the commencement of those provisions.

6. (1) Section 13(1) and paragraph 47(3) of Schedule 10 do not apply where the conviction occurs before the commencement of those provisions.

(2) Section 13(2) applies only in relation to applications made on or after the commencement of that provision.

(3) Section 13(4) and paragraph 47(2) of Schedule 10 do not apply where the acquittal (or, where paragraph (5) of the inserted Article 7A applies, the allowing of the appeal) occurs before the commencement of those provisions.

7. Section 14 applies only in relation to offences committed on or after the commencement of that section.

8. (1) The provisions mentioned in sub-paragraph (2) do not apply—

 (a) in relation to proceedings before the Crown Court or a court-martial, where the accused was arraigned before the commencement of those provisions;

 (b) in relation to proceedings before the Court of Appeal or the Courts-Martial Appeal Court, where the hearing of the appeal began before that commencement.

(2) The provisions are—

 (a) sections 22 and 23;

 (b) section 24 and Schedule 2;

 (c) section 26 and Schedule 3;

 (d) paragraphs 5, 6, 8, 17 to 21, 45, 60 and 61 of Schedule 10.

9. The Schedule inserted by Schedule 2 has effect in relation to any time before the commencement of sections 8 and 37 of the Courts Act 2003 (c. 39)—

(a) as if a reference to a local justice area were to a petty sessions area;

(b) as if a reference to a designated officer were to a justices' chief executive.

10. Each entry in Schedule 11 applies in the same way as the provision of this Act to which it corresponds.

Criminal Procedure (Insanity) Act 1964, ss 4, 5, and 5A as amended[1]

[The text incorporates amendments made to the Criminal Procedure (Insanity) Act 1964 (c 84) before the coming into force by the Domestic Violence, Crime and Victims Act 2004. Please note, these amendments are not yet in force. The amendments will come into force in stages from April 2005. Please see relevant statutory instruments. Repeals made by that Act are shown in italics and amendments in square brackets]

4.—(1) This section applies where on the trial of a person the question arises (at the instance of the defence or otherwise) whether the accused is under a disability, that is to say, under any disability such that apart from this Act it would constitute a bar to his being tried.

(2) If, having regard to the nature of the supposed disability, the court are of opinion that it is expedient to do so and in the interests of the accused, they may postpone consideration of the question of fitness to be tried until any time up to the opening of the case for the defence.

(3) If, before the question of fitness to be tried falls to be determined, the jury return a verdict of acquittal on the count or each of the counts on which the accused is being tried, that question shall not be determined.

(4) Subject to subsections (2) and (3) above, the question of fitness to be tried shall be determined as soon as it arises.

(5) The question of fitness to be tried shall be determined by *a jury and—*

    (a) where it falls to be determined on the arraignment of the accused and the trial proceeds, the accused shall be tried by a jury other than that which determined that question;

    (b) where it falls to be determined at any later time, it shall be determined by a separate jury or by the jury by whom the accused is being tried, as the court may direct.

    [the court without a jury]

(6) *A jury* [The Court] shall not make a determination under subsection (5) above except on the written or oral evidence of two or more registered medical practitioners at least one of whom is duly approved.

4A.—(1) This section applies where in accordance with section 4(5) above it is determined by *a jury* [court] that the accused is under a disability.

(2) The trial shall not proceed or further proceed but it shall be determined by a jury—

    (a) on the evidence (if any) already given in the trial; and

    (b) on such evidence as may be adduced or further adduced by the prosecution, or

---

[1] As substituted by the Criminal Procedure (Insanity and Unfitness to Plead) Act 1991, ss 2–3.

adduced by a person appointed by the court under this section to put the case for the defence, whether they are satisfied, as respects the count or each of the counts on which the accused was to be or was being tried, that he did the act or made the omission charged against him as the offence.

(3) If as respects that count or any of those counts the jury are satisfied as mentioned in subsection (2) above, they shall make a finding that the accused did the act or made the omission charged against him.

(4) If as respects that count or any of those counts the jury are not so satisfied, they shall return a verdict of acquittal as if on the count in question the trial had proceeded to a conclusion.

(5) A determination under subsection (2) above shall be made—

(a) where the question of disability was determined on the arraignment of the accused, by a jury other than that which determined that question; and

(b) where that question was determined at any later time, by the jury by whom the accused was being tried.

[(5) Where the question of disability was determined after arraignment of the accused, the determination under subsection (2) above is to be made by the jury by whom he was being tried.]

5.—*(1) This section applies where—*

(a) a special verdict is returned that the accused is not guilty by reason of insanity; or

(b) findings are recorded that the accused is under a disability and that he did the act or made the omission charged against him.

(2) Subject to subsection (3) below, the court shall either—

(a) make an order that the accused be admitted, in accordance with the provisions of Schedule 1 to the Criminal Procedure (Insanity and Unfitness to Plead) Act 1991, to such hospital as may be specified by the Secretary of State; or

(b) where they have the power to do so by virtue of section 5 of that Act, make in respect of the accused such one of the following orders as they think most suitable in all the circumstances of the case, namely—

(i) a guardianship order within the meaning of the Mental Health Act 1983;

(ii) a supervision and treatment order within the meaning of Schedule 2 to the said Act of 1991; and

(iii) an order for his absolute discharge.

(3) Paragraph (b) of subsection (2) above shall not apply where the offence to which the special verdict or findings relate is an offence the sentence for which is fixed by law.

[5. Powers to deal with persons not guilty by reason of insanity or unfit to plead etc.[2]

(1) This section applies where—

(a) a special verdict is returned that the accused is not guilty by reason of insanity; or

(b) findings have been made that the accused is under a disability and that he did the act or made the omission chargedagainst him.

(2) The court shall make in respect of the accused—

(a) a hospital order (with or without a restriction order);

(b) a supervision order; or

(c) an order for his absolute discharge.

---

[2] Substituted by s 24 of the Act.

(3) Where—

(a) the offence to which the special verdict or the findings relate is an offence the sentence for which is fixed by law, and

(b) the court have power to make a hospital order, the court shall make a hospital order with a restriction order (whether or not they would have power to make a restriction order apart from this subsection).

(4) In this section—

'hospital order' has the meaning given in section 37 of the Mental Health Act 1983;

'prestriction order' has the meaning given to it by section 41 of that Act;

'supervision order' has the meaning given in Part 1 of Schedule 1A to this Act.]

[5A. Orders made under or by virtue of section 5[3]

(1) In relation to the making of an order by virtue of subsection (2)(a) of section 5 above, section 37 (hospital orders etc) of the Mental Health Act 1983 ('the 1983 Act') shall have effect as if—

(a) the reference in subsection (1) to a person being convicted before the Crown Court included a reference to the case where section 5 above applies;

(b) the words after 'punishable with imprisonment' and before 'or is convicted' were omitted; and

(c) for subsections (4) and (5) there were substituted—

'(4) Where an order is made under this section requiring a person to be admitted to a hospital ("a hospital order"), it shall be the duty of the managers of the hospital specified in the order to admit him in accordance with it.'

(2) In relation to a case where section 5 above applies but the court have not yet made one of the disposals mentioned in subsection (2) of that section—

(a) section 35 of the 1983 Act (remand to hospital for report on accused's mental condition) shall have effect with the omission of the words after paragraph (b) in subsection (3);

(b) section 36 of that Act (remand of accused person to hospital for treatment) shall have effect with the omission of the words '(other than an offence the sentence for which is fixed by law)' in subsection (2);

(c) references in sections 35 and 36 of that Act to an accused person shall be construed as including a person in whose case this subsection applies; and

(d) section 38 of that Act (interim hospital orders) shall have effect as if—

(i) the reference in subsection (1) to a person being convicted before the Crown Court included a reference to the case where section 5 above applies; and

(ii) the words '(other than an offence the sentence for which is fixed by law)' in that subsection were omitted.

(3) In relation to the making of any order under the 1983 Act by virtue of this Act, references in the 1983 Act to an offender shall be construed as including references to a person in whose case section 5 above applies, and references to an offence shall be construed accordingly.

(4) Where—

(a) a person is detained in pursuance of a hospital order which the court had power to make by virtue of section 5(1)(b) above, and

---

[3] Inserted by s 24 of the Act.

(b) the court also made a restriction order, and that order has not ceased to have effect,

the Secretary of State, if satisfied after consultation with the responsible medical officer that the person can properly be tried, may remit the person for trial, either to the court of trial or to a prison.

On the person's arrival at the court or prison, the hospital order and the restriction order shall cease to have effect.

(5) Schedule 1A to this Act (supervision orders) has effect with respect to the making of supervision orders under subsection (2)(b) of section 5 above, and with respect to the revocation and amendment of such orders.

(6) In relation to the making of an order under subsection (2)(c) of section 5 above, section 12(1) of the Powers of Criminal Courts (Sentencing) Act 2000 (absolute and conditional discharge) shall have effect as if—

(a) the reference to a person being convicted by or before a court of such an offence as is there mentioned included a reference to the case where section 5 above applies; and

(b) the reference to the court being of opinion that it is inexpedient to inflict punishment included a reference to it thinking that an order for absolute discharge would be most suitable in all the circumstances of the case.'

(2) Before Schedule 2 to the Criminal Procedure (Insanity) Act 1964 (c. 84) insert the Schedule set out in Schedule 2 to this Act.

(3) In section 6 of the Criminal Appeal Act 1968 (c. 19) (substitution of finding of insanity or findings of unfitness to plead etc) and in section 14 of that Act (substitution of findings of unfitness to plead etc), for subsections (2) and (3) substitute—

'(2) The Court of Appeal shall make in respect of the accused—

(a) a hospital order (with or without a restriction order);

(b) a supervision order; or

(c) an order for his absolute discharge.

(3) Where—

(a) the offence to which the appeal relates is an offence the sentence for which is fixed by law, and

(b) the court have power to make a hospital order,

the court shall make a hospital order with a restriction order (whether or not they would have power to make a restriction order apart from this subsection).

(4) Section 5A of the Criminal Procedure (Insanity) Act 1964 ("the 1964 Act") applies in relation to this section as it applies in relation to section 5 of that Act.

(5) Where the Court of Appeal make an interim hospital order by virtue of this section—

(a) the power of renewing or terminating it and of dealing with the appellant on its termination shall be exercisable by the court below and not by the Court of Appeal; and

(b) the court below shall be treated for the purposes of section 38(7) of the Mental Health Act 1983 (absconding offenders) as the court that made the order.

(6) Where the Court of Appeal make a supervision order by virtue of this section, any power of revoking or amending it shall be exercisable as if the order had been made by the court below.

(7) In this section—

"hospital order" has the meaning given in section 37 of the Mental Health Act 1983;

"interim hospital order" has the meaning given in section 38 of that Act;

"restriction order" has the meaning given to it by section 41 of that Act;

"supervision order" has the meaning given in Part 1 of Schedule 1A to the 1964 Act.'

(4) Section 14A of the Criminal Appeal Act 1968 (c. 19) (power to order admission to hospital where, on appeal against verdict of not guilty by reason of insanity, Court of Appeal substitutes verdict of acquittal) is repealed.

(5) Section 5 of the Criminal Procedure (Insanity and Unfitness to Plead) Act 1991 (c. 25) and Schedules 1 and 2 to that Act are repealed.]

Family Law Act 1996, Part IV as amended

[*The text incorporates amendments made to the Family Law Act 1996 (c 27) before the coming into force by the Domestic Violence, Crime and Victims Act 2004. Please note, these amendments are not yet in force. The amendments will come into force in stages from April 2005. Please see relevant statutory instruments. Repeals made by that Act are shown in italics and amendments in square brackets*]

PART IV
FAMILY HOMES AND DOMESTIC VIOLENCE

Rights to occupy matrimonial home

Rights concerning matrimonial home where one spouse has no estate, etc.

30.—(1) This section applies if—
   (a) one spouse is entitled to occupy a dwelling-house by virtue of—
      (i) a beneficial estate or interest or contract; or
      (ii) any enactment giving that spouse the right to remain in occupation; and
   (b) the other spouse is not so entitled.
(2) Subject to the provisions of this Part, the spouse not so entitled has the following rights ('matrimonial home rights')—
   (a) if in occupation, a right not to be evicted or excluded from the dwelling-house or any part of it by the other spouse except with the leave of the court given by an order under section 33;
   (b) if not in occupation, a right with the leave of the court so given to enter into and occupy the dwelling-house.
(3) If a spouse is entitled under this section to occupy a dwelling-house or any part of a dwelling-house, any payment or tender made or other thing done by that spouse in or towards satisfaction of any liability of the other spouse in respect of rent, mortgage payments or other outgoings affecting the dwelling-house is, whether or not it is made or done in pursuance of an order under section 40, as good as if made or done by the other spouse.
(4) A spouse's occupation by virtue of this section—
   (a) is to be treated, for the purposes of the Rent (Agriculture) Act 1976 and the Rent Act 1977 (other than Part V and sections 103 to 106 of that Act), as occupation by the other spouse as the other spouse's residence, and
   (b) if the spouse occupies the dwelling-house as that spouse's only or principal home, is to be treated, for the purposes of the Housing Act 1985 and Part I of the Housing Act 1988, as occupation by the other spouse as the other spouse's only or principal home.

(5) If a spouse ('the first spouse')—

    (a) is entitled under this section to occupy a dwelling-house or any part of a dwelling-house, and

    (b) makes any payment in or towards satisfaction of any liability of the other spouse ('the second spouse') in respect of mortgage payments affecting the dwelling-house, the person to whom the payment is made may treat it as having been made by the second spouse, but the fact that that person has treated any such payment as having been so made does not affect any claim of the first spouse against the second spouse to an interest in the dwelling-house by virtue of the payment.

(6) If a spouse is entitled under this section to occupy a dwelling-house or part of a dwelling-house by reason of an interest of the other spouse under a trust, all the provisions of subsections (3) to (5) apply in relation to the trustees as they apply in relation to the other spouse.

(7) This section does not apply to a dwelling-house which has at no time been, and which was at no time intended by the spouses to be, a matrimonial home of theirs.

(8) A spouse's matrimonial home rights continue—

    (a) only so long as the marriage subsists, except to the extent that an order under section 33(5) otherwise provides; and

    (b) only so long as the other spouse is entitled as mentioned in subsection (1) to occupy the dwelling-house, except where provision is made by section 31 for those rights to be a charge on an estate or interest in the dwelling-house.

(9) It is hereby declared that a spouse—

    (a) who has an equitable interest in a dwelling-Nhouse or in its proceeds of sale, but

    (b) is not a spouse in whom there is vested (whether solely or as joint tenant) a legal estate in fee simple or a legal term of years absolute in the dwelling-house, is to be treated, only for the purpose of determining whether he has matrimonial home rights, as not being entitled to occupy the dwelling-house by virtue of that interest.

Effect of matrimonial home rights as charge on dwelling-house

31.—(1) Subsections (2) and (3) apply if, at any time during a marriage, one spouse is entitled to occupy a dwelling-house by virtue of a beneficial estate or interest.

(2) The other spouse's matrimonial home rights are a charge on the estate or interest.

(3) The charge created by subsection (2) has the same priority as if it were an equitable interest created at whichever is the latest of the following dates—

    (a) the date on which the spouse so entitled acquires the estate or interest;

    (b) the date of the marriage; and

    (c) 1st January 1968 (the commencement date of the Matrimonial Homes Act 1967).

(4) Subsections (5) and (6) apply if, at any time when a spouse's matrimonial home rights are a charge on an interest of the other spouse under a trust, there are, apart from either of the spouses, no persons, living or unborn, who are or could become beneficiaries under the trust.

(5) The rights are a charge also on the estate or interest of the trustees for the other spouse.

(6) The charge created by subsection (5) has the same priority as if it were an equitable interest created (under powers overriding the trusts) on the date when it arises.

(7) In determining for the purposes of subsection (4) whether there are any persons who are not, but could become, beneficiaries under the trust, there is to be disregarded any potential exercise of a general power of appointment exercisable by either or both of the spouses alone (whether or not the exercise of it requires the consent of another person).

(8) Even though a spouse's matrimonial home rights are a charge on an estate or interest in the dwelling-house, those rights are brought to an end by—

(a) the death of the other spouse, or

(b) the termination (otherwise than by death) of the marriage, unless the court directs otherwise by an order made under section 33(5).

(9) If—

(a) a spouse's matrimonial home rights are a charge on an estate or interest in the dwelling-house, and

(b) that estate or interest is surrendered to merge in some other estate or interest expectant on it in such circumstances that, but for the merger, the person taking the estate or interest would be bound by the charge,

the surrender has effect subject to the charge and the persons thereafter entitled to the other estate or interest are, for so long as the estate or interest surrendered would have endured if not so surrendered, to be treated for all purposes of this Part as deriving title to the other estate or interest under the other spouse or, as the case may be, under the trustees for the other spouse, by virtue of the surrender.

(10) If the title to the legal estate by virtue of which a spouse is entitled to occupy a dwelling-house (including any legal estate held by trustees for that spouse) is registered under the Land Registration Act 2002 or any enactment replaced by that Act—

(a) registration of a land charge affecting the dwelling-house by virtue of this Part is to be effected by registering a notice under that Act; and

(b) a spouse's matrimonial home rights are not to be capable of falling within paragraph 2 of Schedule 1 or 3 to that Act within the meaning of that Act affecting the dwelling-house even though the spouse is in actual occupation of the dwelling-house.

(11) *Repealed*

(12) If—

(a) a spouse's matrimonial home rights are a charge on the estate of the other spouse or of trustees of the other spouse, and

(b) that estate is the subject of a mortgage, then if, after the date of the creation of the mortgage ('the first mortgage'), the charge is registered under section 2 of the Land Charges Act 1972, the charge is, for the purposes of section 94 of the Law of Property Act 1925 (which regulates the rights of mortgagees to make further advances ranking in priority to subsequent mortgages), to be deemed to be a mortgage subsequent in date to the first mortgage.

(13) It is hereby declared that a charge under subsection (2) or (5) is not registrable under subsection (10) or under section 2 of the Land Charges Act 1972 unless it is a charge on a legal estate.

Further provisions relating to matrimonial home rights

32. Schedule 4 re-enacts with consequential amendments and minor modifications provisions of the Matrimonial Homes Act 1983.

Occupation orders

Occupation orders where applicant has estate or interest etc. or has matrimonial home rights

33.—(1) If—
  (a) a person ('the person entitled')—
    (i) is entitled to occupy a dwelling-house by virtue of a beneficial estate or interest or contract or by virtue of any enactment giving him the right to remain in occupation, or
    (ii) has matrimonial home rights in relation to a dwelling-house, and
  (b) the dwelling-house—
    (i) is or at any time has been the home of the person entitled and of another person with whom he is associated, or
    (ii) was at any time intended by the person entitled and any such other person to be their home,
  the person entitled may apply to the court for an order containing any of the provisions specified in subsections (3), (4) and (5).
(2) If an agreement to marry is terminated, no application under this section may be made by virtue of section 62(3)(e) by reference to that agreement after the end of the period of three years beginning with the day on which it is terminated.
(3) An order under this section may—
  (a) enforce the applicant's entitlement to remain in occupation as against the other person ('the respondent');
  (b) require the respondent to permit the applicant to enter and remain in the dwelling-house or part of the dwelling-house;
  (c) regulate the occupation of the dwelling-house by either or both parties;
  (d) if the respondent is entitled as mentioned in subsection (1)(a)(i), prohibit, suspend or restrict the exercise by him of his right to occupy the dwelling-house;
  (e) if the respondent has matrimonial home rights in relation to the dwelling-house and the applicant is the other spouse, restrict or terminate those rights;
  (f) require the respondent to leave the dwelling-house or part of the dwelling-house; or
  (g) exclude the respondent from a defined area in which the dwelling-house is included.
(4) An order under this section may declare that the applicant is entitled as mentioned in subsection (1)(a)(i) or has matrimonial home rights.
(5) If the applicant has matrimonial home rights and the respondent is the other spouse, an order under this section made during the marriage may provide that those rights are not brought to an end by—
  (a) the death of the other spouse; or
  (b) the termination (otherwise than by death) of the marriage.
(6) In deciding whether to exercise its powers under subsection (3) and (if so) in what manner, the court shall have regard to all the circumstances including—
  (a) the housing needs and housing resources of each of the parties and of any relevant child;
  (b) the financial resources of each of the parties;
  (c) the likely effect of any order, or of any decision by the court not to exercise its powers under subsection (3), on the health, safety or well-being of the parties and of any relevant child; and
  (d) the conduct of the parties in relation to each other and otherwise.

(7) If it appears to the court that the applicant or any relevant child is likely to suffer significant harm attributable to conduct of the respondent if an order under this section containing one or more of the provisions mentioned in subsection (3) is not made, the court shall make the order unless it appears to it that—

    (a) the respondent or any relevant child is likely to suffer significant harm if the order is made; and

    (b) the harm likely to be suffered by the respondent or child in that event is as great as, or greater than, the harm attributable to conduct of the respondent which is likely to be suffered by the applicant or child if the order is not made.

(8) The court may exercise its powers under subsection (5) in any case where it considers that in all the circumstances it is just and reasonable to do so.

(9) An order under this section—

    (a) may not be made after the death of either of the parties mentioned in subsection (1); and

    (b) except in the case of an order made by virtue of subsection (5)(a), ceases to have effect on the death of either party.

(10) An order under this section may, in so far as it has continuing effect, be made for a specified period, until the occurrence of a specified event or until further order.

Effect of order under s. 33 where rights are charge on dwelling-house

34.—(1) If a spouse's matrimonial home rights are a charge on the estate or interest of the other spouse or of trustees for the other spouse—

    (a) an order under section 33 against the other spouse has, except so far as a contrary intention appears, the same effect against persons deriving title under the other spouse or under the trustees and affected by the charge, and

    (b) sections 33(1), (3), (4) and (10) and 30(3) to (6) apply in relation to any person deriving title under the other spouse or under the trustees and affected by the charge as they apply in relation to the other spouse.

(2) The court may make an order under section 33 by virtue of subsection (1)(b) if it considers that in all the circumstances it is just and reasonable to do so.

One former spouse with no existing right to occupy

35.—(1) This section applies if—

    (a) one former spouse is entitled to occupy a dwelling-house by virtue of a beneficial estate or interest or contract, or by virtue of any enactment giving him the right to remain in occupation;

    (b) the other former spouse is not so entitled; and

    (c) the dwelling-house was at any time their matrimonial home or was at any time intended by them to be their matrimonial home.

(2) The former spouse not so entitled may apply to the court for an order under this section against the other former spouse ('the respondent').

(3) If the applicant is in occupation, an order under this section must contain provision—

    (a) giving the applicant the right not to be evicted or excluded from the dwelling-house or any part of it by the respondent for the period specified in the order; and

    (b) prohibiting the respondent from evicting or excluding the applicant during that period.

(4) If the applicant is not in occupation, an order under this section must contain provision—

    (a) giving the applicant the right to enter into and occupy the dwelling-house for the period specified in the order; and

    (b) requiring the respondent to permit the exercise of that right.

(5) An order under this section may also—

    (a) regulate the occupation of the dwelling-house by either or both of the parties;

    (b) prohibit, suspend or restrict the exercise by the respondent of his right to occupy the dwelling-house;

    (c) require the respondent to leave the dwelling-house or part of the dwelling-house; or

    (d) exclude the respondent from a defined area in which the dwelling-house is included.

(6) In deciding whether to make an order under this section containing provision of the kind mentioned in subsection (3) or (4) and (if so) in what manner, the court shall have regard to all the circumstances including—

    (a) the housing needs and housing resources of each of the parties and of any relevant child;

    (b) the financial resources of each of the parties;

    (c) the likely effect of any order, or of any decision by the court not to exercise its powers under subsection (3) or (4), on the health, safety or well-being of the parties and of any relevant child;

    (d) the conduct of the parties in relation to each other and otherwise;

    (e) the length of time that has elapsed since the parties ceased to live together;

    (f) the length of time that has elapsed since the marriage was dissolved or annulled; and

    (g) the existence of any pending proceedings between the parties—

        (i) for an order under section 23A or 24 of the Matrimonial Causes Act 1973 (property adjustment orders in connection with divorce proceedings etc.);

        (ii) for an order under paragraph 1(2)(d) or (e) of Schedule 1 to the Children Act 1989 (orders for financial relief against parents); or

        (iii) relating to the legal or beneficial ownership of the dwelling-house.

(7) In deciding whether to exercise its power to include one or more of the provisions referred to in subsection (5) ('a subsection (5) provision') and (if so) in what manner, the court shall have regard to all the circumstances including the matters mentioned in subsection (6)(a) to (e).

(8) If the court decides to make an order under this section and it appears to it that, if the order does not include a subsection (5) provision, the applicant or any relevant child is likely to suffer significant harm attributable to conduct of the respondent, the court shall include the subsection (5) provision in the order unless it appears to the court that—

    (a) the respondent or any relevant child is likely to suffer significant harm if the provision is included in the order; and

    (b) the harm likely to be suffered by the respondent or child in that event is as great as or greater than the harm attributable to conduct of the respondent which is likely to be suffered by the applicant or child if the provision is not included.

(9) An order under this section—

    (a) may not be made after the death of either of the former spouses; and

    (b) ceases to have effect on the death of either of them.

(10) An order under this section must be limited so as to have effect for a specified period not exceeding six months, but may be extended on one or more occasions for a further specified period not exceeding six months.

(11) A former spouse who has an equitable interest in the dwelling-house or in the proceeds of sale of the dwelling-house but in whom there is not vested (whether solely or as joint tenant) a legal estate in fee simple or a legal term of years absolute in the dwelling-house is to be treated (but only for the purpose of determining whether he is eligible to apply under this section) as not being entitled to occupy the dwelling-house by virtue of that interest.

(12) Subsection (11) does not prejudice any right of such a former spouse to apply for an order under section 33.

(13) So long as an order under this section remains in force, subsections (3) to (6) of section 30 apply in relation to the applicant—

    (a) as if he were the spouse entitled to occupy the dwelling-house by virtue of that section; and

    (b) as if the respondent were the other spouse.

One cohabitant or former cohabitant with no existing right to occupy

36.—(1) This section applies if—

    (a) one cohabitant or former cohabitant is entitled to occupy a dwelling-house by virtue of a beneficial estate or interest or contract or by virtue of any enactment giving him the right to remain in occupation;

    (b) the other cohabitant or former cohabitant is not so entitled; and

    (c) that dwelling-house is the home in which they [cohabit or a home in which they at any time cohabited or intended to cohabit.][1]

(2) The cohabitant or former cohabitant not so entitled may apply to the court for an order under this section against the other cohabitant or former cohabitant ('the respondent').

(3) If the applicant is in occupation, an order under this section must contain provision—

    (a) giving the applicant the right not to be evicted or excluded from the dwelling-house or any part of it by the respondent for the period specified in the order; and

    (b) prohibiting the respondent from evicting or excluding the applicant during that period.

(4) If the applicant is not in occupation, an order under this section must contain provision—

    (a) giving the applicant the right to enter into and occupy the dwelling-house for the period specified in the order; and

    (b) requiring the respondent to permit the exercise of that right.

---

[1] Replaces 'live together as husband and wife or a home in which they at any time so lived together or intended so to live together' Sch 10, para 34(2).

(5) An order under this section may also—

    (a) regulate the occupation of the dwelling-house by either or both of the parties;

    (b) prohibit, suspend or restrict the exercise by the respondent of his right to occupy the dwelling-house;

    (c) require the respondent to leave the dwelling-house or part of the dwelling-house; or

    (d) exclude the respondent from a defined area in which the dwelling-house is included.

(6) In deciding whether to make an order under this section containing provision of the kind mentioned in subsection (3) or (4) and if so) in what manner, the court shall have regard to all the circumstances including—

    (a) the housing needs and housing resources of each of the parties and of any relevant child;

    (b) the financial resources of each of the parties;

    (c) the likely effect of any order, or of any decision by the court not to exercise its powers under subsection (3) or (4), on the health, safety or well-being of the parties and of any relevant child;

    (d) the conduct of the parties in relation to each other and otherwise;

    (e) the nature of the parties' relationship [and in particular the level of commitment involved in it],[2]

    (f) the length of time during which they have [cohabited],[3]

    (g) whether there are or have been any children who are children of both parties or for whom both parties have or have had parental responsibility;

    (h) the length of time that has elapsed since the parties ceased to live together; and the existence of any pending proceedings between the parties—

        (i) for an order under paragraph 1(2)(d) or (e) of Schedule 1 to the Children Act 1989 (orders for financial relief against parents); or

        (ii) relating to the legal or beneficial ownership of the dwelling-house.

(7) In deciding whether to exercise its powers to include one or more of the provisions referred to in subsection (5) ('a subsection (5) provision') and (if so) in what manner, the court shall have regard to all the circumstances including—

    (a) the matters mentioned in subsection (6)(a) to (d); and

    (b) the questions mentioned in subsection (8).

(8) The questions are—

    (a) whether the applicant or any relevant child is likely to suffer significant harm attributable to conduct of the respondent if the subsection (5) provision is not included in the order; and

    (b) whether the harm likely to be suffered by the respondent or child if the provision is included is as great as or greater than the harm attributable to conduct of the respondent which is likely to be suffered by the applicant or child if the provision is not included.

(9) An order under this section—

    (a) may not be made after the death of either of the parties; and

    (b) ceases to have effect on the death of either of them.

---

[2] Section 2(2) of the Act.
[3] Replaces 'lived together as husband and wife': Sch 10, para 34(3).

(10) An order under this section must be limited so as to have effect for a specified period not exceeding six months, but may be extended on one occasion for a further specified period not exceeding six months.

(11) A person who has an equitable interest in the dwelling-house or in the proceeds of sale of the dwelling-house but in whom there is not vested (whether solely or as joint tenant) a legal estate in fee simple or a legal term of years absolute in the dwelling-house is to be treated (but only for the purpose of determining whether he is eligible to apply under this section) as not being entitled to occupy the dwelling-house by virtue of that interest.

(12) Subsection (11) does not prejudice any right of such a person to apply for an order under section 33.

(13) So long as the order remains in force, subsections (3) to (6) of section 30 apply in relation to the applicant—

(a) as if he were a spouse entitled to occupy the dwelling-house by virtue of that section; and

(b) as if the respondent were the other spouse.

Neither spouse entitled to occupy

37.—(1) This section applies if—

(a) one spouse or former spouse and the other spouse or former spouse occupy a dwelling-house which is or was the matrimonial home; but

(b) neither of them is entitled to remain in occupation—

(i) by virtue of a beneficial estate or interest or contract; or

(ii) by virtue of any enactment giving him the right to remain in occupation.

(2) Either of the parties may apply to the court for an order against the other under this section.

(3) An order under this section may—

(a) require the respondent to permit the applicant to enter and remain in the dwelling-house or part of the dwelling-house;

(b) regulate the occupation of the dwelling-house by either or both of the spouses;

(c) require the respondent to leave the dwelling-house or part of the dwelling-house; or

(d) exclude the respondent from a defined area in which the dwelling-house is included.

(4) Subsections (6) and (7) of section 33 apply to the exercise by the court of its powers under this section as they apply to the exercise by the court of its powers under subsection (3) of that section.

(5) An order under this section must be limited so as to have effect for a specified period not exceeding six months, but may be extended on one or more occasions for a further specified period not exceeding six months.

Neither cohabitant or former cohabitant entitled to occupy

38.—(1) This section applies if—

(a) one cohabitant or former cohabitant and the other cohabitant or former cohabitant occupy a dwelling-house which is the home in which they [cohabit or cohabited],[4] but

(b) neither of them is entitled to remain in occupation—

    (i) by virtue of a beneficial estate or interest or contract; or

    (ii) by virtue of any enactment giving him the right to remain in occupation.

(2) Either of the parties may apply to the court for an order against the other under this section.

(3) An order under this section may—

(a) require the respondent to permit the applicant to enter and remain in the dwelling-house or part of the dwelling-house;

(b) regulate the occupation of the dwelling-house by either or both of the parties;

(c) require the respondent to leave the dwelling-house or part of the dwelling-house; or

(d) exclude the respondent from a defined area in which the dwelling-house is included.

(4) In deciding whether to exercise its powers to include one or more of the provisions referred to in subsection (3) ('a subsection (3) provision') and (if so) in what manner, the court shall have regard to all the circumstances including—

(a) the housing needs and housing resources of each of the parties and of any relevant child;

(b) the financial resources of each of the parties;

(c) the likely effect of any order, or of any decision by the court not to exercise its powers under subsection (3), on the health, safety or well-being of the parties and of any relevant child;

(d) the conduct of the parties in relation to each other and otherwise; and

(e) the questions mentioned in subsection (5).

(5) The questions are—

(a) whether the applicant or any relevant child is likely to suffer significant harm attributable to conduct of the respondent if the subsection (3) provision is not included in the order; and

(b) whether the harm likely to be suffered by the respondent or child if the provision is included is as great as or greater than the harm attributable to conduct of the respondent which is likely to be suffered by the applicant or child if the provision is not included.

(6) An order under this section shall be limited so as to have effect for a specified period not exceeding six months, but may be extended on one occasion for a further specified period not exceeding six months.

Supplementary provisions

39.—(1) In this Part an 'occupation order' means an order under section 33, 35, 36, 37 or 38.

(2) An application for an occupation order may be made in other family proceedings or without any other family proceedings being instituted.

---

[4] Replaces 'live or lived together as husband and wife': Sch 10, para 35.

(3) If—
  (a) an application for an occupation order is made under section 33, 35, 36, 37 or 38, and
  (b) the court considers that it has no power to make the order under the section concerned, but that it has power to make an order under one of the other sections, the court may make an order under that other section.
(4) The fact that a person has applied for an occupation order under sections 35 to 38, or that an occupation order has been made, does not affect the right of any person to claim a legal or equitable interest in any property in any subsequent proceedings (including subsequent proceedings under this Part).

Additional provisions that may be included in certain occupation orders

40.—(1) The court may on, or at any time after, making an occupation order under section 33, 35 or 36—
  (a) impose on either party obligations as to—
    (i) the repair and maintenance of the dwelling-house; or
    (ii) the discharge of rent, mortgage payments or other outgoings affecting the dwelling-house;
  (b) order a party occupying the dwelling-house or any part of it (including a party who is entitled to do so by virtue of a beneficial estate or interest or contract or by virtue of any enactment giving him the right to remain in occupation) to make periodical payments to the other party in respect of the accommodation, if the other party would (but for the order) be entitled to occupy the dwelling-house by virtue of a beneficial estate or interest or contract or by virtue of any such enactment;
  (c) grant either party possession or use of furniture or other contents of the dwelling-house;
  (d) order either party to take reasonable care of any furniture or other contents of the dwelling-house;
  (e) order either party to take reasonable steps to keep the dwelling-house and any furniture or other contents secure.
(2) In deciding whether and, if so, how to exercise its powers under this section, the court shall have regard to all the circumstances of the case including—
  (a) the financial needs and financial resources of the parties; and
  (b) the financial obligations which they have, or are likely to have in the foreseeable future, including financial obligations to each other and to any relevant child.
(3) An order under this section ceases to have effect when the occupation order to which it relates ceases to have effect.

Additional considerations if parties are cohabitants or former cohabitants

41. *Repealed*[5]

---

[5] Schedule 11. The section previously read: '(1) This section applies if the parties are cohabitants or former cohabitants. (2) Where the court is required to consider the nature of the parties' relationship, it is to have regard to the fact that they have not given each other the commitment involved in marriage.'

Non-molestation orders

42.—(1) In this Part a 'non-molestation order' means an order containing either or both of the following provisions—

(a) provision prohibiting a person ('the respondent') from molesting another person who is associated with the respondent;

(b) provision prohibiting the respondent from molesting a relevant child.

(2) The court may make a non-molestation order—

(a) if an application for the order has been made (whether in other family proceedings or without any other family proceedings being instituted) by a person who is associated with the respondent; or

(b) if in any family proceedings to which the respondent is a party the court considers that the order should be made for the benefit of any other party to the proceedings or any relevant child even though no such application has been made.

(3) In subsection (2) 'family proceedings' includes proceedings in which the court has made an emergency protection order under section 44 of the Children Act 1989 which includes an exclusion requirement (as defined in section 44A(3) of that Act).

(4) Where an agreement to marry is terminated, no application under subsection (2)(a) may be made by virtue of section 62(3)(e) by reference to that agreement after the end of the period of the period of three years beginning with the day on which it is terminated.

[(4A) A court considering whether to make an occupation order shall also consider whether to exercise the power conferred by subsection (2)(b).

(4B) In this Part 'the applicant', in relation to a non-molestation order, includes (where the context permits) the person for whose benefit such an order would be or is made in exercise of the power conferred by subsection (2)(b).][6]

(5) In deciding whether to exercise its powers under this section and, if so, in what manner, the court shall have regard to all the circumstances including the need to secure the health, safety and well-being—

(a) of the applicant . . .[7] and

(b) of any relevant child.

(6) A non-molestation order may be expressed so as to refer to molestation in general, to particular acts of molestation, or to both.

(7) A non-molestation order may be made for a specified period or until further order.

(8) A non-molestation order which is made in other family proceedings ceases to have effect if those proceedings are withdrawn or dismissed.

[42A. Offence of breaching non-molestation order[8]

(1) A person who without reasonable excuse does anything that he is prohibited from doing by a non-molestation order is guilty of an offence.

---

[6] Schedule 10, para 36.

[7] The words 'or, in a case falling within subsection (2)(b), the person for whose benefit the order would be made;' repealed by Sch 11.

[8] Inserted by s 1 of the Act.

(2) In the case of a non-molestation order made by virtue of section 45(1), a person can be guilty of an offence under this section only in respect of conduct engaged in at a time when he was aware of the existence of the order.

(3) Where a person is convicted of an offence under this section in respect of any conduct, that conduct is not punishable as a contempt of court.

(4) A person cannot be convicted of an offence under this section in respect of any conduct which has been punished as a contempt of court.

(5) A person guilty of an offence under this section is liable—

    (a) on conviction on indictment, to imprisonment for a term not exceeding five years, or a fine, or both;

    (b) on summary conviction, to imprisonment for a term not exceeding 12 months, or a fine not exceeding the statutory maximum, or both.

(6) A reference in any enactment to proceedings under this Part, or to an order under this Part, does not include a reference to proceedings for an offence under this section or to an order made in such proceedings.

'Enactment' includes an enactment contained in subordinate legislation within the meaning of the Interpretation Act 1978 (c.30).]

Further provisions relating to occupation and non-molestation orders

Leave of court required for applications by children under sixteen

43.—(1) A child under the age of sixteen may not apply for an occupation order or a non-molestation order except with the leave of the court.

(2) The court may grant leave for the purposes of subsection (1) only if it is satisfied that the child has sufficient understanding to make the proposed application for the occupation order or non-molestation order.

Evidence of agreement to marry

44.—(1) Subject to subsection (2), the court shall not make an order under section 33 or 42 by virtue of section 62(3)(e) unless there is produced to it evidence in writing of the existence of the agreement to marry.

(2) Subsection (1) does not apply if the court is satisfied that the agreement to marry was evidenced by—

    (a) the gift of an engagement ring by one party to the agreement to the ther in contemplation of their marriage, or

    (b) a ceremony entered into by the parties in the presence of one or more other persons assembled for the purpose of witnessing the ceremony.

Ex parte orders

45.—(1) The court may, in any case where it considers that it is just and convenient to do so, make an occupation order or a non-molestation order even though the respondent has not been given such notice of the proceedings as would otherwise be required by rules of court.

(2) In determining whether to exercise its powers under subsection (1), the court shall have regard to all the circumstances including—

    (a) any risk of significant harm to the applicant or a relevant child, attributable to conduct of the respondent, if the order is not made immediately;

    (b) whether it is likely that the applicant will be deterred or prevented from pursuing the application if an order is not made immediately; and

    (c) whether there is reason to believe that the respondent is aware of the proceedings but is deliberately evading service and that the applicant or a relevant child will be seriously prejudiced by the delay involved—

        (i) where the court is a magistrates' court, in effecting service of proceedings; or

        (ii) in any other case, in effecting substituted service.

(3) If the court makes an order by virtue of subsection (1) it must afford the respondent an opportunity to make representations relating to the order as soon as just and convenient at a full hearing.

(4) If, at a full hearing, the court makes an occupation order ('the full order'), then—

    (a) for the purposes of calculating the maximum period for which the full order may be made to have effect, the relevant section is to apply as if the period for which the full order will have effect began on the date on which the initial order first had effect; and

    (b) the provisions of section 36(10) or 38(6) as to the extension of orders are to apply as if the full order and the initial order were a single order.

(5) In this section—

'full hearing' means a hearing of which notice has been given to all the parties in accordance with rules of court;

'initial order' means an occupation order made by virtue of subsection (1); and

'relevant section' means section 33(10), 35(10), 36(10), 37(5) or 38(6).

Undertakings

46.—(1) In any case where the court has power to make an occupation order or non-molestation order, the court may accept an undertaking from any party to the proceedings.

(2) No power of arrest may be attached to any undertaking given under subsection (1).

(3) The court shall not accept an undertaking under subsection (1) [instead of making an occupation order] in any case where apart from this section a power of arrest would be attached to the order.

[(3A) The court shall not accept an undertaking under subsection (1) instead of making a non-molestation order in any case where it appears to the court that—

    (a) the respondent has used or threatened violence against the applicant or a relevant child; and

    (b) for the protection of the applicant or child it is necessary to make a non-molestation order so that any breach may be punishable under section 42A.]

(4) An undertaking given to a court under subsection (1) is enforceable *as if it were an order of the court* [the court had made an occupation order or an non-molestation order in terms corresponding to those of the undertaking].

(5) This section has effect without prejudice to the powers of the High Court and the county court apart from this section.

Arrest for breach of order

47.—*(1) In this section 'a relevant order' means an occupation order or a non-molestation order.*

(2) If—
   (a) the court makes *a relevant* [an occupation] order; and
   (b) it appears to the court that the respondent has used or threatened violence against the applicant or a relevant child,

   it shall attach a power of arrest to one or more provisions of the order unless satisfied that in all the circumstances of the case the applicant or child will be adequately protected without such a power of arrest.

(3) Subsection (2) does not apply in any case where *the relevant order* [the occupation order] is made by virtue of section 45(1), but in such a case the court may attach a power of arrest to one or more provisions of the order if it appears to it—
   (a) that the respondent has used or threatened violence against the applicant or a relevant child; and
   (b) that there is a risk of significant harm to the applicant or child, attributable to conduct of the respondent, if the power of arrest is not attached to those provisions immediately.

(4) If, by virtue of subsection (3), the court attaches a power of arrest to any provisions of *a relevant order* [an occupation order], it may provide that the power of arrest is to have effect for a shorter period than the other provisions of the order.

(5) Any period specified for the purposes of subsection (4) may be extended by the court (on one or more occasions) on an application to vary or discharge *the relevant order* [the occupation order].

(6) If, by virtue of subsection (2) or (3), a power of arrest is attached to certain provisions of an order, a constable may arrest without warrant a person whom he has reasonable cause for suspecting to be in breach of any such provision.

(7) If a power of arrest is attached under subsection (2) or (3) to certain provisions of the order and the respondent is arrested under subsection (6)—
   (a) he must be brought before the relevant judicial authority within the period of 24 hours beginning at the time of his arrest; and
   (b) if the matter is not then disposed of forthwith, the relevant judicial authority before whom he is brought may remand him.

   In reckoning for the purposes of this subsection any period of 24 hours, no account is to be taken of Christmas Day, Good Friday or any Sunday.

(8) *If the court has made a relevant order but—*
   (a) has not attached a power of arrest under subsection (2) or (3) to any provisions of the order, or
   (b) has attached that power only to certain provisions of the order,
   [If the court—
   (a) has made a non-molestation order, or
   (b) has made an occupation order but has not attached a power of arrest under subsection (2) or (3) to any provisions of the order, or has attached that power only to certain provisions of the order,]

   then, if at any time the applicant considers that the respondent has failed to comply with the order, he may apply to the relevant judicial authority for the issue of a warrant for the arrest of the respondent.

(9) The relevant judicial authority shall not issue a warrant on an application under subsection (8) unless—

(a) the application is substantiated on oath; and

(b) the relevant judicial authority has reasonable grounds for believing that the respondent has failed to comply with the order.

(10) If a person is brought before a court by virtue of a warrant issued under subsection (9) and the court does not dispose of the matter forthwith, the court may remand him.

(11) Schedule 5 (which makes provision corresponding to that applying in magistrates' courts in civil cases under sections 128 and 129 of the Magistrates' Courts Act 1980) has effect in relation to the powers of the High Court and a county court to remand a person by virtue of this section.

(12) If a person remanded under this section is granted bail (whether in the High Court or a county court under Schedule 5 or in a magistrates' court under section 128 or 129 of the Magistrates' Courts Act 1980), he may be required by the relevant judicial authority to comply, before release on bail or later, with such requirements as appear to that authority to be necessary to secure that he does not interfere with witnesses or otherwise obstruct the course of justice.

Remand for medical examination and report

48.—(1) If the relevant
judicial authority has reason to consider that a medical report will be required, any power to remand a person under section 47(7)(b) or (10) may be exercised for the purpose of enabling a medical examination and report to be made.

(2) If such a power is so exercised, the adjournment must not be for more than 4 weeks at a time unless the relevant judicial authority remands the accused in custody.

(3) If the relevant judicial authority so remands the accused, the adjournment must not be for more than 3 weeks at a time.

(4) If there is reason to suspect that a person who has been arrested—

(a) under section 47(6), or

(b) under a warrant issued on an application made under section 47(8), is suffering from mental illness or severe mental impairment, the relevant judicial authority has the same power to make an order under section 35 of the Mental Health Act 1983 (remand for report on accused's mental condition) as the Crown Court has under section 35 of the Act of 1983 in the case of an accused person within the meaning of that section.

Variation and discharge of orders

49.—(1) An occupation order or
non-molestation order may be varied or discharged by the court on an application by—

(a) the respondent, or

(b) the person on whose application the order was made.

(2) In the case of a non-molestation order made by virtue of section 42(2)(b), the order may be varied or discharged by the court even though no such application has been made.

(3) If a spouse's matrimonial home rights are a charge on the estate or interest of the other spouse or of trustees for the other spouse, an order under section 33 against the other spouse may also be varied or discharged by the court on an application by any person deriving title under the other spouse or under the trustees and affected by the charge.

(4) If, by virtue of section 47(3), a power of arrest has been attached to certain provisions of an occupation order *or non-molestation order*, the court may vary or discharge the order under subsection (1) in so far as it confers a power of arrest (whether or not any application has been made to vary or discharge any other provision of the order).

Enforcement powers of magistrates' courts

Power of magistrates' court to suspend execution of committal order

50.—(1) If, under section 63(3) of the Magistrates' Courts Act 1980, a magistrates' court has power to commit a person to custody for breach of a relevant requirement, the court may by order direct that the execution of the order of committal is to be suspended for such period or on such terms and conditions as it may specify.

(2) In subsection (1) 'a relevant requirement' means—

(a) an occupation order or non-molestation order;

(b) an exclusion requirement included by virtue of section 38A of the Children Act 1989 in an interim care order made under section 38 of that Act; or

(c) an exclusion requirement included by virtue of section 44A of the Children Act 1989 in an emergency protection order under section 44 of that Act.

Power of magistrates' court to order hospital admission or guardianship

51.—(1) A magistrates' court has the same power to make a hospital order or guardianship order under section 37 of the Mental Health Act 1983 or an interim hospital order under section 38 of that Act in the case of a person suffering from mental illness or severe mental impairment who could otherwise be committed to custody for breach of a relevant requirement as a magistrates' court has under those sections in the case of a person convicted of an offence punishable on summary conviction with imprisonment.

(2) In subsection (1) 'a relevant requirement' has the meaning given by section 50(2).

Interim care orders and emergency protection orders

Amendments of Children Act 1989

52. Schedule 6 makes amendments of the provisions of the Children Act 1989 relating to interim care orders and emergency protection orders.

Transfer of tenancies

Transfer of certain tenancies

53. Schedule 7 makes provision in relation to the transfer of certain tenancies on divorce etc. or on separation of cohabitants.

Dwelling-house subject to mortgage

54.—(1) In determining for the purposes of this Part whether a person is entitled to occupy a dwelling-house by virtue of an estate or interest, any right to possession of the dwelling-house conferred on a mortgagee of the dwelling-house under or by virtue of his mortgage is to be disregarded.

(2) Subsection (1) applies whether or not the mortgagee is in possession.

(3) Where a person ('A') is entitled to occupy a dwelling-house by virtue of an estate or interest, a connected person does not by virtue of—

(a) any matrimonial home rights conferred by section 30, or

(b) any rights conferred by an order under section 35 or 36, have any larger right against the mortgagee to occupy the dwelling-house than A has by virtue of his estate or interest and of any contract with the mortgagee.

(4) Subsection (3) does not apply, in the case of matrimonial home rights, if under section 31 those rights are a charge, affecting the mortgagee, on the estate or interest mortgaged.

(5) In this section 'connected person', in relation to any person, means that person's spouse, former spouse, cohabitant or former cohabitant.

Actions by mortgagees: joining connected persons as parties

55.—(1) This section applies if a mortgagee of land which consists of or includes a dwelling-house brings an action in any court for the enforcement of his security.

(2) A connected person who is not already a party to the action is entitled to be made a party in the circumstances mentioned in subsection

(3) The circumstances are that—

(a) the connected person is enabled by section 30(3) or (6) (or by section 30(3) or (6) as applied by section 35(13) or 36(13)), to meet the mortgagor's liabilities under the mortgage;

(b) he has applied to the court before the action is finally disposed of in that court; and

(c) the court sees no special reason against his being made a party to the action and is satisfied—

(i) that he may be expected to make such payments or do such other things in or towards satisfaction of the mortgagor's liabilities or obligations as might affect the outcome of the proceedings; or

(ii) that the expectation of it should be considered under section 36 of the Administration of Justice Act 1970.

(4) In this section 'connected person' has the same meaning as in section 54.

Actions by mortgagees: service of notice on certain persons

56.—(1) This section applies if a mortgagee of land which consists, or substantially consists, of a dwelling-house brings an action for the enforcement of his security, and at the relevant time there is—

(a) in the case of unregistered land, a land charge of Class F registered against the person who is the estate owner at the relevant time or any person who, where the estate owner is a trustee, preceded him as trustee during the subsistence of the mortgage; or

    (b) in the case of registered land, a subsisting registration of—
       (i) a notice under section 31(10);
       (ii) a notice under section 2(8) of the Matrimonial Homes Act 1983; or
       (iii) a notice or caution under section 2(7) of the Matrimonial Homes Act 1967.

(2) If the person on whose behalf—
    (a) the land charge is registered, or
    (b) the notice or caution is entered,
is not a party to the action, the mortgagee must serve notice of the action on him.

(3) If—
    (a) an official search has been made on behalf of the mortgagee which would disclose any land charge of Class F, notice or caution within subsection (1)(a) or (b),
    (b) a certificate of the result of the search has been issued, and
    (c) the action is commenced within the priority period, the relevant time is the date of the certificate.

(4) In any other case the relevant time is the time when the action is commenced.

(5) The priority period is, for both registered and unregistered land, the period for which, in accordance with section 11(5) and (6) of the Land Charges Act 1972, a certificate on an official search operates in favour of a purchaser.

Jurisdiction and procedure etc.

Jurisdiction of courts

57.—(1) For the purposes of this Part 'the court' means the High Court, a county court or a magistrates' court.

(2) Subsection (1) is subject to the provision made by or under the following provisions of this section, to section 59 and to any express provision as to the jurisdiction of any court made by any other provision of this Part.

(3) The Lord Chancellor may by order specify proceedings under this Part which may only be commenced in—
    (a) a specified level of court;
    (b) a court which falls within a specified class of court; or
    (c) a particular court determined in accordance with, or specified in, the order.

(4) The Lord Chancellor may by order specify circumstances in which specified proceedings under this Part may only be commenced in—
    (a) a specified level of court;
    (b) a court which falls within a specified class of court; or
    (c) a particular court determined in accordance with, or specified in, the order.

(5) The Lord Chancellor may by order provide that in specified circumstances the whole, or any specified part of any specified proceedings under this Part is to be transferred to—
    (a) a specified level of court;
    (b) a court which falls within a specified class of court; or
    (c) a particular court determined in accordance with, or specified in, the order.

(6) An order under subsection (5) may provide for the transfer to be made at any stage,

or specified stage, of the proceedings and whether or not the proceedings, or any part of them, have already been transferred.

(7) An order under subsection (5) may make such provision as the Lord Chancellor thinks appropriate for excluding specified proceedings from the operation of section 38 or 39 of the Matrimonial and Family Proceedings Act 1984 (transfer of family proceedings) or any other enactment which would otherwise govern the transfer of those proceedings, or any part of them.

(8) For the purposes of subsections (3), (4) and (5), there are three levels of court—
   (a) the High Court;
   (b) any county court; and
   (c) any magistrates' court.

(9) The Lord Chancellor may by order make provision for the principal registry of the Family Division of the High Court to be treated as if it were a county court for specified purposes of this Part, or of any provision made under this Part.

(10) Any order under subsection (9) may make such provision as the Lord Chancellor thinks expedient for the purpose of applying (with or without modifications) provisions which apply in relation to the procedure in county courts to the principal registry when it acts as if it were a county court.

(11) In this section 'specified' means specified by an order under this section.

Contempt proceedings

58. The powers of the court in relation to contempt of court arising out of a person's failure to comply with an order under this Part may be exercised by the relevant judicial authority.

Magistrates' courts

59.—(1) A magistrates' court shall not be competent to entertain any application, or make any order, involving any disputed question as to a party's entitlement to occupy any property by virtue of a beneficial estate or interest or contract or by virtue of any enactment giving him the right to remain in occupation, unless it is unnecessary to determine the question in order to deal with the application or make the order.

(2) A magistrates' court may decline jurisdiction in any proceedings under this Part if it considers that the case can more conveniently be dealt with by another court.

(3) The powers of a magistrates' court under section 63(2) of the Magistrates' Courts Act 1980 to suspend or rescind orders shall not apply in relation to any order made under this Part.

Provision for third parties to act on behalf of victims of domestic violence

60.—(1) Rules of court may provide for a prescribed person, or any person in a prescribed category, ('a representative') to act on behalf of another in relation to proceedings to which this Part applies.

(2) Rules made under this section may, in particular, authorize a representative to apply for an occupation order or for a non-molestation order for which the person on whose behalf the representative is acting could have applied.

(3) Rules made under this section may prescribe—
  (a) conditions to be satisfied before a representative may make an application to the court on behalf of another; and
  (b) considerations to be taken into account by the court in determining whether, and if so how, to exercise any of its powers under this Part when a representative is acting on behalf of another.
(4) Any rules made under this section may be made so as to have effect for a specified period and may make consequential or transitional provision with respect to the expiry of the specified period.
(5) Any such rules may be replaced by further rules made under this section.

Appeals

61.—(1) An appeal shall lie to the High Court against—
  (a) the making by a magistrates' court of any order under this Part, or
  (b) any refusal by a magistrates' court to make such an order, but no appeal shall lie against any exercise by a magistrates' court of the power conferred by section 59(2).
(2) On an appeal under this section, the High Court may make such orders as may be necessary to give effect to its determination of the appeal.
(3) Where an order is made under subsection (2), the High Court may also make such incidental or consequential orders as appear to it to be just.
(4) Any order of the High Court made on an appeal under this section (other than one directing that an application be re-heard by a magistrates' court) shall, for the purposes—
  (a) of the enforcement of the order, and
  (b) of any power to vary, revive or discharge orders, be treated as if it were an order of the magistrates' court from which the appeal was brought and not an order of the High Court.
(5) The Lord Chancellor may by order make provision as to the circumstances in which appeals may be made against decisions taken by courts on questions arising in connection with the transfer, or proposed transfer, of proceedings by virtue of any order under section 57(5).
(6) Except to the extent provided for in any order made under subsection (5), no appeal may be made against any decision of a kind mentioned in that subsection.

General

Meaning of 'cohabitants', 'relevant child' and 'associated persons'

62.—(1) For the purposes of this Part—
  (a) 'cohabitants' are *a man and a woman who, although not married to each other, are living together as husband and wife* [two persons who, although not married to each other, are living together as husband and wife or (if of the same sex) are in an equivalent relationship]; and
  (b) *'former cohabitants' is to be read accordingly but* ['cohabit' and 'former cohabitants' is to be read accordingly but the latter expression] does not include cohabitants who have subsequently married each other.

(2) In this Part, 'relevant child', in relation to any proceedings under this Part, means—
   (a) any child who is living with or might reasonably be expected to live with either party to the proceedings;
   (b) any child in relation to whom an order under the Adoption Act 1976 or the Children Act 1989 is in question in the proceedings; and
   (c) any other child whose interests the court considers relevant.

(3) For the purposes of this Part, a person is associated with another person if—
   (a) they are or have been married to each other;
   (b) they are cohabitants or former cohabitants;
   (c) they live or have lived in the same household, otherwise than merely by reason of one of them being the other's employee, tenant, lodger or boarder;
   (d) they are relatives;
   (e) they have agreed to marry one another (whether or not that Agreement has been terminated);
   [(ea) they have or have had an intimate personal relationship with each other which is or was of significant duration]
   (f) in relation to any child, they are both persons falling within subsection (4); or
   (g) they are parties to the same family proceedings (other than proceedings under this Part).

(4) A person falls within this subsection in relation to a child if—
   (a) he is a parent of the child; or
   (b) he has or has had parental responsibility for the child.

(5) If a child has been adopted or has been freed for adoption by virtue of any of the enactments mentioned in section 16(1) of the Adoption Act 1976, two persons are also associated with each other for the purposes of this Part if—
   (a) one is a natural parent of the child or a parent of such a natural parent; and
   (b) the other is the child or any person—
      (i) who has become a parent of the child by virtue of an adoption order or has applied for an adoption order, or
      (ii) with whom the child has at any time been placed for adoption.

(6) A body corporate and another person are not, by virtue of subsection (3)(f) or (g), to be regarded for the purposes of this Part as associated with each other.

Interpretation of Part IV

63.—(1) In this Part—
'adoption order' has the meaning given by section 72(1) of the Adoption Act 1976;
'associated', in relation to a person, is to be read with section 62(3) to (6);
'child' means a person under the age of eighteen years;
['cohabit'] 'cohabitant' and 'former cohabitant' have the meaning given by section 62(1);
'the court' is to be read with section 57;
'development' means physical, intellectual, emotional, social or behavioural development;
'dwelling-house' includes (subject to subsection (4))—
   (a) any building or part of a building which is occupied as a dwelling,
   (b) any caravan, house-boat or structure which is occupied as a dwelling, and any yard, garden, garage or outhouse belonging to it and occupied with it;

213

'family proceedings' means any proceedings—

(a) under the inherent jurisdiction of the High Court in relation to children; or

(b) under the enactments mentioned in subsection (2);

'harm'—

(a) in relation to a person who has reached the age of eighteen years, means ill-treatment or the impairment of health; and

(b) in relation to a child, means ill-treatment or the impairment of health or development;

'health' includes physical or mental health;

'ill-treatment' includes forms of ill-treatment which are not physical and, in relation to a child, includes sexual abuse;

'matrimonial home rights' has the meaning given by section 30;

'mortgage', 'mortgagor' and 'mortgagee' have the same meaning as in the Law of Property Act 1925;

'mortgage payments' includes any payments which, under the terms of the mortgage, the mortgagor is required to make to any person;

'non-molestation order' has the meaning given by section 42(1);

'occupation order' has the meaning given by section 39;

'parental responsibility' has the same meaning as in the Children Act 1989;

'relative', in relation to a person, means—

(a) the father, mother, stepfather, stepmother, son, daughter, stepson, stepdaughter, grandmother, grandfather, grandson or granddaughter of that person or of that person's spouse or former spouse, or

(b) brother, sister, uncle, aunt, niece *or nephew* [or nephew or first cousin] (whether of the full blood or of the half blood or by affinity) of that person or of that person's spouse or former spouse,

and includes, in relation to a person who *is living or has lived with another person as husband and wife* [is cohabiting or has cohabited with another person], any person who would fall within paragraph (a) or (b) if the parties were married to each other;

'relevant child', in relation to any proceedings under this Part, has the meaning given by section 62(2);

'the relevant judicial authority', in relation to any order under this Part, means—

(a) where the order was made by the High Court, a judge of that court;

(b) where the order was made by a county court, a judge or district judge of that or any other county court; or

(c) where the order was made by a magistrates' court, any magistrates' court.

(2) The enactments referred to in the definition of 'family proceedings' are—

(a) Part II;

(b) this Part;

(c) the Matrimonial Causes Act 1973;

(d) the Adoption Act 1976;

(e) the Domestic Proceedings and Magistrates' Courts Act 1978;

(f) Part III of the Matrimonial and Family Proceedings Act 1984;

(g) Parts I, II and IV of the Children Act 1989;

(h) section 30 of the Human Fertilisation and Embryology Act 1990.

(3) Where the question of whether harm suffered by a child is significant turns on the

child's health or development, his health or development shall be compared with that which could reasonably be expected of a similar child.

(4) For the purposes of sections 31, 32, 53 and 54 and such other provisions of this Part (if any) as may be prescribed, this Part is to have effect as if paragraph (b) of the definition of 'dwelling-house' were omitted.

(5) It is hereby declared that this Part applies as between the parties to a marriage even though either of them is, or has at any time during the marriage been, married to more than one person.

Protection from Harassment Act 1997, ss 1 to 7 as amended

[The text incorporates amendments made to the Protection from Harassment Act 1997 (c 40), ss 1 to 7 as amended before the coming into force by the Domestic Violence, Crime and Victims Act 2004. Please note, these amendments are not yet in force. The amendments will come into force in stages from April 2005. Please see relevant statutory instruments. Repeals made by that Act are shown in italics and amendments in square brackets]

An Act to make provision for protecting persons from harassment and similar conduct.

[21st March 1997]

Be it enacted by the Queen's most Excellent Majesty, by and with the advice and consent of the Lords Spiritual and Temporal, and Commons, in this present Parliament assembled, and by the authority of the same, as follows:—

England and Wales

Prohibition of harassment

1.—(1) A person must not pursue a course of conduct—
    (a) which amounts to harassment of another, and
    (b) which he knows or ought to know amounts to harassment of the other
(2) For the purposes of this section, the person whose course of conduct is in question ought to know that it amounts to harassment of another if a reasonable person in possession of the same information would think the course of conduct amounted to harassment of the other.
(3) Subsection (1) does not apply to a course of conduct if the person who pursued it shows—
    (a) that it was pursued for the purpose of preventing or detecting crime,
    (b) that it was pursued under any enactment or rule of law or to comply with any condition or requirement imposed by any person under any enactment, or
    (c) that in the particular circumstances the pursuit of the course of conduct was reasonable.

Offence of harassment

2.—(1) A person who pursues a course of conduct in breach of section 1 is guilty of an offence.
(2) A person guilty of an offence under this section is liable on summary conviction to

imprisonment for a term not exceeding six months, or a fine not exceeding level 5 on the standard scale, or both.

(3) *Repealed*

Civil remedy

3.—(1) An actual or apprehended breach of section 1 may be the subject of a claim in civil proceedings by the person who is or may be the victim of the course of conduct in question.

(2) On such a claim, damages may be awarded for (among other things) any anxiety caused by the harassment and any financial loss resulting from the harassment.

(3) Where—

(a) in such proceedings the High Court or a county court grants an injunction for the purpose of restraining the defendant from pursuing any conduct which amounts to harassment, and

(b) the plaintiff considers that the defendant has done anything which he is prohibited from doing by the injunction,

the plaintiff may apply for the issue of a warrant for the arrest of the defendant

(4) An application under subsection (3) may be made—

(a) where the injunction was granted by the High Court, to a judge of that court, and

(b) where the injunction was granted by a county court, to a judge or district judge of that or any other county court.

(5) The judge or district judge to whom an application under subsection (3) is made may only issue a warrant if—

(a) the application is substantiated on oath, and

(b) the judge or district judge has reasonable grounds for believing that the defendant has done anything which he is prohibited from doing by the injunction.

(6) Where—

(a) the High Court or a county court an injunction for the purpose mentioned in subsection (3)(a), and

(b) without reasonable excuse the defendant does anything which he is prohibited from doing by the injunction, he is guilty of an offence.

(7) Where a person is convicted of an offence under subsection (6) in respect of any conduct, that conduct is not punishable as a contempt of court.

(8) A person cannot be convicted of an offence under subsection (6) in respect of any conduct which has been punished as a contempt of court.

(9) A person guilty of an offence under subsection (6) is liable—

(a) on conviction on indictment, to imprisonment for a term not exceeding five years, or a fine, or both, or

(b) on summary conviction, to imprisonment for a term not exceeding six months, or a fine not exceeding the statutory maximum, or both.

Putting people in fear of violence

4.—(1) A person whose course of conduct causes another to fear, on at least two occasions, that violence will be used against him is guilty of an offence if he knows or ought to know that his course of conduct will cause the other so to fear on each of those occasions.

(2) For the purposes of this section, the person whose course of conduct is in question ought to know that it will cause another to fear that violence will be used against him on any occasion if a reasonable person in possession of the same information would think the course of conduct would cause the other so to fear on that occasion.

(3) It is a defence for a person charged with an offence under this section to show that—

    (a) his course of conduct was pursued for the purpose of preventing or detecting crime,

    (b) his course of conduct was pursued under any enactment or rule of law or to comply with any condition or requirement imposed by any person under any enactment, or

    (c) the pursuit of his course of conduct was reasonable for the protection of himself or another or for the protection of his or another's property.

(4) A person guilty of an offence under this section is liable—

    (a) on conviction on indictment, to imprisonment for a term not exceeding five years, or a fine, or both, or

    (b) on summary conviction, to imprisonment for a term not exceeding six months, or a fine not exceeding the statutory maximum, or both.

(5) If on the trial on indictment of a person charged with an offence under this section the jury find him not guilty of the offence charged, they may find him guilty of an offence under section 2.

(6) The Crown Court has the same powers and duties in relation to a person who is by virtue of subsection (5) convicted before it of an offence under section 2 as a magistrates' court would have on convicting him of the offence.

Restraining orders

5.—(1) A court sentencing or otherwise dealing with a person ('the defendant') convicted of an offence *under section 2 or 4* may (as well as sentencing him or dealing with him in any other way) make an order under this section.

(2) The order may, for the purpose of protecting the victim of the offence, or any other person mentioned in the order, from further conduct which—

    (a) amounts to harassment, or

    (b) will cause a fear of violence,

prohibit the defendant from doing anything described in the order.

(3) The order may have effect for a specified period or until further order.

[(3A) In proceedings under this section both the prosecution and the defence may lead, as further evidence, any evidence that would be admissible in proceedings for an injunction under section 3.]

(4) The prosecutor, the defendant or any other person mentioned in the order may apply to the court which made the order for it to be varied or discharged by a further order.

[(4A) Any person mentioned in the order is entitled to be heard on the hearing of an application under subsection (4).]

(5) If without reasonable excuse the defendant does anything which he is prohibited from doing by an order under this section, he is guilty of an offence.

(6) A person guilty of an offence under this section is liable—

    (a) on conviction on indictment, to imprisonment for a term not exceeding five years, or a fine, or both, or

(b) on summary conviction, to imprisonment for a term not exceeding six months, or a fine not exceeding the statutory maximum, or both.

[(7) A court dealing with a person for an offence under this section may vary or discharge the order in question by a further order.]

[5A.—Restraining orders on acquittal

(1) A court before which a person ('the defendant') is acquitted of an offence may, if it considers it necessary to do so to protect a person from harassment by the defendant, make an order prohibiting the defendant from doing anything described in the order.

(2) Subsections (3) to (7) of section 5 apply to an order under this section as they apply to an order under that one.

(3) Where the Court of Appeal allows an appeal against conviction they may remit the case to the Crown Court to consider whether to proceed under this section.

(4) Where—

(a) the Crown Court allows an appeal against conviction, or

(b) a case is remitted to the Crown Court under subsection (3),

The reference in subsection (1) to a court before which a person is acquitted of an offence is to be read as referring to that court.

(5) A person made subject to an order under this section has the same right of appeal against the order as if—

(a) he had been convicted of the offence in question before the court which made the order, and

(b) the order had been made under section 5.]

Limitation

6.—In section 11 of the Limitation Act 1980 (special time limit for actions in respect of personal injuries), after subsection (1) there is inserted—

'(1A) This section does not apply to any action brought for damages under section 3 of the Protection from Harassment Act 1997.'

Interpretation of this group of sections

7.—(1) This section applies for the interpretation of sections 1 to 5.

(2) References to harassing a person include alarming the person or causing the person distress.

(3) A 'course of conduct' must involve conduct on at least two occasions.

(3A) A person's conduct on any occasion shall be taken, if aided, abetted, counselled or procured by another—

(a) to be conduct on that occasion of the other (as well as conduct of the person whose conduct it is); and

(b) to be conduct in relation to which the other's knowledge and purpose, and what he ought to have known, are the same as they were in relation to what was contemplated or reasonably foreseeable at the time of the aiding, abetting, counselling or procuring.

(3) 'Conduct' includes speech.

Useful Addresses

Domestic Violence
24-hour National Domestic Violence Helpline
0808 200 0247

Women's Aid National Office
PO Box 391
Bristol BS99 7WS
0117 944 4411 (office)
www.womensaid.org.uk

Scottish Women's Aid
Norton Park
57 Albion Road
Edinburgh EH7 5QY
0131 475 2372
www.scottishwomensaid.org.uk

Welsh Women's Aid
38–48 Crwys Road
Cardiff CF24 2NN
029 2039 0874
Confidential helpline 0808 801 0800
www.welshwomensaid.org.uk

Jewish Women's Aid
PO Box 2670
London N12 9ZE
020 8445 8060
Helpline 0800 591 203
www.jwauk.cjb.net

Muslim Women's Helpline
020 8904 8193
020 8908 6715

NB: Other specialized helplines can be found through the Women's Aid
National Office

Refuge
2–8 Maltravers Street
London WC2R 3EE
020 7395 7700
www.refuge.org.uk

Refuge for Women with Learning Difficulties
Beverley Lewis House
PO Box 7312
London E15 4TS
020 8522 0675

Rights of Women
52–54 Featherstone Street
London EC1Y 8RT
020 7251 6577
www.rightsofwomen.org.uk

Childline
Freepost 1111
London N1 0BR
020 7650 3200
Helpline 0800 1111

Children's Legal Centre
University of Essex
Wivenhoe Park
Colchester CO4 3SQ
01206 872466
www.childrenslegalcentre.com

National Society for the Prevention of Cruelty to Children (NSPCC)
Weston House
42 Curtain Road
London EC2A 3NH
020 7825 2500
Child Protection Helpline 0808 800 5000
www.nspcc.org.uk

Domestic Violence Intervention Project
PO Box 2838
London W6 9ZE
020 8563 7983
www.dvip.org.uk

Mankind Initiative (Supports male victims of domestic violence)
Municipal Building
Corporation Street
Taunton TA1 4AQ
Helpline 0870 794 4124
www.mankind.org.uk

Men's Aid
PO Box 205
Cheltenham GL51 0YL
01242 691110
support@mensaid.org
www.mensaid.org

Relate
Details of local centres 0845 456 1310
Advice line 0845 130 4016
www.relate.org.uk

Samaritans
The Upper Mill
Kingston Road
Ewell
Surrey KT17 2AF
020 8394 8300
Helpline 0845 790 9090
www.samaritans.org.uk

Shelter National Campaign for the Homeless
88 Old Street
London EC1V 9HU
0845 458 4590
Helpline 0808 800 4444
www.england.shelter.org.uk

Victim Supportline
0845 303 0900
Victim Support
National Office
Cranmer House
39 Brixton Road
London SW9 6DZ
020 7735 9166
www.victimsupport.org.uk

MIND (National Association for Mental Health)
15–19 Broadway
London E15 4BQ
020 8519 2122
Helpline 0845 766 0163
www.mind.org.uk

Index

Page references indicate material appearing in the Appendices

Lightning Source UK Ltd.
Milton Keynes UK
UKOW031011030712